OF TIMES AND RACE

Of TIMES AND RACE

Essays Inspired by John F. Marszalek

Edited by
Michael B. Ballard and Mark R. Cheathem

UNIVERSITY PRESS OF MISSISSIPPI / JACKSON

www.upress.state.ms.us

The University Press of Mississippi is a member of the Association of American University Presses.

Frontis photo by Russ Houston

Copyright © 2013 by University Press of Mississippi
All rights reserved
Manufactured in the United States of America

First printing 2013

∞

Library of Congress Cataloging-in-Publication Data

Of times and race : essays inspired by John F. Marszalek /
edited by Michael B. Ballard and Mark R. Cheathem.
p. cm.
Includes bibliographical references and index.
ISBN 978-1-61703-639-2 (cloth : alk. paper) — ISBN 978-1-61703-640-8 (ebook) 1. African Americans—History—19th century. 2. African Americans—History—20th century. 3. Slavery—United States—History—19th century. 4. United States—History—Civil War, 1861–1865—African Americans. 5. United States—Race relations—Historiography. I. Ballard, Michael B. II. Cheathem, Mark Renfred. III. Marszalek, John F., 1939–
E185.2.O4 2013
973'.0496073—dc23   2012017997

British Library Cataloging-in-Publication Data available

For
John F. Marszalek,
With our esteem, respect, and affection

And to
Jeanne Marszalek,
Thanks for all the feasts

CONTENTS

Preface ix

1. Slavery, Plantation Life, and Debt in Tennessee and Mississippi
   The Example of Andrew Jackson Donelson   3
   MARK R. CHEATHEM

2. Patriots or Traitors
   Unionists in Civil War Mississippi   31
   THOMAS D. COCKRELL

3. The African American Experience in Louisiana's Lafourche Region during the Civil War   55
   STEPHEN S. MICHOT

4. Union Soldiers React to Slaves, Slavery, Freedmen, and Colored U.S. Troops during the Vicksburg Campaign   69
   MICHAEL B. BALLARD

5. Town and Sword
   Black Boxers at Columbus, New Mexico, 1916–1922   89
   HORACE NASH

6. Black Soldiers and the CCC at Shiloh National Military Park   115
   TIMOTHY B. SMITH

7. Challenging the Dunning Orthodoxy
   The Reconstruction Revisionism of Francis Butler Simkins and Robert Hilliard Woody   129
   JAMES SCOTT HUMPHREYS

8. Confronting Race in American History   147
EDNA GREENE MEDFORD

Notes on Contributors   161

Index   163

PREFACE

THIS BOOK IS A TRIBUTE TO JOHN MARSZALEK BY THOSE WHO RECEIVED their doctoral degrees at Mississippi State University under his tutelage. That factual statement does not scratch the surface of the relationship we developed with John during our time in graduate school, a strong relationship that continues to the present.

John was a tough taskmaster, but we do not believe any of us ever feared him. He made clear that he pushed us so that we would never be satisfied with anything less than our best efforts. We soon found that what we were capable of doing far exceeded our expectations, and that knowledge propelled us to accomplish more than we thought possible. He challenged us, and yet he was always there to encourage, to lift up, and, in his own inimitable way, chastise us when we did not do as well as he knew we could. We came to call him "the cheerful assassin," an appellation actually first uttered by one of his colleagues at the university. We embraced it, for the words fit him so well. We had a wooden plaque made with those words etched in, and he immediately hung it from the ceiling of his office. We often wondered what undergraduates and even new graduate students thought and felt when they stopped by to see him for the first time and saw that sign hanging high above his desk.

As important as his academic guidance was his genuine friendship. He also happens to be married to Jeanne Marszalek, who is one of the best cooks ever placed on this earth, and he and she were kind enough to invite us often to their home for one of her always fantastic meals. We watched his three sons grow from very young men into very successful adults. Thanks to the Marszaleks' hospitality, we all became a family, at ease with him and his family and with one another. We felt comfortable sharing our personal situations, for we knew we had not only a sympathetic audience but also a caring one. John and Jeanne listened, and we knew they would find a way, if one existed, to assist us with whatever problems we vocalized, real and imagined.

Long after receiving our degrees, we have kept in touch with him and continued to admire and appreciate him as mentor and friend. We celebrated his publishing and other prominent successes, which he, as might be expected, delayed until his sons were grown and out on their own. His priorities have always had family at the head of the list. He has become one of the truly prominent Civil War historians in the United States, and though we have always had pride in being his doctoral students, we feel all the more so due to the national recognition he has achieved and richly deserves.

He retired, or tried to, as a William L. Giles Distinguished Professor of History at MSU. He has come out of retirement on more than one occasion and is currently executive director of the Ulysses S. Grant Association. His reputation as a scholar and gentleman certainly played a vital role in bringing the U. S. Grant Papers to MSU. His legacy to the university and to the history profession seems to expand every year.

The idea for this book began with Mike Ballard, John's second doctoral student, and all the contributors quickly jumped on board. Others would have joined us, but their schedules made their participation impossible. Those of us who participated faced our own challenges in getting our chapters done, so the project stretched over a much longer period of time than we expected. We know now that we should have had John set a deadline for us, but then the book would not have been a surprise. But it most assuredly would have been completed much sooner. Finally Mark Cheathem, another Marszalek veteran, volunteered to come on board to help. Ballard put the book together, and at last we achieved the momentum to bring this volume to completion.

We chose race as the theme of the book, and our choice is a reflection of one of John's major fields of historical interest. Most of us had not considered race as an imperative in our varying fields of interest. We knew it was a factor, but John's influence helped us to see that more than a factor, it was vital to any area of study in American history. Thus we took a look at our past and present research and evaluated our contributions within the context of race as a thread that has permeated the evolution of the fabric of America. By word and deed, John inspired us in more ways than we could count and many we are likely not aware of. This book is a reflection of his influence; perhaps now he will fully realize how profound his influence was.

None of us had problems addressing race in the essays included in this volume. Beginning with Mark Cheathem's look at Andrew Jackson Donelson's wrestling with issues of slavery and freedom in keeping his plantations going, the racial theme is next addressed by Thomas D. Cockrell as he explores the frequently elusive undercurrent of Unionist sentiment in Mississippi. Stephen Michot explores racial patters in his native Louisiana area of Lafource and finds that blacks served in both armies while dealing with slavery and freedom. Michael Ballard follows the interaction between Union soldiers and slaves, freedmen, and U.S. Colored troops through the course of the Vicksburg campaign, concluding that sympathy for slaves did not outweigh brutal racist behavior by federal soldiers. Horace Nash finds that sports, specifically boxing, mended racial fences long before the twentieth century, while Timothy Smith demonstrates the somewhat surprising role blacks played in Civilian Conservation Corps work on the Civil War battlefield of Shiloh. James Humphreys concludes with an examination of two prominent twentieth-century historians who struggled to combat the racist Dunning school of Reconstruction.

We especially thank Dr. Edna Greene Medford for contributing the closing chapter. A renowned historian, Dr. Medford is an authority on African American history.

We would like to thank Craig Gill, editor-in-chief of the University Press of Mississippi, for his encouragement when we approached him with this project. The two anonymous readers who evaluated the manuscript provided outstanding evaluations, many incorporated in the final versions of the chapters.

OF TIMES AND RACE

1. SLAVERY, PLANTATION LIFE, AND DEBT IN TENNESSEE AND MISSISSIPPI

The Example of Andrew Jackson Donelson

MARK R. CHEATHEM

AS ANDREW JACKSON DONELSON WALKED ALONG THE HUSHPUCKENA River bordering his plantation in Bolivar County, Mississippi, he contemplated suicide. It would be so easy to slide into the water, he thought to himself; Elizabeth and the children would undoubtedly be better off. As he later recounted these thoughts to his wife, he assured her that he had been able to shake off his depression by reminding himself that he could still prove "useful to you & the dear children." Donelson was not able, however, to avoid reminding both himself and Elizabeth that their future depended upon remedying poor decisions that he had made. "Think of nothing but economy and making something," he wrote his wife. "We are too poor to think of anything but making enough to pay for past follies."[1]

Donelson's admonition to his wife was based on a lifetime of debt and unfulfilled economic success, both linked to his attempts at maintaining a profitable plantation. With his uncle, Andrew Jackson, as his role model, Donelson learned what was expected of him as a member of the southern gentry and a prominent Tennessee family: an honorable reputation; ownership of a plantation and slaves; a public career in the military, law, or politics; and a large family. To some degree, he would obtain all of these expectations, but they were accompanied by significant adversity. His first wife, Emily, would die at age twenty-nine, and several of his children died before reaching adulthood or shortly thereafter. His military and law careers ended before they really began, while his political career, though marked by significant achievements, never reached its full potential.

Donelson's attempts to live the life of a southern planter produced some of his deepest disappointments. As successful as his uncle was at being a plantation owner (at least, until Jackson's adopted son, Andrew Jackson Jr., mucked things up), Donelson was unsuccessful, never mastering his finances. Scholars have previously neglected this particular portion of Donelson's life, focusing much of their attention on his political career. It seems important, however, to understand how the influence of a mentor and a region spurred a southerner to continue embracing, even defending, slavery and plantation life despite a consistent record of personal failure. For Donelson, slavery was, in many ways, the institution that both allowed him to pursue his political aspirations and distracted him from giving them his full attention.

Born in 1799, Donelson grew up in Andrew Jackson's household after his father, Samuel, who was Rachel Jackson's brother, died in 1804. As Donelson was growing up, Uncle, as Jackson's wards called him, provided his nephew with a home and private tutors. When Donelson was old enough, Jackson secured him a spot at the United States Military Academy, and when the cadet graduated second in his class in 1820, Donelson found himself appointed as his uncle's aide-de-camp. Both uncle and nephew saw little future in the military for the aspiring young man, so they decided that Donelson should attend law school at Transylvania University in Lexington, Kentucky. Donelson remained there for a short time, but as the 1824 presidential election neared, the two men again made a joint decision; this time, it was that the nephew should serve the uncle as Jackson positioned himself for the presidency.[2]

During these years of tutelage, Donelson learned from Jackson many of the principles to which he would hold throughout his life. Jackson was not shy in giving his nephew advice on numerous topics. He periodically encouraged Donelson to improve his writing, attend assiduously to his studies, avoid "the society of the viper or base character" and immoral women, and preserve his honor. Jackson also passed along his political ideology, particularly his support for a republican government, based on the will of the majority of the people, that preserved liberty.[3]

Donelson also learned from Jackson the importance of slavery in the life of the southern gentry. As a young man on the rise in North Carolina, Jackson had understood the necessity of slave ownership and had acquired his first laborer, a young woman named Nancy, in 1788. By 1794, he owned fifteen, a number that increased to forty-four by 1820. Jackson's treatment of them could be harsh, such as the one runaway slave for whom he offered an extra reward "for every hundred lashes any person will give him, to the amount of three hundred." At the same time, Jackson could also be paternalistically protective, as he was in 1823 when he expressed to Rachel that he wanted the overseer to make sure that the slaves at his plantation, the Hermitage, were "well fed, & warmly cloathed [sic]" and not "in any way oppressed." From his time on Jackson's plantations and his observations of the treatment of slaves, Donelson understood that his own place in the southern gentry was tied directly to slave acquisition and ownership and the successful use of their labor to build a profitable plantation.[4]

Jackson gave Donelson numerous opportunities to become familiar with the acquisition and supervision of slaves. Donelson engaged in buying slaves for his uncle while at Transylvania University. Jackson gave him specific criteria by which to find the best potential workers. Donelson was to look for "three or four likely negro girls from 15 to 20 [years old] ... or one or two boys, from 12 to 18 years old." They had to be "of good charectour, likely and healthy." Donelson was able to identify three young girls and one young boy whom he believed met his uncle's standards for potential slaves at the Hermitage. Financial considerations convinced Jackson to postpone the purchase, but the experience gave Donelson practical experience for his own future slave acquisitions.[5]

Donelson's chance to put his knowledge into personal practice came in 1824, when Jackson gave his nephew a substantial wedding gift: the deed to 348 1/4 acres of land and a male slave named John Fulton. This gift was significant in allowing Donelson to establish a plantation, which he called Springdale, and himself as a member of the gentry. Donelson's father and maternal grandfather had bequeathed hundreds of acres of land to the young man and his brother, Daniel, but their stepfather, James Sanders, was disputing their control over that land. Thus, Jackson's cession of land and slave gave Donelson his first real chance to prove his worth as an independent southern planter. Donelson was not quite independent, however. The land that he received was adjacent to the Hermitage, allowing him to remain at his uncle's disposal. Donelson was also on his uncle's payroll, having given up his law practice to focus on the presidential campaign shortly establishing a firm in downtown Nashville.[6]

Donelson also learned from Jackson the power of the slave master. Shortly after taking office as territorial governor of Florida in 1821, Jackson sent an order to Donelson instructing him to oversee the punishment of a slave named Betty. According to Rachel Jackson, Betty, her personal slave, was "putting on some airs" and disobeying her orders by washing clothing for neighbors. Andrew Jackson was unhappy with her insubordination and wanted Donelson to make sure that she was disciplined. "I have directed [house steward Ephraim A. Blain] that [at] the first disobedience of orders, that she be publicly whipped," he informed Donelson. "She can behave herself if she will & I have told her that publicly whipped she shall be [at] the first offence." Jackson wanted his nephew to "observe her conduct and [at] the first disobedience or impudence under Mr Blain to give her fifty lashes and if he does not perform it, dismiss him, & as soon as I get possession I will order a corporal to give it to her publickly, I am determined to cure her." There is no record of whether Donelson had to carry out Jackson's orders, but the lesson was clear.[7]

Donelson had another opportunity to observe this lesson at the Hermitage, Jackson's Nashville plantation. Jackson owned a male slave named Gilbert, who frequently ran away. During one of Gilbert's flights from the Hermitage, Donelson helped Jackson write a newspaper advertisement for his return, describing the runaway slave as "about thirty years old . . . stout made, very short neck, & broad across the shoulders," with missing teeth and at least two scars. Gilbert's rebelliousness finally cost him his life in August 1827. After being recaptured, Jackson's overseer, Ira Walton, attempted to whip Gilbert. The slave, however, attacked Walton, who in return stabbed him several times, resulting in Gilbert's death. When Jackson heard of the incident, he gathered nine men from the community, including Donelson, to judge if Walton had acted in self-defense. The men determined that he had, and a grand jury subsequently agreed that the overseer was not at fault. The lesson was obvious: the slave, particularly one who challenged the owner's power, was at the bottom of the plantation hierarchy.[8]

The 1820s inculcated in Donelson the expectations of him as a slave owner. Slavery, with all of its dehumanizing aspects, was going to be a part of the fabric of his daily life as a southern planter. Like his uncle, Donelson understood that slavery was indispensable to helping him achieve and preserve his status among the gentry. It provided the order and stability that was necessary for the preservation of a white-dominated southern society. He learned that patriarchy, with its inherent propensity toward violence and exaggerated displays of power, was as much as part of plantation life as was paternalism. Jackson, whom one contemporary considered an "excellent master to his slaves," was the model that Donelson would try to emulate.⁹

While Donelson was able to spend several years enjoying traditional plantation life, Jackson's political career eventually forced him to become an absentee planter. When Jackson won the presidential election of 1828, he asked Donelson and his wife, Emily, who was also Jackson's niece, to accompany him. Being a successful planter required finding a dependable overseer, particularly when one was absent for months at a time, as Donelson would be. On the day that he left for Washington in January 1829, Donelson, along with Jackson, signed a contract with Graves Steele in which they authorized the latter to oversee their plantations that year, with the possibility of extending his service. One of Jackson's business associates, Charles J. Love, informed Donelson that Steele treated the slaves well and that their crops were promising. Relative James G. Martin wrote him otherwise, indicating that while Steele had "little trouble" with Jackson's slaves, he had encountered "some" with Donelson's. Donelson chose to relieve Steele of further duties on his plantation, in part because the overseer wanted more money for managing both plantations. Donelson's next several choices as overseer proved no more satisfactory.¹⁰

Donelson experienced some success as a planter, however, as his purchase of slaves during this period indicates. Before leaving for Washington, Donelson bought seven slaves from his brother-in-law, John C. McLemore. With Jackson's help, he acquired two more slaves (a young boy and girl) in early 1831. From the scattered plantation records that Donelson left, it appears that his slaves suffered the usual maladies. Some even ran away, an action that produced concern among southern planters, including Donelson, who often expressed consternation at the lack of loyalty displayed.¹¹

Donelson discovered that plantation life brought other headaches with it as well. He struggled to keep his Haywood County, Tennessee, plantation, which he had received from Jackson in the mid-1820s in a land exchange, afloat in the early 1830s. Unpaid taxes led the local sheriff to put that plantation up for auction two successive years. Donelson convinced one of his business associates to pay the taxes for him and promised to reimburse him at a future date. Only in his early thirties, Donelson was already finding that owning a plantation and slaves was no guarantee of financial success. Whether he consciously admitted it to himself, he was also realizing that he did not possess the financial acumen that planters found crucial to turning a profit.¹²

Donelson's shortcomings as a planter were unfortunate, especially considering his growing family. Between 1826 and 1834, Andrew and Emily welcomed two sons and two daughters into their family. As his family grew, Donelson believed that "farming," as he called it, promised a more profitable source of future income than any that he had found in working for the government of the United States. Initially, Jackson had written Donelson personal checks to cover his family's expenses while in Washington; this financial support largely ended in March 1833 when his nephew landed a position in the General Land Office signing public land warrants for a monthly salary of $125. Such modest income was insufficient for someone who considered himself a member of elite southern society, although given Donelson's questionable financial decisions, he was fortunate to have it. Still, Donelson was devoted to enhancing his personal fortunes as a planter and providing for his family. With Jackson's help, from 1834 to 1836, he was able to build an attractive Greek Revival mansion on his plantation, renamed Poplar Grove, that attested to his status as an up-and-coming member of the Middle Tennessee gentry.[13]

Jackson left office in 1837, but Donelson had already returned to Tennessee because of Emily's bout with tuberculosis, which eventually led to her death in December 1836. Throughout the rest of the 1830s and into the 1840s, he worked for the Democratic party at the state level and tried his hand at becoming a successful planter. In 1838, he purchased a plantation in Chickasaw County, Mississippi, partially through a loan financed by President Martin Van Buren. Donelson found that the Panic of 1837 and its aftereffects, along with his own faulty decisions, were threatening his future as a planter. By 1840, he was at least $15,000 in debt (and possibly more) and again looked to Van Buren for additional financial help. Jackson even felt compelled to intercede for Donelson, assuring the president that his nephew's plantations, crops, and slaves were worth at least $60,000. Van Buren was able to offer some assistance, but Donelson's tardiness in repaying these loans eventually led the two men to part ways.[14]

Donelson found potential financial relief in another form when he married his second cousin, Elizabeth Martin Randolph, in 1841. Elizabeth was the daughter of Catherine Donelson, Emily Donelson's older sister. In 1835, she had married Meriwether Lewis Randolph, one of Thomas Jefferson's grandsons. Randolph had accepted Jackson's appointment to become the territorial secretary of Arkansas in February 1835, but his premature death two years later left Elizabeth a widow with control over the several thousand acres of Arkansas land. For a man who struggled to make ends meet, this potential wealth undoubtedly played some role in Donelson's decision to pursue Elizabeth.[15]

Andrew and Elizabeth began their marriage at the Poplar Grove plantation and would eventually have eight children together. Donelson's financial problems simply would not go away, however. While working for the Democratic party during the 1844 nominating convention and presidential campaign, during which he supported fellow Tennessean and familiar colleague James K. Polk, Donelson frequently found himself distracted by his debts and plantation problems. At critical political moments, when one would have expected Donelson to enter the fray, he was off in Mississippi looking after his plantation or neglecting campaign duties in order to write requests for more loans. In fact, he was in Mississippi in the late summer of 1844 when President John Tyler selected him to replace the deceased Tilghman A. Howard as chargé d'affaires to the Republic of Texas, a position that would allow Donelson to play a significant role in that country's annexation to the United States.[16]

Donelson accepted the appointment with appropriate reluctance, telling Calhoun that it would come "at a great sacrifice of my private interests." He assured the secretary of state, however, that "[a]s a good citizen ... I could not withhold my aid" and agreed to leave for Texas as soon as he could. As a condition of his acceptance, however, Donelson asked that he be allowed to return home during the winter "to complete the arrangement of my private affairs." His last statement revealed his practical purpose for taking the position: although he supported annexation, Donelson needed the money. His financial problems were well known enough that John C. Calhoun's South Carolina friend, James Hamilton Jr., wrote the secretary of state that "some domestic circumstance [i.e., his financial debts] may make it inconvenient for Major Donelson to accept the mission." In fact, just the opposite was true. Van Buren had already written Donelson that year begging him to pay his long-standing debt. Jackson wrote back that his nephew had accepted the mission, and "[t]he Major requested me to say to you, that as he passed thro[ugh] Neworleans [sic], he would make arrangements, based upon his cotton crop, to remit to his N. York debt six thousand dollars." When Francis P. Blair also wrote Jackson, asking about one of Donelson's bank drafts that "had not been punctually paid, and ...

[was] protested," the general assured his old friend that Donelson would pay the debt. "The Major has had great trouble . . . in mon[e]y Matters [*sic*]," he notified Blair.¹⁷

Even during his months in Texas, Donelson found it impossible to devote his full attention to the important question at hand. In the middle of discussions needed to convince the Texas government to join the United States, he took two leaves of absence to tend to business affairs in Tennessee and Mississippi. Donelson's financial circumstances were so pressing that Jackson suggested selling the Mississippi plantation as a way to pay off his debts. Donelson rejected his uncle's proposition, still hoping to turn the plantation into a profit maker. Jackson's situation was not much better. "Poverty stares us in the face," the General lamented. Low cotton prices undermined any chance that Donelson had of making a profit, and Jackson's own financial problems meant he would be unable to help his nephew pay off his creditors.¹⁸

To secure him a more profitable government appointment, there was considerable discussion of Donelson taking over the *Washington Globe*, the Democratic newspaper in the nation's capital, or of President-elect Polk placing him in his cabinet. Neither of these ideas resulted in Donelson's appointment, however, partly by his own choice but largely because of Jackson's interference. As Donelson wrote Polk during discussions about the cabinet appointment, "My only ambition is to repair now, by a life of economy, the mistakes of early years, and lay up, if possible, something for the education of my children, and the support of old age." Weeks later, in rejecting the offer of the *Globe*'s editorship, he reiterated to the new president his concern about his personal finances. His "chief solicitude" now, Donelson told Polk, was "to repair the losses to which I have been subjected by a long connection with politics. In this respect[,] my position has been unfortunate, borne along as you have been aware by circumstances from which I could not separate without apparent harshness to the Genl [Jackson]."¹⁹

Donelson was referring in this letter to his complicated relationship with his uncle. The man who had raised him to be a profitable member of the southern gentry had lost faith in his nephew over the years. The change in their relationship resulted from the infamous Eaton affair of Jackson's first administration, a scandal involving the controversial marriage of John H. Eaton, Jackson's close friend and choice for the secretary of war post, and Margaret O'Neale Eaton, a notorious Washington widower. The scandal split Jackson's advisors, with some supporting the president and Eaton, while others, including Donelson, took the opposing side. Jackson and Donelson barely tolerated living together during this scandal, periodically exchanging angry letters and conversations over the course of a year. To justify their opposing stances, both men employed arguments that centered on the concept of honor, an important code of conduct that undergirded southern society.[20]

While the rift was eventually resolved, Jackson and Donelson never completely reconciled; yet, they also could not live without each other. Jackson continued to rely on his nephew to maintain his correspondence and write speeches for him, and Donelson continued to look for his uncle's help to advance as a politician and as a planter. That assistance came less and less often in monetary form, which may have forced Donelson to look for other sources of credit, such as Martin Van Buren, to increase his chances of success. He may also have devoted so much attention to his personal affairs to prove to his uncle that he had inculcated the lessons of his childhood and early adulthood regarding the planter class—namely, independence, masculinity, and patriarchy.

Jackson's death in June 1845 decisively severed their strained relationship. In what must have been a devastating blow to Donelson's expectations regarding his own economic future, Jackson's final will, last amended in June 1843, bequeathed to him only a sword given to the Hero of New Orleans by the state of Tennessee. His uncle's original will, composed in 1833, had left to Donelson land, slaves, cash, and the sword. In the end, however, everything of monetary value went to Andrew Jackson Jr., Jackson's adopted son, something that the General said he did because it was what Rachel would have wanted. The ceremonial sword and Jackson's admonition to use it "in support and protection of our glorious Union" did nothing to alleviate Donelson's precarious finances.[21]

Donelson seemed even more intent on proving himself as a planter after Jackson died. To do so, however, he had to find a source of capital that would get him back on his feet financially. That source appeared in the form of an appointment as minister to Prussia, which promised to pay him an annual salary of $9,000, plus an extra $9,000 to cover moving and other expenses. This remuneration would be double that of Donelson's Texas mission, and he confidently predicted to Elizabeth that "with the same economy that we have practiced [sic], something will be made by the movement."[22]

This appointment and its accompanying salary came at a fortuitous time, as creditors were once again pressing Donelson for payment. He considered selling his Mississippi plantation in 1845 but decided that the low price of cotton made it unprofitable to do so at the time. Finding no financial salvation in Mississippi, Donelson turned to another possible source of income: the Arkansas land that Elizabeth had brought into their marriage. Efforts to sell part of that land, however, netted him only $906, none of it in cash and most of it paid in installments stretched over four years. This amount was hardly the windfall that Donelson had expected, and he was forced to resort to taking out new loans to pay off old creditors, a recourse to which he had repeatedly turned over the years to stay solvent.[23]

Despite his experience as chargé to Texas, Donelson was ill prepared to take on the task at the American legation in Berlin, even without the revolutionary events that would envelop the German states during his tenure. He made his job more difficult by spending much of his time and energy worrying about his personal investments back in the States. Shortly after arriving in Berlin, Donelson received warnings from relatives that his finances back home were dangerously weak. Daniel, who was overseeing his brother's business while he was away, wrote Donelson that he needed to send $10,000 immediately to begin paying off his debts, which he estimated at $17,300. Daniel advised his brother to secure a $25,000 loan, which he could then use, with the profits from the year's cotton crop, to stabilize his position. His brother-in-law, James G. Martin Jr., reported that while the cotton crop looked promising, he had been unable to sell more land in Arkansas. By July 1847, Daniel was warning his brother that he either had to sell some of his property or mortgage his land and property to pay off debts that had risen to nearly $25,000.[24]

With these warnings in mind, Donelson began clamoring for a leave of absence to return to the United States, but he had to settle for meetings in London with old friend Robert Armstrong, who tried unsuccessfully to obtain more loans for him. Daniel must have secured some money for his brother, or perhaps cotton crops made a larger profit than expected; in either case, Donelson let the issue lie until February 1848, when he requested a two-month leave of absence, claiming that he barely possessed enough money to enable his son, Jackson, to purchase passage to Berlin. Polk denied Donelson's request because of the outbreak of the French Revolution but promised him that, if the situation in Europe calmed by the summer, he could return for a short time. In relating his difficulties to Jackson, Donelson was uncharacteristically introspective. He strongly advised his son to take care of his finances, even telling him to record daily expenditures to keep from accruing debt. "Let it be your maxim in the commencement of your career to live within your means," he told his oldest son. "Consider that the basis of all morality and religion. The fatal error in my life was to be seduced into habits which were beyond my income."[25]

Donelson continued to grouse about the lack of a leave, even after the German states were thrown into chaos by their own revolutions in March and April. When the German states began discussing unification that spring and summer, he was astute enough to ask for an additional, concurrent diplomatic post to the provisional government in Frankfort. Donelson hoped that his salary would double, from $9,000 to $18,000, and that he would receive an extra outfit of $9,000. The additional money would not only defray the expenses that Donelson faced while trying to sustain what was now a family of eight, but it would also allow him to pay his debts in the United States. After conferring with President Polk, Secretary of State James Buchanan gave him the additional post but without the expected additional compensation. Donelson's disgruntlement with this arrangement would eventually poison his relationship with Buchanan and his successor, John M. Clayton. The minister's recall in October 1849 was a relief for all involved.[26]

Donelson returned to a nation debating slavery, an issue about which he had said very little in his private or public lives until that point. That he had said little is not surprising when one considers that many antebellum southerners unquestioningly accepted its existence until it was attacked by northern abolitionists or foreign observers intent on pointing out the United States' hypocrisy. While in the German states during the Mexican-American War of 1846–48, Donelson had found some occasion to defend the institution in discussions with politicians there. For example, when Alexander von Humboldt, Prussian king Friedrich Wilhelm IV's personal advisor, had identified slavery as a potential obstacle to United States success in its war with Mexico, Donelson had set him straight: "[I]f let alone, it [expansion] will be found to be the amelioration of a necessary servitude, in the direction of which the U. States ought to be applauded rather than censured." Donelson further bragged that, by employing slave labor, his nation "will have accomplished more for the black race than all the nations of the earth can ever expect to do for the same race, existing as a separate people in Africa." Instead of slavery threatening the American republic, he argued, it strengthened the United States by spreading its institutions to a "less-enlightened" people and keeping republican government, for white men, intact.[27]

Rather than critically evaluate his own region and its own employment of slavery, Donelson instead found hypocrisy among northern abolitionists and Whig party members. In 1848, when John C. Calhoun had sent Donelson his speech opposing American involvement on the Yucatan Peninsula, the American minister had replied, "the institution of slavery[,] if abandoned in the Tropical regions[,] will leave the Anglo Saxon as incapable there of maintaining his true character as it has left the Spaniard in Mexico." "The only inquiry," Donelson declared, "is whether it is better for humanity that that portion of the world should relapse into a savage negro & Indian state, or be gradually improved by permitting the white man to continue the civilization which he is capable of enforcing as a legitimate superior of the negroe [sic] or Indian."[28]

Donelson's criticism of those politically opposed to slavery gave a clear indication of his view of African American slaves. The self-righteous claims by northern free-soilers, such as his former friend Van Buren, that they were helping both African Americans and whites rang hollow to Donelson. Legislation touting "free soil" was, to him, "an idle boast, not benefitting [sic] the black race but punishing the white man who has had the humanity to protect it[.]" Donelson's time in Germany had "satisfied" him "that this institution of ours called slavery, has had an agency in shaping our institutions which few of us in the South even sufficiently appreciate."

> The presence of the black race in the United States enabled the white man to treat as his equal all his own race. A basis was thus formed for liberty as broad as the population; and hence popular sovereignty was a reality, not a fiction. The absence of such a basis in Europe is the secret of the failure of all its attempts to found popular institutions.... This is only saying that in my judgement [sic], if slavery be an evil as recognized by us in the South, it is one which has been sent by Providence, and our Northern friends ought long ago to have learned that their remedies for it, even if successful, would only doom them as well as ourselves to dangers far more threatening to our common liberty and prosperity.[29]

Shortly after Donelson's return in 1850, then, when southerners called together the Nashville Convention to debate congressional legislation limiting slavery's expansion, Donelson found himself in a tenuous position. Like his uncle, he had for years been a staunch and outspoken supporter of the Union, but as a southern planter dependent on slave labor for his well-being, he had more than just Unionist ideology to consider. In 1850, fifty-year-old Donelson held sixty-six slaves and owned 1,200 acres, valued at $47,000 in Tennessee, plus an unknown number of slaves on his Mississippi plantation. Owning slaves was a normal part of Donelson's life and livelihood, and like many wealthy southerners, he based his defense of slavery on two fundamental tenets: the inferiority of Africans and the necessity of their enslavement to preserve republican principles, including the sanctity of the Union.[30]

As the most well-known relative of the late Andrew Jackson, who had stared down the nullifiers in 1832–33, Donelson must have known that he would be expected to play a prominent role in the regional meeting near his home. A meeting of interested Davidson County men resulted in his appointment as president of their delegation and his selection as a state delegate to the larger convention. Mindful of his close association with northern politicians, Donelson denied that the convention delegates intended to "interfere with slavery as it was regulated by the framers of the constitution." He believed northerners understood that "neither their true interests nor those of their country can be advanced by any imitation of the conduct of foreign nations," such as Great Britain, toward slavery.[31]

Moderate delegates probably expected Donelson to help fashion a compromise suitable for comparison to the one that ended the Nullification Crisis. Instead, Donelson disappeared during the convention's two meetings in June and November, not making a public statement until after Henry Clay and Stephen Douglas had formulated the Compromise of 1850 and the Nashville delegates were wrapping up their last session. Seeing the conversation moving in a decidedly fire-eating direction, Donelson introduced resolutions calling for adherence to the compromise legislation by both North and South and supporting secession only when the federal government became "the instrument of intolerable tyranny and oppression." When it appeared that delegates were going to ignore his suggestions and approve a preamble and resolutions that denounced the compromise legislation and implicitly advocated secession, Donelson angrily demanded the floor to speak. The convention chair rejected his plea, however, and closed the meeting.[32]

A few days later, a group of Davidson County Unionists from both parties, led by Donelson and several others, met in Nashville. Donelson was a member of the resolutions committee that composed nine resolutions, based on those that he had presented at the convention, passed by the assembly. The audience called for Donelson to speak, which he agreed to do. In a speech filled with republican imagery and references to his uncle, he denounced divisive politics that sought the dismembering of the Union. Nevertheless, Donelson could not completely escape the pull of his social class and its dependence on the institution of slavery. He admitted that secession, horrible as the thought was to him, might one day take place if northern politicians attempted to abolish slavery. When they did, he believed there would be "revolution" and a reshaping of the United States' government: "The sword then becomes the arbiter." No one could predict how such a revolution would conclude, but Donelson warned that ancient and modern history taught that "the objects of war are generally lost by the efforts of war." Secession, then, should be avoided if possible; southerners would not find their answer in that course of action, he concluded.[33]

Donelson continued these themes the next year when he took over the editorship of the *Washington Union*. During his thirteen-month tenure as editor of this influential national newspaper, Donelson, through his avowed platform based on the Constitution and the Union, attempted to steer the Democratic party toward moderation and away from the secessionist impulse that was becoming more prevalent within the party, while at the same time battling Millard Fillmore's Whig administration. Unfortunately for Donelson, he found it difficult to please any of his party's factions, and the job that he thought would make him a substantial amount of money to pay off his nearly $40,000 debt ended abruptly in May 1852 with Donelson and his financial partner, Robert Armstrong, under congressional investigation for improperly receiving government contracts. This unceremonious end embittered Donelson against the Democratic party, prompting him eventually to seek other political associates in the Know-Nothing, or American, party.[34]

From late 1852 to early 1855, Donelson focused on "the cares and vexations incident to the return to a farmer[']s life." The Tulip Grove plantation was producing well, he informed his oldest son, despite the sickness that had stricken his slaves and others in the neighborhood. The news from his plantation in Chickasaw County, Mississippi, was just as satisfactory. Donelson predicted that in two years, he would be completely free of debt and able to take care of his wife and children for the rest of their lives. His confidence was such that he rejected an offer to sell the Mississippi plantation. Later that year, however, it became clear that the crops would fail, so he changed his mind, eventually selling the Chickasaw County land and slaves.[35]

Donelson returned to politics in 1855 when he began campaigning for the Know-Nothing party. The party's general reluctance to address the slavery issue helped ameliorate Donelson's own conflicting thoughts on the institution's divisiveness. His campaign speeches doggedly attacked threats to the Union, particularly singling out President Franklin Pierce and the Democratic presidential nominee in 1856 and Donelson's former political ally, James Buchanan. They were effective enough to garner Donelson the vice presidential slot on the Know-Nothing ticket, which was headed by Millard Fillmore, the former president whom he had attacked for months while serving as the *Union* editor. This ticket failed to carry the day against Buchanan and the Republican party nominee, John C. Frémont. With the Democrats in control of the presidency and the influence of the Know-Nothings waning, Donelson retreated from national politics.

Following the 1856 election, Donelson spent the next few years once again occupied in efforts to salvage his financial situation. In early 1857, Donelson purchased 1,579 acres of land in the Australia Landing/Duncan community of Bolivar County, Mississippi, located in the delta region of the state, southwest of Memphis. Situated on the east bank of the Hushpuckena River, this plantation reportedly cost Donelson $46,358, an enormous sum of money considering his financial travails.[36]

Donelson, however, was committed to making a living as a planter, traveling between his Tulip Grove and Bolivar County plantations throughout 1857. He was reminded frequently that the life of the planter was not always pleasant or easy. For one thing, slaves were not always submissive. In June 1857, Donelson reported to Elizabeth that one of his slaves, a man named Payman, had assaulted the overseer at the Bolivar County plantation, when the latter "corrected" the former's pregnant wife by whipping her. "Payman slipped up behind him [the overseer] and struck him in the head several blows leaving him senseless on the ground," Donelson recounted. The overseer was slowly recovering from the assault, but Payman had run away. The overseer's "accident," as Donelson described it, had caused the other slaves to slow down their work, and he was having considerable difficulty keeping them under his control. "The negroes have a plenty [*sic*] to eat and to wear. They have coffee and molasses, and vegetables of every description, yet they are not satisfied," he remarked incredulously, "and I fear that I shall find some of them in the woods in a few days." The problem, according to Donelson, was that in Mississippi, "they miss the groggeries in our neighborhood, and have no chance to steal." Overall, he concluded, "the amount of land necessary to make it [his plantation] profitable, and the difficulty of managing the negroes, are quite discouraging." Later that fall, he observed to his wife that "the negroes have improved a little, but they take fresh chills nearly as fast as I send them to the field." These illnesses may have been real, as Donelson supposed, or, more likely, they were an indication of indirect rebellion on the part of the slaves.[37]

Donelson also discovered that national economic cycles and past indebtedness made plantation life difficult to manage. Pressured to pay his personal debts and state property taxes, which by his account were enormous, and disowned by Middle Tennessee family and friends who considered him a traitor to the Democratic party, in early 1857, Donelson placed his Tulip Grove plantation on the market. He eventually found a buyer in April 1858 in the person of Mark R. Cockrill, a successful wool producer, who purchased Donelson's 1,063 acres in Tennessee for $53,000. In addition to paying off some of his many debts, Donelson also hoped to use the profit from the sale of the Tulip Grove land to finance the Mississippi plantation that he had recently purchased. After finalizing the sale, Donelson moved his family to Memphis, where Elizabeth and the children stayed while he traveled between the city and the Bolivar County plantation.[38]

The Panic of 1857 undermined Donelson's optimism about success in Mississippi. He had wanted to keep his land because of its potential profitability, believing that its value would soon exceed fifty dollars per acre. While selling the Tulip Grove land, Donelson also explored the possibility of doing the same with his Mississippi plantation, "one of the best in the South," but he abandoned the idea when it became apparent he could not find a buyer willing to pay the requested price of forty dollars per acre. (Donelson was overly optimistic in his appraisal, as the average value of an acre of Bolivar County land in 1860 was only $29.03.)[39]

Donelson found time in the midst of farming life to make one last foray into national politics. In 1859, he joined the Opposition party in Tennessee, which supported the Constitutional Union ticket in the 1860 presidential election. Elected as a state delegate from Tennessee, Donelson traveled to Baltimore, where he helped nominate John Bell, his and Andrew Jackson's old nemesis, and Edward Everett. Bell and Everett ran against two separate Democratic tickets, headed by Stephen A. Douglas and John C. Breckenridge, and the Republican nominee, Abraham Lincoln. Donelson believed that if voters elected the Bell-Everett tandem, then "the country will be restored to its ancient traqnquility [sic]. The laws will be enforced. All sectional controversy will cease, and the prosperity and welfare of the people will be secured." He was unable to prove his argument, as Lincoln and the Republicans carried the day, and several southern states moved to secede.[40]

As Tennesseans watched their fellow southerners leaving the Union, Donelson continued to urge caution and support for the Union. He also reportedly stated that "if the Rebellion was carried out, and a civil war broke out," then he would be "bound by interest to follow the fortunes of the South." At the same time, he also warned southerners that "the Rebellion would be the overthrow of Slavery on the american [sic] continent." Once South Carolina troops fired on Fort Sumter and Lincoln issued a call for 75,000 militia troops from those states still in the Union to resist this insurrection, however, Donelson was forced to choose sides and, with the majority of Tennesseans, he left the United States. "You know how earnestly I have endeavored to avert the calamities which have come upon us," he reminded his daughter, Mary. "But it has all been in vain. Sectional animosity has at last destroyed the Union, and no alternative is left the patriot but the assertion of the rights which belong to a free people. When the invader comes[,] we must meet him as we did the British in the Revolutionary War." Donelson warned her to "prepare ... for the trials to which you may be subjected by the folly of those Demagogues who have brought the present ruin upon the country." He seemed not to recognize the role of slavery in precipitating the conflict and his own decision to support secession.[41]

Throughout the war, Donelson enjoyed a relatively friendly relationship with the United States and its military representatives, while his association with the Confederate States slowly deteriorated. Union soldiers allowed him to move freely between Memphis and his Bolivar County plantation, although there were times when he had to ask Union officers for permission to travel. On one occasion in late 1862, Donelson mentioned his displeasure with "Lincolnites" who visited his slaves and likely gave them news of the impending Emancipation Proclamation. In January 1865, as the war neared an end, he complained that United States soldiers and refugees, both black and white, were tearing down fences and "interfer[ing] with our comforts" and would leave the South "desolated." Otherwise, his complaints about the United States military occupation of his state and region were few.[42]

Donelson saved his harshest comments for Confederate soldiers and their government. In August 1862, Confederate officials had him arrested, reportedly for his continuing call for an end to the war. Donelson also hated the Confederate policy of burning cotton and taking farm animals to keep them from Union troops, which affected him personally. Both acts were common occurrences that compelled him to hide his cotton bales in order to salvage something for the market. In 1864, he complained to his oldest daughter, "[t]he Confederates have injured me more than the Yankees, by burning my cotton and pressing my stock." Donelson's frustration with the Confederate government increased as the war progressed. "The foolish policy of the Confederate Govt in burning cotton and destroying our stock in the bottom has damaged me immensely. I have lost by this policy more than 300 bales of cotton and all the Negroes which they pressed from me under the pretences of carrying provisions to Vicksburgh [sic]." In the Mississippi Delta region, Confederate "bushwhackers and Guerillas [argue] that it is better to destroy crops than to let the Yankees get them. They are very willing themselves to take the cotton and trade it for supplies," Donelson bitterly grumbled, "but seem to forget that the families who are dependent for their support upon this cotton ought to have the benefit of it."[43]

Donelson obviously resented the effect of Confederate policy on his economic potential, but his complaints did not always mesh with reality. The Civil War years were, in fact, some of his most profitable. Ironically, concerns about moving his crops, especially cotton, to market disappeared as the war lengthened. Early in 1864, he believed that cotton prices, which were at sixty cents per pound, would net him a profit of $10,000 on that year's crop. In August 1864, he confidently predicted that, if he could keep the Confederates from destroying his cotton crop, it would "make me as much money as I want." It is unclear whether or not Donelson made the profit that he expected, but either way, he still owed enormous debts, which were alleviated somewhat in November 1864 by a significant inheritance of Middle Tennessee land from his brother-in-law and cousin, William Donelson.⁴⁴

Worse than losing cotton and slaves were the personal losses that Donelson experienced as a result of the war. His estranged brother and Confederate brigadier general, Daniel, died near Knoxville in April 1863. In September of that year, Donelson's son, John, was killed at the Battle of Chickamauga, after having fought at Shiloh and suffering a wound at Murfreesboro. Five months later, his son-in-law, John Wilcox, died in Richmond, Virginia, of a heart condition, no doubt exacerbated by the stress of fighting. The biggest blow came in January 1864, when Donelson's son, Daniel, a Confederate soldier, was murdered in De Soto County, Mississippi, while on furlough, allegedly for his horse and boots. The murderer, reportedly a Confederate soldier or bushwhacker, left Daniel's body on the side of the road, where it lay for three months before Donelson learned of his death and traveled from nearby Memphis to recover it. Daniel's murder was never solved.⁴⁵

The end of the war was in many ways a relief to Donelson. He did find it necessary afterward to defend his conduct during the war. On the one hand, some individuals had accused him of betraying his principles by becoming a rabid secessionist; on the other hand, some accused him of conveying contraband for the United States. "I have been represented as lately a member of the Confederate Congress, an active secessionist . . . [and] a refugee to the Federal lines seeking the protection of the Amnesty Oath of President Lincoln," Donelson informed readers of the *Memphis Argus*. "All such statements are unfounded and unjust." Federal troops had allowed him to travel freely to his Bolivar County plantation and "to purchase and transport such articles of necessity as would enable me to support the negroes who chose to remain with me."⁴⁶

Donelson approved of the social and political changes in Tennessee and the nation, but he still urged moderation. In September 1865, he gave his public support to President Andrew Johnson, who now represented the moderates. Donelson was not quite moderate on the issue of African American freedom, however. He publicly stated his satisfaction with the Freedmen's Bureau, but in 1866, according to one historian, he ignored attempts by conservative Unionists to use his name in support of their campaign to attract black voters. Donelson's final political foray, in fact, focused on the issue of African American suffrage, a subject about which he gave ambivalent signs. In 1867, he was elected as a delegate to a meeting of Davidson County Conservatives, where he became one of three vice presidents of the Conservative state convention. The Conservatives' speeches seemingly indicated that they supported black suffrage, which they actually opposed, and the restoration of republican government, which Donelson undoubtedly approved. Conservatives lost the fall elections by large margins, and Donelson finally retired from political life.[47]

Now solely a farmer, Donelson found the transition from slave labor to free labor difficult to accept, both politically and personally. In 1869, after watching Mississippi's "negroe loving [sic] democracy" put African Americans in office, he told Elizabeth that it was "terrible to contemplate the future if what is called democracy in the south [sic] succeeds in giving office and power to the negroe [sic]." With two farms to maintain (one in Mississippi, one in Tennessee), realizing a profit in what was a difficult period for any southern farmer to grow crops, while also paying former slaves wages, stretched Donelson's finances to their limits. His oldest living son, Martin, resided in nearby Duncan, Mississippi, and attempted to help his busy father, who traveled among Bolivar County, Nashville, and Memphis. Donelson often complained to Martin and Elizabeth that African American workers on the Mississippi plantation were troublesome. Local whites, including one man who was hired to oversee the farm's operation, "put it into their head that something is due to them for service in past years." "They would steal all that we have if not watched," he assured Elizabeth. Still, their discontent threatened to impede Donelson's attempts at farming, so he was forced to "deal liberally" with them.[48]

Much of Donelson's worrying about his labor force was tied directly to his concern about his plantation's profitability. He often vacillated, sometimes from one week to the next, over whether or not his ventures would be a success or a failure. His crops, which included corn, potatoes, wheat, and cotton, seemed to net him but little profit. By 1870, his debts were once again approximately $10,000 and probably higher. With his African American help expressing their dissatisfaction, Donelson considered employing immigrant Chinese workers, who would work at a cheaper rate, or even renting out his land to former slaves.[49]

The anxiety of worrying about past mistakes and troublesome labor, combined with persistent health problems, finally taxed Donelson's body beyond its limitations. On the afternoon of June 25, 1871, he became ill and left his Bolivar County plantation for Memphis to receive medical treatment. The next evening, Donelson died. His life ended as he had always lived it, however—in debt. Creditors forced Elizabeth, who died only two months later, to vacate the Bolivar County plantation in order to sell it; her late husband had left $26,000 in debts that needed paying. Not surprisingly, at the time of his death, Donelson was still battling the financial demons that had shadowed him all his adult life.[50]

Notes

A version of this chapter was previously published as Mark R. Cheathem, "Slavery, Plantation Life, and Debt in Antebellum Tennessee and Mississippi: The Example of Andrew Jackson Donelson," *West Tennessee Historical Society Papers* 61 (2007): 32–61.

1. Andrew J. Donelson to Elizabeth R. Donelson, June 19, 1869, Andrew Jackson-Jackson Donelson Collection, Joint University Libraries, Nashville, Tennessee (hereafter cited as JDC).
2. For background on Donelson's childhood, education, and career, see Robert B. Satterfield, "Andrew Jackson Donelson: A Moderate Nationalist Jacksonian" (Ph.D. diss., Johns Hopkins University, 1961); and Mark R. Cheathem, *Old Hickory's Nephew: The Life of Andrew Jackson Donelson* (Baton Rouge: Louisiana State University Press, 2007).
3. Andrew Jackson to Andrew J. Donelson, February 24, 1817, in Harold D. Moser, David R. Hoth, and George H. Hoemann, eds., *The Papers of Andrew Jackson, Volume IV, 1816–1820* (Knoxville: University of Tennessee Press, 1994), 91–92. Following initial citation, these volumes hereafter cited as *PAJ*.
4. Hendrik Booraem, *Young Hickory: The Making of Andrew Jackson* (Dallas: Taylor, 2001), 127–28, 185–86; "Record of Slave Sale," November 17, 1788, and "Tax Assessment," October 1, 1798, in Sam B. Smith and Harriet Chappell Owsley, eds., *The Papers of Andrew Jackson, Volume I, 1770–1803* (Knoxville: University of Tennessee Press, 1980), 15, 210–11; "Advertisement for Runaway Slave," [September 26, 1804], in Harold D. Moser, Sharon Macpherson, and Charles F. Bryan Jr., eds., *The Papers of Andrew Jackson, Volume II, 1804–1813* (Knoxville: University of Tennessee Press, 1984), 40–41; Andrew Jackson to Rachel Jackson, December 11, 1823, in Moser, Hoth, and Hoemann, eds., *Papers of Andrew Jackson*, 4:324–25; Robert V. Remini, *Andrew Jackson and the Course of American Empire, 1767–1821*, Vol. 1 (New York: Harper and Row, 1977), 133–34; and Matthew S. Warshauer, "Andrew Jackson: Chivalric Slave Master," *Tennessee Historical Quarterly* 65 (Fall 2006): 202–28.
5. Andrew Jackson to Andrew J. Donelson, March 21, 1822, May 2, 1822, June 28, 1822, in Harold D. Moser, David R. Hoth, and George H. Hoemann, eds., *The Papers of Andrew Jackson, Volume V, 1821–1824* (Knoxville: University of Tennes-

see Press, 1996), 163–64, 177–78, 195–96; Andrew Jackson to Andrew J. Donelson, April 1, 1822, and April 12, 1822, Andrew J. Donelson Papers, Library of Congress, Washington, D.C. (hereafter cited as DLC); and Andrew J. Donelson to Andrew Jackson, December 14, 1822, Andrew Jackson Papers, Scholarly Resources, Wilmington, Delaware (hereafter cited as JSR).

6. Andrew Jackson to John Coffee, October 24, 1823 (fn. 4), in Moser, Hoth, and Hoemann, eds., *PAJ*, 5:311; and Atkins, *Emily Donelson*, 109.

7. Andrew Jackson to James C. Bronaugh, July 3, 1821, in Moser, Hoth, and Hoemann, eds., *PAJ*, 5:66–67; and Andrew Jackson to Andrew J. Donelson, July 3, 1821, DLC.

8. Andrew Jackson to Egbert Harris, April 13, 1822, in Moser, Hoth, and Hoemann, eds., *PAJ*, 5:170–71; Advertisement for runaway slave, [September 1824], JSR; and Andrew Jackson to William Faulkner, August 28, 1827, Andrew Jackson to Andrew Hays, August 30, 1827, Andrew Hays to Andrew Jackson, August 31, 1827, Andrew Jackson to William B. Lewis, September 1, 1827, in Harold D. Moser and J. Clint Clifft, eds., *The Papers of Andrew Jackson, Volume VI, 1825–1828* (Knoxville: University of Tennessee Press, 2002), 384, 385–86, 386–87, 387.

9. Memorandum, [January 1, 1825], in Moser and Clifft, eds., *PAJ*, 6:3–5; Bertram Wyatt-Brown, "Andrew Jackson's Honor," *Journal of the Early Republic* 17 (Spring 1997): 18; Bertram Wyatt-Brown, *Southern Honor: Ethics and Behavior in the Old South* (New York: Oxford University Press, 1982), 16; Dickson D. Bruce Jr., *Violence and Culture in the Antebellum South* (Austin: University of Texas Press, 1979), 137; and Chase C. Mooney, *Slavery in Tennessee* (Bloomington: Indiana University Press, 1957), 91.

10. Agreement Among Andrew Jackson, Andrew J. Donelson, and Graves W. Steele, January 19, 1829, and Andrew Jackson to Andrew J. Donelson, August 22, 1829, in John Spencer Bassett and J. Franklin Jameson, eds., *Correspondence of Andrew Jackson*, 7 vols. (Washington, D.C.: Carnegie Institute of Washington, 1926–35), 4:2–3, 65–66; Andrew J. Donelson to Emily T. Donelson, July 26, 1829, Martin Van Buren to Andrew J. Donelson, July 27, 1829, Andrew Jackson to Andrew J. Donelson, August 22, 1829, and August 26, 1829, Charles J. Love to Andrew J. Donelson, August 22, 1829, Agreement Between Andrew J. Donelson and Archibald Pool, October 22, 1829, and Emily T. Donelson to Andrew J. Donelson, October 4, 1830, October 30, 1830, and November 30, 1830, DLC; Robert V. Remini, *Andrew Jackson and the Course of American Freedom, 1822–1832*, Vol. 2 (New York: Harper and Row, 1981), 250–51; and Satterfield, "Moderate Nationalist Jacksonian," 42–43, 101.

11. Bill of Sale between JCM and Andrew J. Donelson, January 5, 1829, William Watson to Andrew J. Donelson, June 13, 1829, [?] to Andrew J. Donelson, October 27, 1830, Andrew J. Donelson to Emily T. Donelson, January 15, 1831, February 6, 1831, June 10, 1831, Andrew J. Donelson's order to purchase slaves, June 14, 1831, [D. F. Armstrong?] to Andrew J. Donelson, December 6, 1832, DLC; Andrew J. Donelson to [Lewis Jones], March 7, 1831, and June 21, 1831, Arthur Holbrook Collec-

tion, Milwaukee County Historical Society, Milwaukee, Wisconsin; Peter J. Parish, *Slavery: History and Historians* (Boulder, Colo.: Westview Press, 1989), 64–66; James Oakes, *The Ruling Race: A History of American Slaveholders* (New York: Knopf, 1982; Vintage, 1983), 188–90.

12. Andrew Jackson to Andrew J. Donelson, August 22, 1829, in Bassett and Jameson, eds., *Correspondence of Andrew Jackson*, 4:2–3, 65–66; Andrew J. Donelson to Emily T. Donelson, July 26, 1829, Martin Van Buren to Andrew J. Donelson, July 27, 1829, Andrew Jackson to Andrew J. Donelson, August 22, 1829, and August 26, 1829, Charles J. Love to Andrew J. Donelson, August 22, 1829, DLC; Remini, *Course of American Freedom*, 250–51; and Satterfield, "Moderate Nationalist Jacksonian," 42–43, 101.

13. Satterfield, "Moderate Nationalist Jacksonian," 55–56, 113; Edward Livingston to Andrew J. Donelson, March 7, 1833, DLC; Stephen S. Lawrence, "Tulip Grove: Neighbor to the Hermitage," *Tennessee Historical Quarterly* 26 (Spring 1967): 8–14; and Pauline Wilcox Burke, *Emily Donelson of Tennessee*, ed. Jonathan M. Atkins (Knoxville: University of Tennessee Press, 2001), 266–67, 274–75.

14. Deed of sale to Andrew J. Donelson, November 26, 1838, DLC; Satterfield, "Moderate Nationalist Jacksonian," 189–92; [Andrew J. Donelson to Martin Van Buren], April 3, 1837 [fragment], JCM to [Andrew J. Donelson], January 8, 1839, DLC; Andrew Jackson to Martin Van Buren, May 2, 1839, and Andrew Jackson to Martin Van Buren, May 21, 1840, Martin Van Buren Papers, Library of Congress, Washington, D.C. (hereafter cited as VLC); and Martin Van Buren to Andrew J. Donelson, December 23, 1839, Andrew Jackson to Martin Van Buren, February 15, 1840, DLC.

15. Jonathan Daniels, *The Randolphs of Virginia* (Garden City, N.Y.: Doubleday, 1972), 265–67; Pauline Wilcox Burke, *Emily Donelson of Tennessee*, 2 vols. (Richmond, Va.: Garrett and Massee, 1941), 2:62–63, 67–70, 72, 84, 99–102, 122; Tax records, 1842–49, Andrew J. Donelson Papers, Tennessee State Library and Archives, Nashville, Tennessee; and Entries in the journal of James G. Martin Jr., 1843–1846, DLC.

16. John Tyler to Andrew Jackson, September 17, 1844, in Bassett and Jameson, eds., *Correspondence of Andrew Jackson*, 6:319–20; Robert Armstrong to James K. Polk, September 25, 1844 [summary], Jeremiah George Harris to James K. Polk, September 26, 1844, Andrew Jackson to James K. Polk, September 26, 1844, in Wayne Cutler, Robert G. Hall II, and Jayne C. DeFiore, eds., *Correspondence of James K. Polk: Volume VIII, September–December 1844* (Knoxville: University of Tennessee Press, 1993), 120, 127–28, 129–30; and Annie Middleton, "Donelson's Mission to Texas in Behalf of Annexation," *Southwestern Historical Quarterly* 24 (1921): 251.

17. Andrew J. Donelson to John C. Calhoun, October 2, 1844, in Clyde N. Wilson, Shirley Bright Cook, and Alexander Moore, eds., *The Papers of John C. Calhoun: Volume XX, 1844* (Columbia: University of South Carolina Press, 1991), 16–17; Andrew Jackson to Francis P. Blair, October 17, 1844, in Bassett and Jameson, eds., *Correspondence of Andrew Jackson*, 6:325; Andrew Jackson to Martin Van Buren,

October 2, 1844, and October 22, 1844, VLC; Martin Van Buren to Andrew J. Donelson, October 5, 1844, Francis P. Blair and John C. Rives to Andrew J. Donelson, October 30, 1844, DLC; Account statement between Andrew J. Donelson and Martin Van Buren, [May 28, 1846?], Martin Van Buren Papers (Chadwyck-Healey Collection), Library of Congress, Washington, D.C. (hereafter cited as VCH); and Satterfield, "Moderate Nationalist Jacksonian," 256.

18. Elizabeth R. Donelson to Andrew J. Donelson, January 1, 1845, January 17, 1845, and February 3, 1845, JDC; Andrew Jackson to Elizabeth R. Donelson, January 16, 1845, Andrew J. Donelson to H. McLeod, January 21, 1845, and Andrew Jackson to Andrew J. Donelson, February 10 [16?], 1845, in St. George L. Sioussat, ed., "Selected Letters, 1844–1845, from the Donelson Papers," *Tennessee Historical Magazine* 3 (1917): 149, 149–50, 151–52; Andrew J. Donelson to John C. Calhoun, January 27, 1845, and January 30, 1845, in Wilson, Cook, and Moore, eds., *Papers of John C. Calhoun*, 21:211–14, 232–33; Andrew Jackson to Andrew J. Donelson, [February 16, 1845?], in Bassett and Jameson, eds., *Correspondence of Andrew Jackson*, 6:367–68; and Satterfield, "Moderate Nationalist Jacksonian," 278.

19. Andrew J. Donelson to James K. Polk, February 1, 1845, February 15, 1845, and March 18, 1845, in Wayne Cutler and Robert G. Hall II, eds., *Correspondence of James K. Polk: Volume IX, January–June 1845* (Knoxville: University of Tennessee Press, 1996), 80, 103–4, 205–7.

20. Mark R. Cheathem, "The Ass in Lion's Skin: The Role of Patriarchy, Honor, and Conflict in Andrew J. Donelson's Relationship with Andrew Jackson," Paper presented at the 2005 Society for Historians of the Early American Republic meeting, Philadelphia, Pennsylvania. See also, John F. Marszalek, *The Petticoat Affair: Manners, Mutiny, and Sex in Andrew Jackson's White House* (New York: Free Press, 1997), and Charles Faulkner Bryan Jr., "The Prodigal Nephew: Andrew Jackson Donelson and the Eaton Affair," *East Tennessee Historical Society Publications* 50 (1978): 92–112.

21. Andrew Jackson's will, September 30, 1833, Andrew Jackson Papers, Library of Congress, Washington, D.C.; Andrew Jackson's will, June 7, 1843, in Bassett and Jameson, eds., *Correspondence of Andrew Jackson*, 6:220–23; and Robert V. Remini, *Andrew Jackson and the Course of American Democracy, 1833–1845*, Vol. 3 (New York: Harper and Row, 1984), 483–85.

22. Andrew Jackson to James K. Polk, May 26, 1845, in Cutler and Hall, eds., *Correspondence of James K. Polk*, 9:410–11; James Buchanan to Andrew J. Donelson, April 26, 1846, in Diplomatic Instructions, German States, Volume 14, Department of State, National Archives II, College Park, Maryland; Andrew J. Donelson to James K. Polk, February 20, 1846, James K. Polk Papers, Library of Congress, Washington, D.C. (hereafter cited as PLC); and Andrew J. Donelson to Elizabeth R. Donelson, February 22, 1846, DLC.

23. Martin Van Buren to Andrew J. Donelson, July 10, 1845, and October 8, 1845, and T. Beckman to Andrew J. Donelson, March 9, 1846, DLC; Andrew J. Donelson to James K. Polk, November 4, 1845, December 20, 1845, PLC; Satterfield, "Moderate

Nationalist Jacksonian," 340–41; Arkansas land tax receipts, n.d., Andrew J. Donelson to John P. Heiss, January 16, 1846 [promissory note], Andrew J. Donelson to William M. Gwin, May 14, 1846 [promissory note], Note by John P. Beckman, May 23, 1846, and Henry Horn to Andrew J. Donelson, May 20, 1846, DTL; and Martin Van Buren to Andrew J. Donelson, April 15, 1846, VLC.

24. Daniel S. Donelson to Andrew J. Donelson, August 3, 1846, September 4, 1846, and July 3, 1847, Bettie M. Donelson Papers, Tennessee State Library and Archives, Nashville, Tennessee (hereafter cited as BDP); and James G. Martin Jr., to Andrew J. Donelson, December 9, 1846, DTL.

25. Andrew J. Donelson to James K. Polk, February 22, 1848, PLC; Andrew J. Donelson to Jackson Donelson, March 5, 1848, JDC; James K. Polk to Andrew J. Donelson, April 2, 1848, in St. George L. Sioussat, ed., "Letters of James K. Polk to Andrew J. Donelson, 1843–1848," *Tennessee Historical Magazine* 3 (1917): 72–73; Andrew J. Donelson to James Buchanan, November 16, 1846, December 22, 1846, and May 15, 1847, James Buchanan Papers, Historical Society of Pennsylvania, Philadelphia, Pennsylvania (hereafter cited as JBP); Andrew J. Donelson to James Buchanan, November 16, 1846, and June 24, 1847, in Despatches from United States Ministers to the German States and Germany, Prussia, Volume 4, Department of State Archives, National Archives II, College Park, Maryland (hereafter cited as DSA); and J. N. Armstrong to Andrew J. Donelson, November 12, 1846, Robert Armstrong to Andrew J. Donelson, n.d. [April 27, 1847], and July 9, 1847, DLC.

26. Andrew J. Donelson to James Buchanan, April 3, 1848, DLC; Andrew J. Donelson to James Buchanan, June 30, 1848, July 1, 1848, and July 15, 1848, in Despatches, Prussia, 4, DSA; James Buchanan to Andrew J. Donelson, July 24, 1848, August 3, 1848, August 7, 1848, and August 15, 1848, in John Bassett Moore, ed., *The Works of James Buchanan*, 8 vols. (Philadelphia: J. B. Lippincott, 1909), 8:130–31, 150–51, 152–54, 167–69; Diary entry, August 5, 1848, in Milo M. Quaife, ed., *The Diary of James K. Polk During His Presidency, 1845 to 1849*, 4 vols. (Chicago: A. C. McClung, 1910), 4:53–58; Andrew J. Donelson to James Buchanan, November 26, 1848, March 11, 1849, July 21, 1849, JBP; John M. Clayton to Andrew J. Donelson, March 19, 1849 [two despatches], in Diplomatic Instructions, German States, Volume 14, DSA; Andrew J. Donelson to John M. Clayton, March 29, 1849, June 3, 1849, and June 4, 1849, in Despatches from United States Ministers to the German States and Germany, Prussia, Volume 5, DSA; James Buchanan to Andrew J. Donelson, June 29, 1849, in St. George L. Sioussat, ed., "Selected Letters, 1846–56. From the Donelson Papers," *Tennessee Historical Magazine* 3 (1917): 266–67; Andrew J. Donelson to John M. Clayton, August 12, 1849, and August 20, 1849, in Despatches from United States Ministers to the German States and Germany, Federal Government of Germany, Volume 1, DSA.

27. Andrew J. Donelson to James Buchanan, December 22, 1846, and January 8, 1847, JBP; Second annual message, December 8, 1846, in James D. Richardson, ed., *The Messages and Papers of the Presidents, 1789–1897*, 10 vols. (Washington, D.C.: Government Printing Office, 1896–99), 4:471–506; and Andrew J. Donelson to James

Buchanan, September 28, 1846, October 24, 1846, February 4, 1847, and February 20, 1847, DLC.
28. Andrew J. Donelson to John C. Calhoun, March 3, 1848, and July 8, 1848, in Clyde N. Wilson, Shirley Bright Cook, and Alexander Moore, eds., *The Papers of John C. Calhoun: Volume XXV, 1847–1848* (Columbia: University of South Carolina Press, 1999), 221–23, 572–74.
29. Andrew J. Donelson to John C. Calhoun, September 27, 1848, in Chauncey S. Boucher and Robert P. Brooks, eds., *Correspondence Addressed to John C. Calhoun, 1837–1849*, in *Annual Report of the American Historical Association for the Year 1929* (Washington, D.C.: Government Printing Office, 1930), 475–77; and Andrew J. Donelson to James Buchanan, December 14, 1848, and July 21, 1849, JBP.
30. Thelma Jennings, *The Nashville Convention: Southern Movement for Unity, 1848–1850* (Memphis, Tenn.: Memphis State University Press, 1980), 78, 94–97, 130–33, 237 (appendix B); Jonathan M. Atkins, *Parties, Politics, and the Sectional Conflict in Tennessee, 1832–1861* (Knoxville: University of Tennessee Press, 1997), 166–67; and Nashville *Daily Union*, May 7, 1850.
31. Nashville *Daily Union*, April 13, 1850, May 7, 1850, and September 26, 1850; *Republican Banner and Nashville Whig*, May 7, 1850; Jennings, *Nashville Convention*, 78, 94–97, 130–33, 233–50 (appendix B); St. George L. Sioussat, "Tennessee, the Compromise of 1850, and the Nashville Convention," *Mississippi Valley Historical Review* 2 (December 1915): 323–24; and Atkins, *Parties, Politics, and Sectional Conflict*, 166–67.
32. Jennings, *Nashville Convention*, 194–97; *Republican Banner and Nashville Whig*, November 15, 1850, November 19, 1850, and November 20, 1850; and *Nashville Daily Union*, November 19, 1850, and November 22, 1850.
33. Nashville *Daily Union*, 19 November 1850, 22 November 1850, 25 November 1850, and 26 November 1850; and *Republican Banner and Nashville Whig*, November 19, 1850, and November 25, 1850.
34. Satterfield, "Moderate Nationalist Jacksonian," 428.
35. Andrew J. Donelson to [Jackson Donelson], September 9, 1852, Andrew J. Donelson to Elizabeth R. Donelson, October 10, 1853, JDC; and J. M. Coffman to Andrew J. Donelson, December 4, 1852, and n.d. [1853], Andrew J. Donelson to Jackson Donelson, January 8, 1853, B. H. Shepherd and A. J. Shepherd to Andrew J. Donelson, January 28, 1853, W. F. Dowd to Andrew J. Donelson, November 14, 1853, Bartlett Sims to Andrew J. Donelson, November 16, 1853, Gray A. Chandler to Andrew J. Donelson, December 29, 1853, DLC.
36. Loyce Braswell Miles, "Duncan, Mississippi: The Origins and Survival of a Town," *Journal of the Bolivar County Historical Society* 5–7 (March 1983): 13; Florence Warfield Sillers et al., comp., *History of Bolivar County, Mississippi* (Jackson, Miss.: Hederman Brothers, 1948), 137; Andrew J. Donelson to Elizabeth R. Donelson, January 26, 1857, February 11, 1857, February 13, 1857, February 19, 1857, and June 8, 1857, JDC; and Andrew J. Donelson to Elizabeth R. Donelson, March 14, 1857, DLC.

37. Andrew J. Donelson to Elizabeth R. Donelson, June 7, 1857, June 9, 1857, October 17, 1857, and November 21, 1857, JDC.
38. Sarah Jackson to Andrew Jackson III, January 16, 1857, and April 15, 1858, Ladies' Hermitage Association, Nashville, Tennessee; and Lawrence, "Tulip Grove," 16.
39. Andrew J. Donelson to Elizabeth R. Donelson, January 19, 1858, January 24, 1858, January 30, 1858, February 4, 1858, and May 6, [1858], Andrew J. Donelson to [John Donelson], November 24, 1858, JDC; and Anna Alice Kamper, "A Social and Economic History of Ante-Bellum Bolivar County, Mississippi" (M.A. thesis, University of Alabama, 1942), 50–51.
40. Speech of Andrew J. Donelson [at Baltimore], May 1860, quoted in Satterfield, "Moderate Nationalist Jacksonian," 541–42; and Speech of Andrew J. Donelson speech [at Memphis], June 4, 1860, in *Republican Banner and Nashville Whig*, June 8, 1860.
41. Satterfield, "Moderate Nationalist Jacksonian," 544–45; Nashville *Republican Banner*, January 22, 1861; Andrew J. Donelson to Editor, January 19, 1861, in Memphis *Bulletin*, n.d., Andrew J. Donelson to Editor, March 15, [1861], in *Nashville Union and American*, n.d., Andrew J. Donelson to Mary E. Donelson (Wilcox), May 24, 1861, DLC; and A. Clark Denson to Andrew Johnson, July 2, 1862, in Leroy P. Graf, Ralph W. Haskins, and Patricia P. Clark, eds., *The Papers of Andrew Johnson: Volume 5, 1861–1862* (Knoxville: University of Tennessee Press, 1979), 527–29.
42. Andrew J. Donelson to Elizabeth R. Donelson, March 22, 1861 [1862], Andrew J. Donelson to Stephen A. Hurlbut, May 29, 1863, Andrew J. Donelson to Mary E. Donelson (Wilcox), August 27, 1864 and January [6?], 1865, DLC; and Elizabeth R. Donelson to John Donelson, December 2, 1862, Andrew J. Donelson to John Donelson, December 4, 1862, Andrew J. Donelson to Elizabeth R. Donelson, [?] 17, 1863, JDC.
43. Andrew J. Donelson to Mary E. Donelson (Wilcox), August 27, 1864, and January [6?], 1865, DLC; Andrew J. Donelson to John Donelson, December 4, 1862, Andrew J. Donelson to Elizabeth R. Donelson, [?] 17, 1863, JDC; and Stephen V. Ash, *When the Yankees Came: Conflict and Chaos in the Occupied South, 1861–1865* (Chapel Hill: University of North Carolina Press, 1995), 17.
44. Andrew J. Donelson to Mary E. Donelson (Wilcox), September 28, 1861, August 27, 1864, and January [6?], 1865, Andrew J. Donelson to Elizabeth R. Donelson, March 22, 1861 [1862], Andrew J. Donelson to H. Windly, April 8, 1865, Promissory note from Andrew J. Donelson and Elizabeth R. Donelson to Harry Smith, May [?], 1865, DLC; Andrew J. Donelson to John Donelson, December 4, 1862, Andrew J. Donelson to Elizabeth R. Donelson, [?] 17, 1863, March 23, 1864, Andrew J. Donelson to A. W. [William Alexander] Donelson, August 13, 1864, and Promissory note from Andrew J. Donelson and Elizabeth R. Donelson to Harry Smith, May [?], 1865, JDC; and Leroy P. Graf, Ralph W. Haskins, and Patricia P. Clark, eds., *The Papers of Andrew Johnson: Volume 6, 1862–1864* (Knoxville: University of Tennessee Press, 1983), 193.

45. Frank Moore, comp., *The Rebellion Record*, 6 vols. (New York: G. P. Putnam, 1861–66), 6:38, 64; Andrew J. Donelson to Mary E. Donelson (Wilcox), September 28, 1861, August 27, 1864, and January [6?], 1865, John Donelson to Elizabeth R. Donelson, February 2, 1863, Newspaper obituaries of John S. Donelson, n.d., Newspaper obituaries of John A. Wilcox, n.d., Affidavit by S. W. White, July 16, 1864, DLC; and Elizabeth R. Donelson to John Donelson, December 2, 1862, Andrew J. Donelson to John Donelson, December 4, 1862, Elizabeth R. Donelson to Andrew J. Donelson, [9?] October 1863, and Andrew J. Donelson to A. W. [William Alexander] Donelson, August 13, 1864, JDC.
46. Andrew J. Donelson to Editor, February 5, 1865, in Memphis *Argus*, n.d., DLC.
47. Memphis *Argus*, April 4, 1865; Nashville *Republican Banner*, September 5, 1865, quoted in Robert B. Satterfield, *Andrew Jackson Donelson: Jackson's Confidant and Political Heir* (Bowling Green, Ky.: Hickory Tales, 2000), 190; Satterfield, "Moderate Nationalist Jacksonian," 553; Davidson M. Leatherman to Andrew Johnson, December 10, 1865, in Paul H. Bergeron, ed., *The Papers of Andrew Johnson: Volume 9, September 1865–January 1866* (Knoxville: University of Tennessee Press, 1991), 501–2; Andrew J. Donelson to the editor, Augusta *Weekly Constitutionalist*, September 20, 1865, quoted in E. Merton Coulter, *The South during Reconstruction, 1865–1877* (Baton Rouge: Louisiana State University Press and the Littlefield Fund for Southern History of the University of Texas, 1947), 78; Nashville *Republican Banner*, April 2, 1867, and April 17, 1867; and Paul H. Bergeron, Stephen V. Ash, and Jeanette Keith, *Tennesseans and Their History* (Knoxville: University of Tennessee Press, 1999), 161–66.
48. Andrew J. Donelson to [?], December 13, [1865?] and Andrew J. Donelson to Elizabeth R. Donelson, September 11, 1869, DLC; Andrew J. Donelson to Martin Donelson, December 12, 1868, March 10, 1869, and April 1, 1869, and Martin Donelson to Andrew J. Donelson, January 2, 1869, DTL; and Andrew J. Donelson to Elizabeth R. Donelson, December 22, 1868, February 18, 1869, June 19, 1869, June 21, 1869, August 6, 1869, and September 13, 1870, JDC.
49. Andrew J. Donelson to [Martin Donelson and William Alexander Donelson], May 24, 1867, Andrew J. Donelson to Martin Donelson, November 24, 1868, December 6, 1868, December 12, 1868, December 14, 1868, December 15, 1868, December 18, 1868, January 2, 1869, March 10, 1869, April 1, 1869, April 26, 1869, and August 16, 1870, and Martin Donelson to Andrew J. Donelson, January 20, 1869, DTL; Andrew J. Donelson to Elizabeth R. Donelson, December 22, 1868, February 18, 1869, June 19, 1869, June 21, 1869, July 16, 1869, August 6, 1869, August 22, 1869, August 23, 1869, September 3, 1869, and September 4, 1869, JDC; and Andrew J. Donelson to [Martin Donelson?], July 15, 1869, Andrew J. Donelson to Elizabeth R. Donelson, September 11, 1869, DLC.
50. William C. Miller to G.W. Curry, June 26, 1871, DLC; Memphis *Daily Appeal*, June 27, 1871; Nashville *Republican Banner*, June 27, 1871, June 28, 1871, and June 30, 1871; and James C. Cobb, *The Most Southern Place on Earth: The Mississippi Delta and the Roots of Regional Identity* (New York: Oxford University Press, 1992), 75.

2. PATRIOTS OR TRAITORS

Unionists in Civil War Mississippi

THOMAS D. COCKRELL

AFTER EXTENSIVE STUDY OF MOST ALL OTHER AREAS OF THE AMERICAN Civil War, a small group of historians are giving more attention to the topic of Unionism and the activities of Unionists in the southern states. At present, there seems to be somewhat of a dearth of published information, most of which originated three decades ago, maybe one of the earliest being Georgia Lee Tatum's *Disloyalty in the Confederacy* (1934). Therefore, this chapter is not intended to exhaust every aspect of Unionists in Mississippi or reach any definitive conclusions. The purpose is to cover, to some degree, those areas of the state and classes of citizens who chose to remain loyal to the Union or resist the Confederacy, thereby providing more information for even broader studies yet to come. In Mississippi, as in Alabama, most of the Unionists lived in the northern part of the state with some in the Piney Woods region, and a few in Natchez. Similar areas in North Carolina's Piedmont and the Big Thicket area of east Texas compared in philosophy with Unionist areas of Mississippi, perhaps due in part to several Jones County residents moving from the Piney Woods region to Texas. Most were non-slaveholding farmers. Some owned many slaves and others held patriotic views due to ancestral loyalty to the concept of the Union. One Virginia Unionist said "he felt like a sane man in a mad house." Historians even disagree as to what definition may be placed on the term Unionist. Those who opposed secession or came to support the Union during the war with "uncompromising devotion" may not be classified with those who opposed the Confederacy for other reasons or were apathetic about the war. However, in all areas, Unionism was to some degree inherently tied to the secession movement that gained momentum from 1850 to the presidential election of 1860.[1]

After the Compromise of 1850, Unionists throughout the South did well in the congressional elections of 1851, gaining thirteen seats as opposed to only five for the States' Rights Democrats. In Mississippi, John A. Quitman, known as the leading "fire-eater" in the state and dubbed the "Father of Secession," bowed out of the gubernatorial race, presenting an opportunity for Jefferson Davis to replace him on the States' Rights ticket. However, Davis lost the election to the Unionist, Henry S. Foote, and Unionists' seats in the state Senate numbered twenty-one compared to eleven for the States' Rights Democrats. Unionists also gained control of the House of Representatives in the state by an impressive 63 to 35 margin.[2]

In 1850, most Mississippians apparently believed leaving the Union would be of little or no benefit. What changed the South's nationalism to overwhelming sectionalism over the next decade was a series of events, mostly related to the expansion of slavery from the Kansas-Nebraska Act in 1854 to the Lincoln-Douglas Debate in 1858 and the presidential election of 1860. As the 1850s moved along, the average citizen in the state took the states' rights position, which allowed unrestricted expansion of slavery, to be the absolute and only answer. One newspaper columnist wrote, it was "so often sounded in their ears that they had become somewhat accustomed to it." In 1859, Mississippi overwhelmingly elected a "fire-eater" governor, John J. Pettus of Kemper County. Regionwide, the States' Rights Democrats had driven home the concept that if slavery was threatened, then all southerners would suffer due to the resulting economic consequences and social deterioration. Abraham Lincoln's election in 1860 was all they needed to convince the majority to secede.[3]

The strongest opposition to disunion in 1860–1861 came from an unlikely alliance of delegates in the northeastern hill counties and the old Whig areas along the Mississippi River. As seemed to be the case in Alabama, this strange coalition of poor upcountry non-slaveholding farmers and large slaveholding planters in the Delta indicated that Mississippians may have agreed in principle, but their views on Unionism varied significantly. Many poor subsistence farmers saw no need to secede since their plight would be the same in or out of the Union, and they would probably end up fighting a war in which they saw no personal gain. The large planter saw his slaves protected by the Constitution and feared he would lose everything if the South left the Union and lost a war that could, and probably would, follow. William J. Minor of Natchez vigorously worked to persuade other planters and state officials to avoid secession that "would lead to war and war to emancipation."[4]

Of the one hundred delegates elected statewide to the January 7, 1861, convention who would decide Mississippi's fate, fifty-six were professional men, small slaveholders, or non-slaveholders. Forty-four owned at least twenty slaves, which placed them in the planter class, but only ten owned over one hundred slaves. On January 9, the vote was eighty-four to fifteen to leave the Union. Instead of the large planters, it would appear that the middle-class professionals, small slaveholders, and non-slaveholders who believed in the "righteousness of slavery" led Mississippi out of the Union, mistakenly believing it could be done peacefully. Without their vote, Mississippi would have remained loyal to the Union. Scattered throughout the state, the anti-Unionists in this group inflamed the secession fervor. One account of a typical delegate was a young man already holding an honored position in society but whose "real hopes lay in the future."[5] In other words, he aspired to be a wealthy slave owner, an accomplishment by which the white South measured success and a means for ascending the social structure. As the *Vicksburg Sun* printed in 1860, "A large plantation and [slaves] are the [ultimate goal] of every Southern gentleman's ambitions."[6]

The northeastern counties of Tishomingo, Tippah, and Itawamba had populations that were 66 percent non-slaveholding, but even there in the delegate vote on secession, Tishomingo was divided, Tippah voted for it, and Itawamba voted against it. As one observer wrote, "Unionism in northeast Mississippi in 1860 was not prepared to oppose the secessionists with force," although their delegates were Union men "who believed that secession would be but another grievance and no remedy."[8]

Threats and intimidation by the secessionists in order to control the election of delegates began early and with earnest against ordinary citizens in most areas of the state. The Reverend John H. Aughey of Choctaw County in central Mississippi, who went to the polls and proudly voted against secession, did so "amidst the frowns, murmurs, and threats of the judges and bystanders" urging him to do just the opposite. Matthew J. Babb of Tishomingo County voiced his fear of being arrested if he failed to stop "talking against secession."[9]

Both sides had the opportunity to be heard when Mississippi's secession convention met in Jackson in January 1861. The ensuing debate included three propositions offered by Unionists or cooperationists (those who wanted to secede only in cooperation with other southern states) that would have delayed action, but they all failed. One of these included a request that the ordinance be delayed until it was ratified by the voters. It failed to pass by a vote of seventy to twenty-nine, eliminating any opportunity for the people to be heard. Oppose secession as they might, Unionists in the state were outvoted and their pleas for Mississippi to remain loyal to the Union were ignored.[10]

As cooperationists acquiesced and signed the document, one pro-Unionist newspaper prophetically warned, "It may prove a fatal, an [ir]retrievably fatal error" to interpret such as submission, an indication that not all opponents of secession would blindly follow the secessionists into the pending catastrophe.[11] For the most part, those who were loyal to the Union either chose to remain silent or reluctantly gave in. Of the one hundred delegates, only two refused to sign the secession ordinance; John W. Wood of Attala County and Dr. J. J. Thornton of Rankin County. Unionists correctly accused fire-eaters of "buying votes, trickery, and false promises."[12]

In some pro-Unionist areas of the state, citizens often found themselves misrepresented and even betrayed by their delegates. Jones County in the Piney Woods region elected John H. Powell, a cooperationist over the pro-secession candidate John M. Baylis by a vote of 166 to 89. When the alternatives to secession failed to pass, Powell joined the overwhelming majority and voted for secession, either from intimidation or the desire to present a united effort. His decision enraged the citizens of Jones County, who hanged their delegate in effigy for his defection. This incident prompted the belief of the infamous Newton Knight (who would later lead his own version of war against the Confederacy) that support for the Confederacy by Jones residents was, by default, purely voluntary since Powell failed to honor the wishes of his constituents, an opinion shared by many of Knight's neighbors. Knight's ideas may not have been patriotically inspired, but they certainly confirmed his belief in individualism, a liberty later reflected during the war when Knight stated that "if they had a right to conscript me when I did not want to fight the Union, I had a right to quit when I got ready."[13]

With the January 9 decision, Mississippi became the second state to secede, and the state joined the Confederate States of America on March 29. Unionists in the state who previously had hoped for a peaceful solution had to decide what their role would be in this new government. Unionists saw their support diminish. Some eventually gave in, including some of the state's premier leadership, linking their fate with that of Mississippi and the Confederacy, as the editor of the *Vicksburg Daily Whig* had indicated in January 1861, saying he would "abide its fate, be it for weal or be it for woe." Many just yielded to the inevitable as one delegate said, "It was manifest to the most superficial observer that the die had been cast already, and that civil war was upon us."[14]

Others would express and act upon their pro-Union sentiments in a variety of ways. Members of the clergy, who voiced their sentiments for peace and for the Union in sermons, often paid a high price for their loyalty, especially if they became actively vocal in public affairs. Reverend James A. Lyon, pastor of First Presbyterian Church in Columbus, Mississippi, repeatedly denounced secession. Lyon rebuked what he called the "wicked unprincipled demagogues, who have brought the country to its present ruin." He blamed the southern people for the war, declaring that their "only hope was in repentance." He prayed publicly throughout the war for the success of the armies without specifying for which side he was praying, creating a complicated dilemma for his critics. Lyon was called "Abolitionist," "Black Republican," and "Traitor." As a result, by February 1862, Confederates not only attacked his church and its leadership but also the minister's family members as well. His son, Theodoric, an officer in the Confederate army, was even brought up for court-martial in the fall of 1863, presumably as part of an attack against his father.[15]

Another minister, James Pelan of the Presbyterian Church in Macon, located in Noxubee County, Mississippi, in the rich black prairie belt along the Alabama border, was threatened with lynching if he did not cease his anti-Confederate tendencies. He failed to heed the warnings and would-be assassins shot him as he walked near his home. Learning of his eventual recovery, the assailants later went to his residence, where under pretenses of a friendly visit, they shot and killed the minister in the presence of his wife, who had offered them supper. As they drew their weapons, they told Pelan, "all the supper we want is to kill you, you infernal Unionist and abolitionist."[16]

Some Mississippi Unionists chose to join federal units and openly fight for the Union. Records indicate that over 100,000 white southerners fought in Union military units during the course of the war. William Franks and several of his neighbors enlisted in the First Alabama Cavalry Volunteers

(USA), at Glendale, Mississippi, on December 15, 1862, under Union general Grenville M. Dodge. In fact, more than 2,000 southern hill country men joined the unit at some time during the war. For a few months, the unit participated in scouting expeditions in northern Mississippi, and they fought against the Confederates at Bear Creek in Alabama and accompanied General William T. Sherman to Atlanta in 1864. Franks left the service in 1863 in order to take his family to Cairo, Illinois, for five years. Franks made this decision because northwest Alabama and northeast Mississippi suffered severely during the war and several Unionists were either shot or hanged. Returning to Corinth in 1868, the family quickly moved to McNairy County, Tennessee, and at the end of Reconstruction, they settled permanently in Itawamba County.[17]

General Ulysses S. Grant saw pro-Union sentiment in north Mississippi as something worth cultivating as he made his way toward Vicksburg in December of 1862. He attempted to rectify the "poor job of reaping sympathy for the Union" that his troops had demonstrated among potential Unionists. Likewise, President Lincoln desired for Unionists in the South to unite in a coordinated resistance against the Confederacy. However, widespread support never came to fruition. While W. I. Morris, a spy from Vicksburg, reported that 8,000 troops had left for Tennessee on April 10, 1863, Grant complained about "imperfect and scarce intelligence" from the locals. Those who were dedicated Unionists often kept quiet for fear of reprisals by Confederates when the Union army left the area. Others quietly voiced their anti-Confederate sentiments, feeling betrayed by Jefferson Davis and the Confederate government.[18]

Apathy, regret, and resentment all played a role in how people dealt with being torn emotionally due to having to face their neighbors whose views were different in such trying times. Such apathy regarding either the Union or the Confederacy was exemplified by Joel Harvey of Attala County, who proudly announced at Pilgrim's Rest Church, "I don't owe allegiance to Jeff Davis or Abe Lincoln." Then there were those who were simply afraid of reprisals from local authorities as one Unionist said of his friends, "I am sorry to state that many professed Union men changed their politics and became sadly adulterated with the fire of secession." Vicksburg had fallen to the Union partly due to Confederate mistakes and command inefficiency, but most Mississippians were reluctant to "point fingers at their own kind." They chose to vociferously blame everything on the invading federals and their "hard-war attitudes."[19] Organizing uniform widespread resistance would not be easy for the Unionists of Mississippi.

Some of the most ominous threats to Unionists came from the numerous Confederate vigilance committees operating in virtually every county during the war. These vigilantes served the dual purpose of harassing the disloyal whites and controlling potential slave insurrections. They often performed extralegal interrogations of anyone suspected of pro-Unionist or anti-Confederate sympathies. They were encouraged to "use a stiff limb and a strong rope" by the leadership at the secession convention. One of these vigilance committees summoned the Reverend John H. Aughey to appear before them. Unable to satisfy his inquisitors, he became a target for more aggressive behavior. Aughey wrote, "self-constituted vigilante committees sprang up all over the country, and a reign of terror began." After two attempts failed to kill him at French Camp, he decided to flee the area in constant fear for his life. He later wrote "the vigilantes had my name on their list of proscribed persons, and if recognized my fate would be sealed."[20] Shortly after his safe arrival in Tishomingo County, he expressed his belief "that the great heart of the county still beat true to the music of the Union." A hundred Unionists apparently confirmed his belief when they flocked to the banks of the Tennessee River in February 1862 to welcome Union gunboats passing through. Later, Confederates did arrest him and while in the Central Military Prison at Tupelo, he wrote a petition to United States secretary of state, William H. Seward, dated July 11, 1862, in which he and thirty-seven other prisoners complained about the treatment of those who were loyal to the Union. Later, he managed to escape and make his way to federal lines. Consequently, he turned from mere Unionist sympathizer to outright anti-Confederate informant providing intelligence to Union general William S. Rosecrans about Confederate strength and activities at Tupelo in 1862.[21]

Levi H. Naron of Chickasaw County, a future Union spy in northern Mississippi and western Alabama, also faced encounters with a vigilance committee because of his Unionist views and activities. After secession, Naron arrived home one evening and while stabling his horse he said, "I found myself surrounded by a body of men, who ordered me to accompany them . . . stating that I should appear before the vigilance committee." Only after a long, heated, and terrifying exchange of words, and at one point even escaping a noose around his neck, was Naron finally released. Leaving his home in Chickasaw County in central Mississippi, Naron made his way to Corinth, but continued on to Pittsburg Landing across the Tennessee border when he learned that federal troops were gathering prior to the Battle of Shiloh on April 6–7, 1862. There he met General William Tecumseh Sherman. "It was he who gave me the name of Chickasaw, by which I am so well known in his army," Naron dictated after the war to Union veteran Richard W. Surby of Chicago.[22]

An unknown but apparently significant number of southerners assumed a more covert role in the war. While by day they appeared to be loyal Confederates, by night they changed allegiance and gave support to people like Naron. There were "good Union men residing in the South, without whose assistance many of my plans would have proved failures," Naron relayed in his memoirs. He added, "while laying in the woods, waiting for my scouts to report, my meals were brought to me by a young lady, and I promised that . . . her services would be greatly rewarded." He followed through with his promise later at Corinth, saying he "knew of no better way to remunerate her than to offer her my heart and my hand, which she at once accepted." Her name was Mary Hannah Lee, a native of Alabama, and Naron's second wife. His first wife, Sarah Kellum, died in 1863 in Girard, Illinois, shortly after Naron took his family there for safety.[23]

Naron remained in Mississippi after the war, but when federal troops were removed after Reconstruction, he realized that he could not stay due to the animosity held toward him by his neighbors, many of whom probably had suffered the loss of family and property due to his military operations. He and his family moved to Pratt County, Kansas, in 1878 where he purchased land and became involved in politics. He sought and obtained a pension from the United States Government for his services as chief of scouts, his most prized accomplishment, indicated by the inscription on his tombstone: "Served 3 years and 8 mos. as Chief of Scouts."[24]

Testimonials from Union generals under whom Naron served attest to the magnitude of his contributions to their efforts. General Benjamin H. Grierson said Naron had "proven his loyalty and devotion to the cause of our country by his acts, and the sacrifices of property which he has made." General William S. Rosecrans called Naron's behavior that of which "became an honest, brave, loyal and reliable citizen of the United States," and General Grenville M. Dodge recalled Naron's service as "daring, bold and shrewd, he rendered me most valuable services."[25]

Naron undoubtedly sacrificed greatly for the position he held and the stand he took. He was ostracized by his neighbors and former friends for obvious reasons. Some even threatened to hang him on occasion. He lost his first wife after the long and arduous journey through enemy lines to Illinois. He suffered from wounds that he received in the performance of his duty. He had to leave his home and property which were confiscated by the Confederates, and almost unbearably for him, he faced alienation (if not retaliation) from his brother, George, a captain in the Confederate army.[26]

General Grenville M. Dodge employed many spies like Naron throughout the war in Mississippi. As U. S. Grant moved toward Vicksburg and planned the siege of the city, Dodge employed large numbers of operatives, mostly southern Unionists, to gather intelligence. He even gave some spies the discretion to "go right in and get to General Grant at Vicksburg instead of coming to me." Some of these spies were women, such as Mississippians Jane Featherstone and Mary Malone, who supplied important information. Often affectionately referring to his spies as "his boys," Dodge also "felt a fatherly duty to protect [females] in this dangerous line of work." After the capture of one of his female operatives, the general even thought of "abducting a Confederate officer's wife and holding her hostage until the enemy released his spy." While scouts made an average of $50 for their services, spies often made between $250 to $500 due to the hazardous nature of their service and depending on the information they provided.[27]

Other Unionists across the state continued to be intimidated and threatened throughout the war even in areas like northeastern Mississippi where Unionism was common. E. J. Sorrell of Tishomingo County claimed that "all Union men were threatened in a general way." Terry Dalton recalled that almost all Unionists in that county (speaking of the southern portion of Tishomingo that later became Prentiss County) suffered from some kind of damage, either personal or property, as a result of their Unionist sympathy. M. A. Higginbottom, a resident of Corinth in what was then Tishomingo County (later Alcorn), said that "it was a common expression that every man who would not side with the Confederacy 'ought to be hung.'" Higginbottom lived there until 1864 when he, like Naron, volunteered for service in the Union army, later joining the Federal Secret Service as a spy. A farmer in Tippah County, Samuel Beaty, had his property destroyed and lost his right to vote due to his Unionist sympathies.[28]

Across much of north Mississippi, punishment was quick and harsh for Unionists at the hands of both military and civilian Confederates. Yet faithful allegiance to the Union was not deterred as was evidenced when local inhabitants warned who they assumed were Union soldiers that rebel cavalry was operating in the area as they approached Holly Springs in December 1862. Apparently they had mistaken Earl Van Dorn's Confederates for federals. Armistead Burwell, after visiting Vicksburg in August 1863, wrote Abraham Lincoln that he believed thousands of Mississippians wanted the restoration of the Union but knew no way to safely express their views.[29]

In the watershed counties of the Pearl and Big Black Rivers in central Mississippi, anti-Confederate disillusionment may have been difficult to distinguish from pro-Union sentiment. There deserters from the Confederate army found refuge, aid, and comfort from a large number of the citizenry. In 1863, fugitive slaves in Choctaw County complained that the woods were "so full of runaway white men that there was no room for them." Attala, Winston, and Leake counties were also overwhelmed by deserters seeking the safety of the forests where they received help from the people who lived there.[30] In Attala County, Unionist Jason Niles recorded in his diary accounts of a man named Henry Gray who said that demagogues ran the Confederacy and Jefferson Davis was its first king. One Jim Shuler actually shot himself to escape military service against the Union.[31]

Jones County launched the greatest open resistance against the Confederacy, even resorting to force of arms, but whether it was Unionism or not seems in question. The Piney Woods area of Mississippi had its own version of disloyalty, and the most famous account of dissension was in the person of Newton Knight. Some have mistakenly claimed that the Civil War dissidence in the county led to the term "Free State of Jones." Apparently the term "Free State" was used to describe the area even before the Civil War began, but the term was inevitably attributed to the county during and after the war and perhaps for good reason. According to Jones residents, the term came about when the county government collapsed in the 1830s. It was then that all county officers failed to legally qualify due to the depopulated condition of the county following the migration northward of large numbers of the citizenry when the Choctaw and Chickasaw cessions opened new land for settlement in 1830 and 1832, respectively.[32] Another possibility of the term was the description of individualism of

Jones residents by their neighbors in surrounding counties who said Jones folks "went to church barefooted, dressed in a way they saw fit, and carr[ied] their guns to use in case any game might cross their paths." They went on to say the "entire freedom of the citizens of Jones County [departed] from the arbitrary rules of society and the restraints of fashion recognized elsewhere."[33]

Newton Knight, a farmer and shoemaker before the war, enlisted in the service of the Confederacy on July 29, 1861, but he was shortly discharged due to concern over his dying father. After passage of the Conscription Act on April 16, 1862, he joined the army again. The "Twenty [Slave] Law"[34] passed by the Confederate Congress on October 11 of that same year caused Knight to question the fairness of a law that appeared to allow the rich to escape military service while the poor were dying on the battlefield. As a result, according to Ben Graves, a descendant of pro-Confederate slaveholders in Jones County, Knight "called himself a Union man and was a full-fledged Republican."[35]

Some local sources revealed another reason for Knight's break with the Confederates after their cavalry apparently confiscated his mother's horse on one of their raids. A failed attempt by Knight to retrieve the horse from military headquarters infuriated him. After the Union victories at Iuka in September and Corinth in October 1862, Knight attained a furlough and went home. He formed a military company of his own comprised mostly of fellow deserters. Knight attempted to join federals at Memphis, Vicksburg, and New Orleans to form a legitimate regiment in the Union army but was unable to do so. In fact, the Jones County Scouts were organized in October 1863 made up of men from Jones and the surrounding counties. They pledged themselves "to stay together and obey all orders from the government of the United States." Although Union general U. S. Grant promised they would be mustered into service, it never happened, which was not uncommon. The First Georgia State Troops Volunteers, organized in 1864, was the only official Union force in that state. In Alabama, the First Alabama Cavalry was one of few and the best-known unit. Knight later reflected, "We'll all die guerrillas, I reckon. Never could break through the rebels to jine [sic] the Union Army. The Johnny Rebs busted up the party they sent to swear us in." Knight's followers increased their raids of local Confederate storehouses, and eventually the company grew to an estimated 125 members who obtained arms and supplies by raiding wagons from Confederate supply trains passing through the community. They also pillaged neighboring areas and intimidated local citizens. Knight's most famous accomplice was Rachel Knight, a former slave of Knight's grandfather. Their alliance bound them for the rest of their lives. Together they created a "multiracial community" with Rachel bearing several of Knight's children.[36]

County officials were frightened witless by threats from these ruffians. This outlawry soon gave rise to rumors that the deserters in Jones County had seceded from the state and the Confederacy, but according to one resident the "fellows that cried secede were afraid that the [deserters] [Knight's followers] would kill them; so [the secessionists] left. There was no sheriff, assessor, or tax collector." It would appear that instead of seceding from the Confederacy, however, Knight's outlaws simply wanted to control the county.[37]

In August 1863, Confederate general Braxton Bragg ordered Major Amos McLemore to Jones County to return deserters to the ranks. Two months later on October 5, while the major was in the company of several Confederate officers at the home of Mississippi Confederate representative Amos Deason, an unknown assailant shot and killed him. Most people speculated it was Newton Knight's bullet, but the *Louisville Daily Journal* did not name the assailant, only reporting that McLemore "was on duty at Ellisville, Miss., gathering up conscripts and deserters." Although Knight never confessed, he did say of the incident, "we stayed out in the woods minding our own business until the Confederate army began sending raiders after us with bloodhounds ... then we saw we had to fight."[38] Finally, in 1864, the Confederate military brought the area back under control.

On February 29, 1864, when Major General William T. Sherman was regrouping after his Meridian campaign, he wrote to Major General Henry Halleck concerning Jones County saying "a declaration of independence" had been issued "by certain people who were trying to avoid Southern conscription, and lie out in the swamps. I promised them countenance, and encouraged them to organization for mutual defense." Even Sherman appeared to be under the impression that Jones County had seceded from the Confederacy. He was not alone. The belief was widespread. Even after the war, one former Unionist and Jones County delegate to the 1865 Mississippi Constitutional Convention, Thomas G. Crawford, told a former Confederate, "yes, sir, we did secede from the Confederacy, and, sir, we fought them [the Confederates] like dogs, we killed them like devils, we buried them like asses—yes, like asses, sir."[39]

Not surprisingly, the Jones County disloyalty was embellished in newspapers in Natchez, New Orleans, and New York in 1864. After the war it lived on and was greatly exaggerated in 1886 by J. Norton Galloway, historian of the U.S. Sixth Army Corps, in the *Magazine of American History*. He claimed Knight had 10,000 followers and that at a convention held in Ellisville, Jones County seceded from the State of Mississippi and the Confederacy in late 1862, quoting the ordinance itself, which said in part: "That we sever the union existing between Jones county and the State of Mississippi and proclaim our independence of said State, and of the Confederate States of America." According to Goode Montgomery in the *Publications of the Mississippi Historical Society* in an article in 1904, this was an erroneous claim and the ordinance was fictitious. Harvard University professor Albert Bushnell Hart expounded on the validity of this thesis of secession in the *New England Magazine* and even quoted Galloway. He later acknowledged his error in a letter to Montgomery on February 8, 1904, saying, "the article on Jones County . . . was printed in the [magazine] for December 1891. But I feel doubtful now whether the evidence is sufficiently weighty to be so stated." Nevertheless, myth became legend and whether fact or fiction, Newt Knight came to be viewed by many as a folk hero, "Robin Hood of the Piney Woods," and leader of the "Free State of Jones."[40]

Clearly Jones County resisted the Confederate government with arms, but an overlooked rebellion in Tishomingo County was going on as well. Dissension escalated to such a point by mid-war, that the Confederates eventually ended any efforts to collect taxes in the county. Federal authorities allowed Unionists there to use the railroads for personal and business reasons in exchange for help against guerrilla bands in the county. By the end of the war, anti-Confederates dominated county politics, and perhaps another "Free State" was in the making. Motivations in Tishomingo were more clearly defined where people outwardly supported the Union, whereas in Jones County, they were definitely more anti-Confederate in tone.[41]

Such disloyalty to the southern cause in Jones County soon spread to surrounding counties in the Piney Woods area and central Mississippi as well, including the women who lived there, while women apparently supported Confederate troops and remained loyal to the cause in much of the state. Union sergeant Richard W. Surby, who participated in Colonel Benjamin H. Grierson's raid through central Mississippi in 1863, encountered some women who lived in the Piney Woods region north of Jones County. After learning they were Yankee soldiers, the women welcomed them in and fed them, proudly showed them a U.S. flag, and berated Confederate conscription laws. With so many men away at war, women often found themselves in the lead where social unrest was concerned, protesting inflated prices and encouraging their men to return home. Judge Robert S. Hudson of Leake County, whose district also included the counties of Yazoo, Holmes, Attala, and Madison, complained to both President Jefferson Davis and Governor Charles Clark in 1864 about female disloyalty in central Mississippi. He strongly recommended that the "most radical and severe treatment" be used against anti-Confederate "women and noncombatants." He called disloyal women "rotten hearted" and "far worse than the men."[42]

The disloyalty of these women against the Confederacy resulted from hunger, illness, and abuse often caused by Confederate soldiers. Such sentiment apparently stemmed more from personal rather than political motivation; nevertheless, these women often encouraged their husbands and sons to desert, creating great consternation for the Confederate leadership. Furthermore, it suggested both personal and political motivation for desertion to troops who needed little encouragement. Over the four-year period of the war out of the 78,000 Mississippians who enlisted, as many as fifty-six officers and over 11,600 enlisted men from the state deserted from the Confederate army.[43]

While the middle class struggled between loyalties, many of the large slaveholding class did not. Located in large measure in the Mississippi Delta, especially in the Natchez area where many built magnificent pillared mansions, these men hoped if not believed loyalty to the Union might somehow save their fortunes.

By far the largest planter in the state in the 1850s was Stephen Duncan of Natchez, who once served as president of the Bank of the State of Mississippi as well as a delegate to the 1832 Mississippi Constitutional Convention. Duncan moved to Natchez in 1808 from Carlisle, Pennsylvania. He owned sugar and cotton plantations in Louisiana, and cotton plantations in Adams and Issaquena counties in Mississippi. By 1851, he owned over 1,000 slaves and the Issaquena property alone was worth an estimated one million dollars.[44]

Unlike many Yankees who came south, he never accepted southern political views and when the threat of secession loomed over the state, "political battles ... pushed him to take a position." In a letter written in 1860, he said, "If the Union is dissolved, I, for one, would be for selling out my possessions immediately. Any man of sense and reflection cannot fail to see that after disunion, we would be in no better condition in any one respect, and almost in all respects infinitely worse." He went on to warn that "our taxes alone would consume more than one quarter of our products; for under a Southern republic there would be no premium collected from imports, but all [revenue would be] derived from direct taxation and to an enormous extent."[45] He was as good as his word, consequently investing much of his capital in northern railroads and midwestern land.

When war came, Duncan gave no support to the Confederacy, although he initially leaned toward it due to the circumstances in which he found himself. Due to his fear for the safety of his investments in the South he abandoned "Auburn," his antebellum home in Natchez in the spring of 1863, leaving his sons in charge of the southern holdings, and moved to New York City where he remained until his death in January 1867. His loyalty to the Union, however, did not prevent losses on his property in the South at the hands of federal troops.[46]

Mary Duncan, wife of Duncan's son, Henry P. Duncan, in a letter to Abraham Lincoln on May 24, 1863, complained to the president of the damages rendered to their nine plantations north of Vicksburg in Issaquena County. She wrote, "owing to the depredations of the Union troops and the enormous loss in [slaves], millions would hardly cover our losses, consequently it is somewhat natural that we should ask due protection for the fragment that remains of a once princely fortune." She informed Lincoln that both she and her husband had warrants for their arrests issued by the Confederate government and, they often had to "conceal" themselves due to their "well-known loyalty."[47]

Mary's complaints appeared at best petty and at the least insensitive considering the fact that so much of her family's wealth remained intact throughout and after the war while many of her neighbors' losses were extremely severe. It may have simply reflected her lack of knowledge about the overwhelming destruction others had suffered or it may have revealed the belief by this group of Unionists that they should somehow escape the ravages of war and live as though nothing was different.

Another Unionist, Haller Nutt, unlike Duncan, was a native Mississippian, born in Jefferson County in 1816. In 1860, he began construction on a luxurious mansion called "Longwood" in Natchez. The home was never actually finished, since the northern workmen returned home when the war began, and the family was forced to maintain living quarters exclusively on the ground level. Although Nutt presumably had protection papers as a loyal citizen of the United States, it did not prevent Union troops from pillaging the property and removing material which was on hand to finish the construction of the house. Nutt owned forty-three thousand acres and over eight hundred slaves and was described as one of "the most prominent and influential Union men in [Natchez]." Union general Walter Q. Gresham often wrote his wife of his visits to Longwood and the many times he and his officers had dined there.[48]

A correspondent for the *New York Herald*, James W. Latham, reported in 1863, "Mr. Nutt has lost, since the occupation of Natchez, by our forces, one million five hundred thousand dollars." Throughout the war, Nutt witnessed over three million dollars of cotton burned or confiscated by Union troops indiscriminately exerting punitive measures against the Confederate war effort. Troops burned at random without checking on whose property the cotton was located. Soldiers also damaged his steamboats and other business enterprises scattered over six plantations. What the federals did not take, the Confederates did, leaving Nutt financially ruined and emotionally distressed.[49]

While Duncan sat out much of the war securing most of his wealth in the safety of New York City, Nutt remained in Natchez and endured the misfortune of watching his wealth be taken from him by both armies. Perhaps as a result, his widow had a substantially more legitimate claim against the government than was warranted by the Duncan heirs.

Julia Nutt sued the federal government for losses after the war, and according to the United States quartermaster general, the claim totaled a little less than $257,000 since the damage to the plantation crops could not be determined. Federal courts awarded several payments over a span of years, but the total was less than $100,000, not nearly enough to finish construction of the house and provide for the children and their education. In later years she wrote her son, Prentiss, "We all look like a broken down southern family. Only family pride [is] keeping us going."[50]

Another Unionist, Kate Minor, widow of John Minor of Natchez who died in 1869, also fought for compensation in the amount of $64,155. When questioned by the claims commissioners, Kate had trouble convincing them that she and her husband were completely loyal to the Union throughout the war. Among the fourteen witnesses on her behalf between

1871 and 1877 were Julia A. Nutt and General Walter Gresham, who traveled in Unionist circles in Natchez. She pointed out further evidence of John's loyalty with his resignation from the Adams (County) Troop as it began preparations to join Robert E. Lee's Army of Northern Virginia. Former Confederate general William T. Martin testified before the committee saying, "John Minor had disgraced himself. I looked upon it in the light of an officer resigning in the face of the war."[51]

Kate received only $13,072 from the government since there was no proof of who took what and when they took it, and the commission could not determine with any certainty the steadfastness of the family's loyalty to the Union. Under these conditions, she was fortunate to get any settlement whatsoever since only 44 claims of the 152 submitted by Mississippians were ever settled. Like other large planters, the Minors' main concern was the preservation of their property and wealth, which superseded any other allegiance.[52]

The loyalty of the upper class appeared to some degree conditional or perhaps more self-serving than patriotic. In fact, there is no evidence that Unionists of Natchez took any of the actions undertaken by Unionists in other areas of the state such as "destroying rebel property, joining the Union army, [or] spying." They provided no help for the Confederacy, but apparently none for the Union, either, other than their cordial relationships with federal officers. As one observer commented, "Their kind of Unionism manifested itself chiefly in avoiding conscription in the Confederate army, resisting rebel impressments, and continuing as best they could to carry on their lives as they always had in spite of the tumult swirling around them."[53]

One group of Unionists often overlooked is African Americans. Often their role was determined by geographic location regarding Union troop movements. A large number would eventually enlist in the service of the United States Army. Both slaves and free blacks participated in isolated civil unrest along with non-slaveholding white farmers indicating more evidence of a not so "Solid South" as was once believed.[54]

After emancipation changed the status of former slaves from "contraband" to "freedmen," President Lincoln wished to initiate the establishment of the United States Colored Troops (USCT). Adjutant General Lorenzo Thomas accepted the challenge to recruit and enlist this new source of manpower for the Union, which would weaken the South and strengthen the North simultaneously. His goal was a reduction in the inordinate numbers of freedmen who followed and burdened Union armies by enlisting as many of the followers as possible into useful service. For his efforts, he met substantial resistance from many in the military. General Andrew Jackson Smith said he would hang Thomas if he came into his camp and mentioned such an idea. He went on to reveal his opposition to abolition, saying, "If Jesus Christ was to come down and ask [me ... to] be an abolitionist ... I would say no! Mr. Christ, I beg to be excused ... I would rather go to hell."[55]

Opposition notwithstanding, an estimated 25,000 African Americans from Mississippi served in northern military units during the course of the war including nine regiments and two light artillery companies. Many of these soldiers were former slaves who either made their way to federal lines or were from areas brought under Union control as the war progressed. At Milliken's Bend, Louisiana, on June 7, 1863, the First Mississippi Volunteers of African Descent fought well in spite of receiving their weapons only one day before the battle. Hand-to-hand fighting there ranked among "one of the bloodiest small engagements of the war." The unit's losses numbered 35 percent killed or wounded. Assistant Secretary of War Charles A. Dana later recalled that "the bravery of the blacks in the battle at Milliken's Bend completely revolutionized the sentiment of the army with regard to the employment of negro troops."[56]

The Third U.S. Colored Cavalry, formerly the First Mississippi Cavalry of African Descent, operated out of Vicksburg from October 17, 1863, until being mustered out of service on January 26, 1866. This unit, seeing several engagements with the enemy, was a very busy regiment. It participated in the second raid through Mississippi by Brigadier General Benjamin H. Grierson (in which Levi Naron was the scout) from December 21, 1864, to January 5, 1865. Another unit was the Third Mississippi Volunteers of African Descent organized on May 20, 1863, a result of the success of Thomas's Mississippi Valley recruiting initiative. A somewhat surprised secretary of war, Edwin M. Stanton, wrote Thomas that his success gave him "great pleasure."[57] Lincoln, Stanton, and other national leaders began to understand their plan was working. They also came to appreciate that under extremely challenging conditions, black troops fought out of pride for their newfound freedom while also fighting for the release of those yet to be free.

Unionist activity in Mississippi varied from outright armed conflict to secret meetings and covert actions to simply being friendly to Union officers. Some Union sympathizers undoubtedly did nothing at all from fear. Unionism, although appearing to be widespread throughout much of the state, exhibited more activism in some regions than in others such as the extreme northeastern and central Mississippi counties and the Piney Woods region. The Unionists themselves were never united, partly due to distance, but also due to the divergence in motivations of the several groups with varying agendas. Nevertheless, in all areas of the state, whether majority slaveholding, majority non-slaveholding, or in between, many Union patriots were willing to make significant sacrifices, even to the death.

Upper-class patriotism in Natchez, such as it was, may have been understandably more from fear of losing wealth than from allegiance to the Union, although many of them also paid a high price for their decision. One could argue that the most loyal of the Unionists among the farmers of Mississippi were the poor who gave aid and comfort to spies often at great sacrifice to themselves and their families, while realizing that they could possibly be no better off serving either of the belligerent powers. Middle-class professionals and yeomen-class farmers were torn between loyalty to the Union or siding with the majority who favored secession.

Rebels against the Confederacy in Jones County had different reasons for their actions, perhaps more from the desire to desert and take over the county in which they lived than either love of the Union or disloyalty to the Confederacy. African Americans who served in the military and civilians alike had a personal stake in fighting for the new freedom the Union offered even though there was no promise of equality in response to their efforts.

Two areas that definitely need more research are the role of white Mississippians who served in the Union army and free blacks and their role in civil disorder and aid to the Union cause. Both of these groups would give more insight into how widespread Unionism was in the state.

A general consensus regarding Unionist motivation is difficult to summarize. It could narrow down to plain and simple personal conviction. They were never able or willing to cooperate in a systematic resistance that Abraham Lincoln envisioned for the South. Perhaps it was a lost opportunity that would have made a difference in shortening the war. A significant number of people from all classes in Mississippi worked against the Confederacy and aided the Union cause in ways and by means available to them. Their service will never be fully appreciated by the nation, but what they did should be remembered. The sacrifices they made complimented and strengthened Union soldiers who served and died on the field of battle, indicating that Mississippi Unionists were, depending which side of the conflict viewed them, both patriots to the United States and traitors to the Confederacy.

Notes

1. "Unionism," *Encyclopedia of Alabama*, http://www.encyclopediaofAlabama .org/face/Article.jsp?id=h-1415 (accessed January 12, 2011); "Southern Unionists as Traitors to the Confederacy," *Cenantua's Blog*, http://cenantua.wordpress .com/2008/06/11/southern-unionists-as-traitors-to-the-confederacy; "Unionists," *New Georgia Encyclopedia*, http://www.georgiaencyclopedia.org/nge/Article .jsp?id=h-3753 (accessed June 18, 2010); Victoria E. Bynum, *The Long Shadow of the Civil War: Southern Dissent and Its Legacy* (Chapel Hill: University of North Carolina Press, 2010), 5.
2. James L. Hutson, *Southerners against Secession: The Arguments of the Constitutional Unionists in 1850–51* (Kent, Ohio: Kent State University Press, 2000), 285; James Wilford Garner, "The First Struggle over Secession in Mississippi," *Publications of the Mississippi Historical Society* (hereafter cited as *PMHS*), IV (Harrisburg, Pa.: Harrisburg Publishing Company, 1901), 102.
3. Ben Wynne, *Mississippi's Civil War: A Narrative History* (Macon, Ga.: Mercer University Press, 2006), 17–18; (Jackson, Miss.) *Mississippian*, March 7, 1851; John K. Bettersworth, review of Percy Lee Rainwater, *Mississippi: Storm Center of Secession, 1856–1861* (Baton Rouge, 1938), in the *Journal of Mississippi History* [hereafter cited as *JMH*] 1 (1939): 64.
4. William J. Minor Diary, XIV, December 20, 1860, William Minor Family Papers, Department of Archives, Louisiana State University, Baton Rouge, Louisiana; J. Carlyle Sitterson, *Sugar Country: The Cane Sugar Industry in the South, 1753–1950* (Lexington: University of Kentucky Press, 1953), 205.
5. Richard A. McClemore, ed., *A History of Mississippi*, 2 vols. (Hattiesburg, Miss., 1973), 1:442; Ralph A. Wooster, "The Membership of the Mississippi Secession Convention of 1861," *JMH* 16 (1954): 248, 257.
6. *Vicksburg Sun*, April 9, 1860; Robert W. Dubay, *John Jones Pettus, Mississippi Fire-Eater: His Life and Times, 1813–1867* (Jackson: University Press of Mississippi, 1975), 84–85.
7. Thomas H. Wood, "A Sketch of the Mississippi Secession Convention of 1861—Its Membership and Work," *PMHS* 6 (1902): 91–104.
8. Mary Floyd Sumners, "Politics in Tishomingo County, 1836–1860," *JMH* 27 (1966): 151.
9. M. Shannon Mallard, "I Had No Comfort to Give Thee," *North and South* 6 (May

2003): 79, 83; McClemore, *History of Mississippi*, 1:443; John H. Aughey, *Tupelo* (Lincoln, Neb., 1888), 46.
10. Wood, "A Sketch of the Mississippi Secession Convention," 100; Westley F. Busbee Jr., *Mississippi: A History* (Wheeling, Ill.: Harlan-Davidson, 2005), 132.
11. William J. Cooper and Thomas E. Terrill, *The American South: A History* (New York: McGraw-Hill, 1996), 323.
12. Dubay, *John Jones Pettus*, 87; *Mississippi Journal of the State Convention* (1861), 86–88; *Vicksburg Daily Whig*, December 25, 1860; *Natchez Weekly Courier*, December 27, 1860.
13. *New Orleans Item*, March 20, 1921; Goode Montgomery, "Alleged Secession of Jones County," *PMHS* 8 (1904): 14; Victoria Bynum, *The Free State of Jones: Mississippi's Longest Civil War* (Chapel Hill: University of North Carolina Press, 2001), 98; Rainwater, *Storm Center of Secession*, 198–200.
14. *Vicksburg Daily Whig*, January 23, 1861; Wooster, "The Membership of the Mississippi Secession Convention," 251; Wood, "Sketch of the Mississippi Secession Convention," 93.
15. McClemore, *History of Mississippi*, 1:516–17; *Journal of Rev. James A. Lyon, 1861–1870*, Mississippi Department of Archives and History (hereafter cited as MDAH), Jackson, Mississippi, 30–31; David B. Chesebrough, "Dissenting Clergy in Confederate Mississippi," *JMH* 55 (1993): 125; John K. Bettersworth, ed., "Mississippi Unionism: The Case of the Reverend James A. Lyon," *JMH* 1 (1939): 37–52; James W. Silver, *Confederate Morale and Church Propaganda* (New York: W. W. Norton, 1957), 20.
16. Chesebrough, "Dissenting Clergy," 119; Mallard, "I Had No Comfort to Give Thee," 80–83; Timothy B. Smith, *Mississippi in the Civil War: The Home Front* (Jackson: University Press of Mississippi, 2010), 182–84.
17. "Unionists," *New Georgia Encyclopedia*; Terry Thornton, "Hill Country Unionism: Civil War Revisited," *Itawamba History Review*, January 20, 2008; Frank Moore, *The Rebellion Record* (New York: Putnam, 1863), 400.
18. Michael B. Ballard, *Vicksburg: The Campaign That Opened the Mississippi* (Chapel Hill: University of North Carolina Press, 2004), 113, 417; U. S. Grant to Colonel J. C. Kelton, July 6, 1863, Grant Papers, 8:485, in William B. Feis, *Grant's Secret Service: The Intelligence War from Belmont to Appomattox* (Lincoln: University of Nebraska Press, 2002), 145.
19. McClemore, *History of Mississippi*, 1:529; Thomas D. Cockrell and Michael B. Ballard, eds., *Chickasaw, A Mississippi Scout for the Union: The Civil War Memoir of Levi H. Naron* (Baton Rouge: Louisiana State University Press, 2005), 10; Ballard, *Vicksburg*, 421; Mark Grimsley, *Hard Hand of War: Union Military Policy toward Southern Civilians* (Cambridge: Cambridge University Press, 1995), 142–43; John K. Bettersworth, *Confederate Mississippi: The People and Politics of a Cotton State in Wartime* (Baton Rouge: Louisiana State University Press, 1934), 223.
20. McClemore, *History of Mississippi*, 1:519; Aughey, *Tupelo*, 47, 280–81; Chesebrough, "Dissenting Clergy," 121–22.

21. *War of the Rebellion: A Compilation of the Official Records of the Union and Confederate Armies* (hereafter cited as *OR*), 130 vols. (Washington, D.C.: Government Printing Office, 1880–1901), ser. I, VII: 155–56; Aughey, *Tupelo*, 280–81.
22. Cockrell and Ballard, *Chickasaw*, 15.
23. Ibid., 106.
24. Wesley M. Naron, *The Narons: A 202 Year History, 1779–1981* (Chickasaw County Library, Houston, Mississippi), 76–79, 199.
25. Cockrell and Ballard, *Chickasaw*, 171–72.
26. Mallard, "I Had No Comfort to Give Thee," 84; James R. Atkinson, "Levi H. Naron: An Uncompromising Unionist from Mississippi," Unpublished essay, Atkinson Papers, Special Collections, Mitchell Memorial Library, Mississippi State University, Mississippi State, Mississippi.
27. Feis, *Grant's Secret Service*, 166–68.
28. Mallard, "I Had No Comfort to Give Thee," 79, 83.
29. Ballard, *Vicksburg*, 123, 417.
30. *Diary of Jason Niles*, February 3, 1863, in McClemore, *History of Mississippi*, 1:520.
31. Ibid., 1:520–21.
32. Montgomery, "Alleged Secession," 15.
33. Ibid.
34. The law as originally passed was called "The Twenty Negro Law" and gave exemption from military service to one white man for every twenty slaves on a plantation, which enforced the concept of "a rich man's war and a poor man's fight."
35. McClemore, *History of Mississippi*, 1:522–24; John S. Bowman, ed., *The Civil War Almanac* (New York: Gallery Books, 1983), 95, 116; B. D. Graves Narrative, Hebron Community Meeting, June 17, 1926, Lauren Rogers Museum of Art, Laurel, Mississippi.
36. Bynum, *The Free State of Jones*, 98–99; Bowman, *The Civil War* Almanac, 115; Bynum, *Long Shadow of the Civil War*, 8, 85; "Unionists," *New Georgia Encyclopedia*; "Unionism," *Encyclopedia of Alabama*.
37. Address of Mattie P. Bush, February 17, 1912, Rogers Museum, Laurel, Mississippi; Sally Jenkins and John Stauffer, *The State of Jones: The Small Southern County That Seceded from the Confederacy* (New York: Doubleday, 2009), 8. (It would appear that Professors Stauffer and Jenkins have resurrected the argument of nineteenth-century Harvard professor Albert Bushnell Hart, who originally stated the certainty of Jones County secession from the Confederacy but later recanted that assumption in a letter to Goode Montgomery in 1904; see n. 40.)
38. *New Orleans Item*, March 20, 1921; *Louisville Daily Journal*, November 11, 1863; Jenkins and Stauffer, *State of Jones*, 135.
39. Major General William T. Sherman to Major General Henry Halleck, February 29, 1864; *OR*, ser. 2, 32:498–99; Bynum, *Long Shadow of the Civil War*, 10; *Adams* [County, Mississippi] *Sentinel*, September 26, 1865.
40. McClemore, *History of Mississippi*, 1:522; J. Norton Galloway, "A Confederacy within a Confederacy," *Magazine of American History* 16 (November 1886):

387–90; Montgomery, "Alleged Secession," 13–22; Albert Bushnell Hart to Goode Montgomery, February 8, 1904, in Montgomery, "Alleged Secession," 19.
41. Mallard, "I Had No Comfort to Give Thee," 85.
42. Bynum, *Long Shadow of the Civil War*, 3–4; R. S. Hudson to Jefferson Davis, March 14, 1864, *OR*, ser. 1, 32:626; R. S. Hudson to Governor Charles Clark, June 25, 1864, Governors' Papers, MDAH, Jackson, Mississippi; Bynum, *The Free State of Jones*, 94–95.
43. Ella Lonn, *Desertion during the Civil War* (New York: Century Co., 1928), 231.
44. Herbert Weaver, *Mississippi Farmers, 1850–1860* (Nashville: Vanderbilt University Press, 1945), 120; McClemore, *History of Mississippi*, 1:348–49.
45. Stephen Duncan Papers, Department of Archives, Louisiana State University, Baton Rouge, Louisiana; Dunbar Rowland, *Mississippi: The Heart of the South*, 2 vols. (1925), 1:554.
46. *Biographical and Historical Memoirs of Mississippi*, 2 vols. (Chicago: Goodspeed Publishing Company, 1891), 1:676; Martha Jane Brazy, *An American Planter: Stephen Duncan of Antebellum Natchez and New York* (Baton Rouge: Louisiana State University Press, 2006), 151.
47. Mary Duncan to Abraham Lincoln, May 24, 1863, Abraham Lincoln Papers, Library of Congress, Manuscript Division, Washington, D.C., http://www.rootsweb.ancestry.com/~msissaq2/duncan.html (accessed August 2010).
48. Alma K. Carpenter, "Haller Nutt: A Correction," *JMH* 60 (1998): 150–51; Matilda Gresham, *Life of Walter Quinton Gresham, 1832–1895*, 2 vols. (Chicago, Ill.: Rand McNally & Company, 1919), 1:246–47; *Biographical and Historical Memoirs*, 2:520; Ezra J. Warner, *Generals in Blue: Lives of the Union Commanders* (Baton Rouge: Louisiana State University Press, 1964, 1992), 188–89.
49. *The Southern Reporter* (St. Paul, Minn.: West Publishing Company, 1904), *Nutt v. Forsythe et al.*, 36: 247–48; *Nutt v. U. S. Supreme Court* (1888); Joanne V. Hawks, "Julia A. Nutt of Longwood," *JMH* 57 (1994): 299; Carpenter, "Haller Nutt," 150.
50. Julia A. Nutt to Sergeant Prentiss Nutt (Knut), February 24, 1893, Nutt Family Papers, MDAH, Jackson, Mississippi; Ina Mae Ogletree McAdams, *The Building of Longwood* (Austin: University of Texas Press, 1972), 110–24.
51. Rebecca M. Dresser, "Kate and John Minor: Confederate Unionists of Natchez," *JMH* 64 (2002): 189, 191; Petition of Katherine S. Minor, August 30, 1871, Records of the Southern Claims Commission, Records of the General Accounting Office, Record Group 217, National Archives and Records Administration, Washington, D.C., Testimony of William T. Martin, December 12, 1877; Ezra J. Warner, *Generals in Gray: Lives of the Confederate Commanders* (Baton Rouge: Louisiana State University Press, 1959, 1987), 214–15.
52. Dresser, "Kate and John Minor," 213; Frank W. Klingberg, *The Southern Claims Commission* (Berkeley and Los Angeles: University of California Press, 1955), 116.
53. Dresser, "Kate and John Minor," 200; Horace S. Fulkerson, "A Civilian's Recollections of the War Between the States," *Mississippi Valley Historical Review* 24 (December 1937): 360.

54. Bynum, *Long Shadow of the Civil War,* 3–5.
55. David Slay, "Abraham Lincoln and the United States Colored Troops of Mississippi," *JMH* 70 (2008): 68–72; *OR,* ser. III, 4:734; Warner, *Generals in Blue,* 502–3.
56. John David Smith, ed., *Black Soldiers in Blue: African-American Troops in the Civil War* (Chapel Hill: University of North Carolina Press, 2002), xv–xvi, 55; Charles A. Dana, *Recollections of the Civil War* (New York: Collier Books, 1898, 1963), 93; Slay, "United States Colored Troops," 75; Wynne, *Mississippi's Civil* War, 127.
57. Smith, *Black Soldiers in Blue,* 258, 291–94; Edwin Stanton to General Lorenzo Thomas, May 15, 1863, *OR,* ser. 2, 3:214; Cockrell and Ballard, *Chickasaw,* 140; *OR,* ser. I, 45 (1), 844–75; Wynne, *Mississippi's Civil* War, 166. (Accounts vary as to the date for the end of the second raid by Grierson from January 5 to January 13, 1865, which probably only indicates that the activities associated with it by the Third USCC ended several days later than the actual raid itself.)

3. THE AFRICAN AMERICAN EXPERIENCE IN LOUISIANA'S LAFOURCHE REGION DURING THE CIVIL WAR

STEPHEN S. MICHOT

IF THE ABUNDANCE OF LITERATURE AND POPULARITY WERE THE SOLE measure, the American Civil War was principally fought and won east of the Appalachian Mountain chain. Granted, new attention in recent years has been devoted to military operations west of the Appalachians, and there is perhaps even a consensus now among Civil War scholars that the Civil War was actually won and lost in the western theater of operations. Still, the amount of attention the western theater receives, not to mention the Trans-Mississippi, has been minuscule in comparison to the attraction of Robert E. Lee's battles and campaigns in the East.

When considering the role of African Americans in the Civil War, the focus remains on the East. No one would deny the overdue attention to African Americans raised by the movie *Glory*.[1] The fact remains, however, that the Fifty-fourth Massachusetts and their famous charge against Fort Wagner occurred in the East, and having mustered into service after January 1863,[2] it was definitely not "the first black regiment to fight for the North."[3] When it comes to standard scholarship on African Americans, the assertions continue. Dudley Taylor Cornish writes in his classic work, *The Sable Arm*, that the November 3–10, 1862, raids along the Georgia and Florida coasts represent the "first use of ... colored troops as a military force against the Confederacy."[4] Herman Hattaway and Archer Jones repeat this contention in *How the North Won* when stating that "this first use of blacks as a military force against the Confederacy concluded as a splendid success."[5] But are these factual statements? We can perhaps blame Hollywood and Internet blogs on misinformation about the Fifty-fourth Massachusetts. But did the paradigm of Civil War historians examine all available sources before they came to their conclusions, or did they reference eastern theater sources because of the popularity of the Virginia theater?

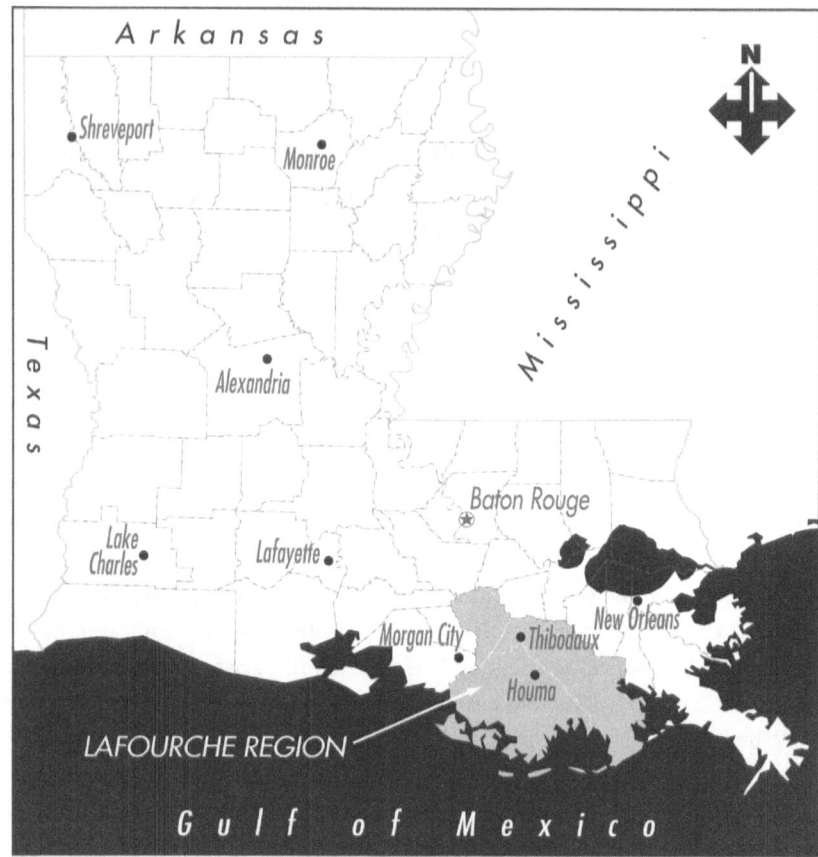

Map by Bill Pitts

Two historians who addressed the experiences of African Americans west of the Appalachians are Lawrence Hewitt and James Hollandsworth. In his 1987 work on Port Hudson, Hewitt recounts the futile assaults of the Louisiana Native Guards against the Confederate bastion. Hollandsworth, in his study of the Native Guards, chronicles the Civil War history of the black regiment, which officially mustered into Union service on September 27, 1862, in New Orleans as the "first (official Negro units) on the rolls." In as dramatic and glorious a charge as anything Hollywood could dream up, the role of the Native Guards at Port Hudson on May 27, 1863, represented the first large-scale use of African Americans in a major battle, occurring some two months prior to the Fifty-fourth's July 18, 1863, assault on Fort Wagner.[6]

Aside from Port Hudson, what else happened in Louisiana that illuminates the role of black troops in the war? The Lafourche region in Louisiana, the focus of this chapter, is an arable land intermixed with bayous, lakes, swamps, and marshes typical of the Louisiana gulf coast region. Lying roughly between the lower Mississippi and Atchafalaya river systems, the region is intersected by Bayou Lafourche, which branches off from the Mississippi River at Donaldsonville, some sixty-five miles above New Orleans. Comprising the core parishes of Lafourche, Assumption, and Terrebonne, and parts of several others, the region is located just southwest of New Orleans, making it a part of the Trans-Mississippi theater. During the antebellum period, the Lafourche region attracted a diversity of settlers including Native Americans, colonial French, Acadians, Hispanics, Germans, Irish, and Italians, as well as free and enslaved Africans. Its plantation sugar cane economy, demographics, and location next to New Orleans determined that the region would be of strategic significance during the American Civil War.[7]

The African American experience in the Lafourche region was primarily associated with a plantation sugar cane crop economy. In 1860, there were over one thousand agricultural farming operations in Assumption, Lafourche, and Terrebonne parishes. According to the 1860 Census records, the three-parish population totaled 41,000 people. Within this population aggregate, 1,200 were slaveholders, 315 were free blacks, and over half (21,000) were African American slaves. While most of the slaves resided on the large plantations, a majority of the slaveholders were not planters, but white yeoman farmers owning 5 or fewer slaves. On the large plantations, a social stratification of occupations existed. At the top were the owners or overseers, followed by slaves, including drivers, house servants, skilled slaves, and unskilled fieldhands. Occupation and skill determined degrees of privilege and lifestyle. For example, some skilled slaves were allowed to earn income by hiring themselves out during the slow months or on Sundays. Others were given passes to the nearby towns for the day as long as they returned by curfew. The status of the yeoman's slave was often the same as that of the family with whom he or she worked and lived. Free blacks, some of whom were slaveholders, tended to hold highly skilled trades positions in Lafourche society.[8] It was upon this society that the war fell in 1862.

In April 1862, New Orleans, a major port city of the South, fell to Union forces under the command of naval captain David Farragut and Major

General Benjamin Butler, commander of the Department of the Gulf. With the fall of New Orleans, the adjacent Lafourche was destined to experience military action. For the next several months, both Confederate and Union forces were content with conducting small raids or foraging expeditions into the Lafourche. In the summer of 1862, General Butler concentrated on grander operations against Baton Rouge and a weakly held, but strongly fortified Vicksburg. By late August, however, Butler was forced to fall back on New Orleans due to an influx of Confederate forces into the Lafourche and the threat this posed to New Orleans and all Union operations north of New Orleans on the Mississippi River.[9] Butler wrote,

> I am preparing for the defense of New Orleans, and I shall hold it too. Baton Rouge has been evacuated. . . . I could have held it till doomsday so far as the enemy were concerned, . . . but the whole rebel army of the Southwest are concentrating to move upon me, and I am not in condition to cut my force in halves.[10]

As part of Butler's scheme to beef up forces in the Department of the Gulf, he adopted a plan to recruit African Americans. This was not as unusual as it may first appear. African Americans fought with George Washington during the American Revolution and with Andrew Jackson at the Battle of New Orleans in 1815. Louisiana free blacks serving in the state's Corps d'Afrique were the last organized rebel forces standing in defense of New Orleans upon Farragut's arrival. Only an order to "stand down" prevented any bloodshed between black Confederates and white Union soldiers. There were even prior unauthorized northern efforts to arm blacks as with the case of Major General David Hunter in South Carolina in May 1862, and Butler's subordinate brigadier general John Phelps near New Orleans in July 1862. Both of these efforts came without President Abraham Lincoln's approval, and thus all regiments formed were subsequently dismissed without seeing service or receiving recognition.[11]

On August 22, 1862, with the de facto approval of Secretary of the Treasury Salmon Chase, Benjamin Butler issued General Order No. 63, ordering the enrollment of the ex-Confederate free colored militiamen of Louisiana into Union service. The first regiment that formed on September 27, 1862, was a thousand strong, and became known as the First Louisiana Native Guards. Several other 1,000-man Native Guard regiments (made up of free blacks and ex-slaves) were soon to follow. In all, 15,000 African Americans from the lower Mississippi River valley were recruited into federal service, and many were from the Lafourche region.[12]

It is interesting to denote the specifics of Butler's General Order. Its call for Louisiana's free black militiamen was recognition of the prior existence of African Americans in the service of a Confederate state. George Denison, a New Orleans customs official, exclaimed as much in a letter to Secretary Chase when he wrote, "By accepting a regiment which had already been in Confederate service, he [Butler] left no room for complaint that the Government were arming the negroes." The initial transition from Louisiana's Corps d'Afrique into Butler's Native Guards was basically a matter of switching uniforms and re-arming, with the exception of incoming contrabands and officers. Whereas Confederate Louisiana recognized black officers over its free black units, black Union regiments were all eventually officered by whites.[13]

Butler's initial opinion on arming blacks did not rank very high. He believed that it was "ludicrous" to train blacks in the manual of arms and in firing muskets. Butler felt that African Americans were best suited for manual labor, and had himself utilized contraband slaves to that effect in both Virginia and Louisiana. During his summer 1862 Vicksburg campaign, Butler had used slaves in an unsuccessful attempt to dig a diversion channel around the bastion's defenses, a failed method used by Ulysses S. Grant one year later at Vicksburg. Butler also conscripted slaves to build fortifications, drainage ditches, and levees. It seems that General Butler altered his stance on the subject primarily out of political ambition and to claim popular credit for recruiting African Americans.[14]

By October 1862, Butler felt sufficiently strong to seize the initiative and launch an attack to clear out the Lafourche region. His plan of attack was three-pronged and included (1) the descent of his main force of five regiments from Donaldsonville on the Mississippi River down Bayou Lafourche; (2) a direct approach from New Orleans along the New Orleans, Opelousas, and Great Western Railroad by two regiments; and (3) a one-regiment naval expedition via the Gulf and the Atchafalaya spillway to cut off any retreat at Brashear City, the N.O.O. & G.W.'s railhead. Butler's invasion force numbered over 5,000 men. In what is perhaps the first official use of black Union troops in a Civil War military operation, the First Louisiana Native Guards, along with the white Eighth Vermont regiment, were a part of the second line of advance along the railway.[15]

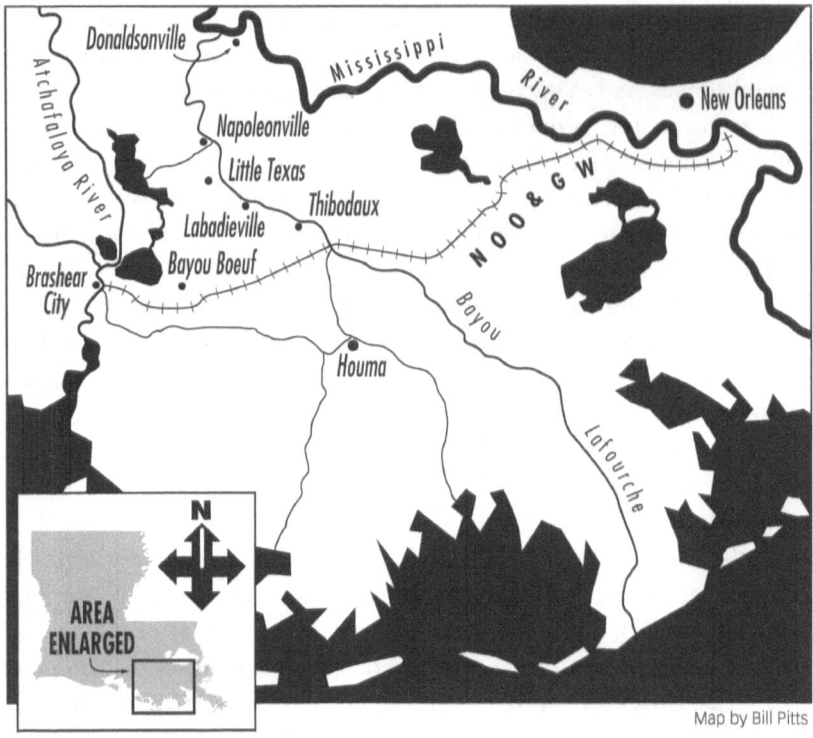

Map by Bill Pitts

With Colonel Stephen Thomas in command, the Native Guards advanced cautiously over the next several days, brushing aside enemy scouts and repairing tracks and bridges as they went. Even in places where the tracks were not sabotaged, the grass had grown so high and thick that the locomotive could not make headway. Thomas had his men literally pulling up miles of grass. Thomas did not want to advance his infantry outside the range of his artillery guns that were affixed on a flat rail car in front of the slowly advancing locomotive. A functioning rail line back to New Orleans also represented a logistical safety net for sustaining Butler's entire operation once the Lafourche region was secured. In addition, the rails would serve to rapidly ship sugar, cotton, and other spoils of war out of the region to await oceanic shipment to Butler's home state and personal benefactors in Massachusetts.[16]

Stiff enemy opposition was expected at a German settlement known as des Allemands, situated approximately halfway between New Orleans and the heart of the Lafourche region. As the Union forces approached des Allemands, they deployed into battle lines with the Eighth Vermont on the right side of the tracks and the Native Guards on the left. Captain James Ingraham of the Native Guards thought of his men as being anxious and showing courage.[17] Thomas addressed his men bestowing glowing words of God and glory amid threats of shooting anyone who flinched. The anticipation of a fight was in vain, however, when the Native Guards found the enemy camp deserted and a 475-foot bridge burnt. The Confederates, having recently been defeated on October 27, 1862, by the Union main force at the Battle of Labadieville, and being aware of the converging Union advance, retreated all available forces across the Atchafalaya and out of the Lafourche region. Despite the admirable work of the Native Guards, the slow advance of Thomas's wing failed to cut off the Confederates' line of retreat. Thomas's refusal to detach himself from the protection of his rail-transported artillery allowed the Confederates to withdraw relatively intact and to return to fight the following year.[18]

The Native Guards continued their important repair work all the way to Brashear City. After several weeks, they had, in part, repaired over eighty miles of rail, telegraph, and bridge lines, effectively opening the Lafourche region from the Mississippi River to the Atchafalaya. The Native Guards, having also been stationed as checkpoint guards along the rail lines, were credited with intercepting dozens of wandering Confederate stragglers. While the federals listed 261 prisoners captured in the days following the Lafourche campaign, the Confederates reported over 400 missing. Most of these were recent militia conscripts, who had been unwillingly conscripted into Confederate service, and who now refused to leave home and hearth by crossing the Atchafalaya to the west. For example, over 200 of the 300 recent conscripts facing the Native Guards at des Allemands failed to show up at Brashear City. Many of them fell into the hands of the Native Guards, not during the Confederate retreat, but in a vain effort at doubling back down the tracks to return home.[19]

The possibility that these Confederate captives included African American soldiers and laborers must also be considered. Donald Evertt, in his study on Louisiana's antebellum free colored population, argues that hundreds of free blacks had joined the Louisiana militia in 1861 at the onset of war. H. E. Sterkx, in his book-length study, mentions the formation of free colored military units in Point Coupee, Natchitoches, and New Orleans. Even the veteran Confederate Crescent Regiment, which had fought at Shiloh and Labadieville, had advertised for "colored teamsters" earlier in the year.[20]

Years after the war, the testimonials of many illiterate ex-slaves were recorded in the trials conducted by the Southern Claims Commission and the French and American Claims Commission, both of which oversaw compensation to loyal Unionists and French nationalists for property damaged or lost at the hands of Union armies during the war. John Rainey, an ex-slave of a Lafourche planter, testified that on November 3, 1862, "an armed [Union] squad came on the place about sun-set and took the horses out of the field."[21] James Allen was a slave hired out to work on a flatboat traveling Bayou Lafourche when Union soldiers stopped them at Napoleonville in late October 1862:

> When the Federal troops came from up the bayou going down they stopped at the boat and came on board and ordered me to leave the boat together with the other hands who was working on the boat; they then discharged the cargo . . . and placed them in wagons and carried them away. . . . They then set fire to the boat and burnt it up; I know they were United States soldiers by their uniforms and flags.[22]

Following the 1862 Lafourche campaign, complaints began to mount of plundering by the Native Guard's rank and file. Pillaging was not limited to black soldiers, nor necessarily unauthorized. Butler's white and black regulars accompanied by emancipated slaves went from plantation to plantation and homestead to homestead stealing and destroying at will. Butler did not hesitate to order some of the new black recruits into the fields to harvest the autumn sugar cane crop. Early freezes were threatening a potential cash windfall for the general, and he lost little time in exploiting the labor potential of his newly uniformed soldiers while others carried out official acts of confiscation. The orders were carried out, but not without much expected grumbling on the part of the recently emancipated soldiers.[23]

Relationships between white Union soldiers and newly freed slaves ranged from cordial to mischievous to outright criminal. As the presence of the Union army became commonplace and as more and more plantation owners fled the region, many slaves simply walked away from their old homes placing freedom above the security of food, shelter, and clothing. With no place to go, most ex-slaves sought refuge in the army camps where soldiers put them to tasks carrying knapsacks, cooking, and doing odd jobs. Freedmen were subjected to tricks, robbery, and beatings. There were so many runaways in camp, recalled a New Hampshire volunteer, that each soldier could have his own servant who can "be very attentive for a week, and then each needs an every day strap admonition in order that he shall attend to his business."[24]

Camp life nights were described as entertaining and jubilant. African Americans were noted for their musical talent, dance customs, and, among females, flirtations. Apparently, it was quite common for white Union soldiers to bed with African American females during their tour of duty in the Lafourche region. One soldier noted that "not infrequently these sable nymphs would be led off by a partner in uniform" after a night of "tripping the light fantastic toe."[25] Sometimes, soldiers took privileges with black females that were not condoned. Charges of rape were not prevalent in the contemporary literature, but not entirely unheard of. Union commander of the Lafourche district between January and March 1864, Acting General Edward L. Molineux, wrote home about drunken Union soldiers, robbery, indecorous conduct toward females, and crimes "too revolting to name." In early 1864, twelve soldiers of the 159th New York Infantry Regiment, while pillaging a plantation near Thibodaux, raped a twelve-year-old black girl in the presence of her parents. Molineux noted that he would not hesitate to court-martial and imprison soldiers for such crimes even though "such things are passed over in some regiments."[26]

In the summer of 1863, in an attempt to relieve Port Hudson, Confederate forces returned to the Lafourche region in force.[27] During this time, Confederate units rounded up hundreds of previously freed ex-slaves—their fate most likely being a return to a condition of slave labor on the planation or in the Confederate army. Confederate colonel James P. Major, commanding a cavalry brigade during operations in the Lafourche, June 1863, reported:

> At Bayou Goula took commissary and quartermaster's stores; destroyed Federal plantations; recaptured over 1,000 negroes, stolen by [Gen. Nathaniel] Banks from planters living in Saint Landry and Rapides Parishes; found them starving and in great destitution; kept the men, and left women and children.[28]

Following the fall of Vicksburg and Port Hudson in July, however, Confederate forces had once again retreated from the region. A period of Union occupation fell over the Lafourche district. Under Union occupation, African Americans were still sought as plantation laborers and as soldiers. In August 1864, General Nathaniel Banks (Butler's replacement) ordered the enlistment of all able-bodied blacks between eighteen and forty years of age into U.S. service. General Order No. 100 gave Union recruiters free access to plantations for the purpose of filling quotas. By October 1864, General E. R. S. Canby (Banks's replacement) modified Banks's order to encourage volunteerism among blacks rather than rely solely upon a draft. In March 1865, Congress created the Freedmen's Bureau in part to regulate the employment of ex-slaves who had been compelled under the Black Codes to work the plantations as wage earners. In some cases, the Bureau oversaw the leasing of confiscated farmlands to the freedmen.[29]

The Civil War, however, was not over. Throughout 1864 and 1865, guerrilla warfare raged across the Lafourche district. While federal forces controlled the urban centers, Confederate guerrilla bands roamed the rural countryside. Confederate guerrilla raids and bushwhacking against Union patrols or anyone sympathizing with Union authorities were commonplace. Union forces retaliated by indiscriminately robbing, arresting, or even shooting marauders and collaborators. It was truly a no-man's land that lacked any official rules of engagement from either side.[30]

African Americans witnessed the guerrilla war in the Lafourche from both sides. The Seventy-fifth and Ninety-third U.S. Colored Infantry Regiments and the Eleventh U.S. Colored Heavy Artillery all participated as part of the Union dragnet to disrupt and capture Confederate guerrillas. On November 17, 1864, the Ninety-third Infantry participated in an operation to seek out and destroy a local guerrilla encampment. En route, Confederate guerrillas intercepted the Union patrol on Bayou Portage in the Atchafalaya basin, but were unable to protect their refuge. Black Union troops helped destroy the guerrillas' living quarters and large quantities of provisions and equipment before withdrawing.[31] The following year on April 4, 1865, the Seventy-fifth Infantry, Ninety-third Infantry, and the Eleventh Heavy Artillery were among a large Union contingent that attempted to block the escape route of a one-hundred-man guerrilla force that had crossed the Atchafalaya into the Lafourche region. After traversing swamps and bayous, Union forces succeeded in capturing sixteen Confederate guerrillas and recovering sixty mules taken from federal plantations. Moreover, a Confederate smuggling operation in foods, medicine, arms, and mail between Union-held New Orleans and Confederate territory west of the Atchafalaya River was disrupted.[32]

Almost assuredly, some of the Confederate guerrillas were of African descent. It would not be unreasonable for free blacks, some of whom were slaveholders and who had previously made up Louisiana militia units, to have continued the fight as guerrillas. In the case of individual black servants, many would still have taken the field in the service of their owners. By the autumn of 1864, Louisiana Confederate governor Henry Allen was urging the enlistment of "every able-bodied black" into the Confederate army since it was better to be fighting "with us than against us."[33] During the April 1865 raid, Union forces captured the undoubtedly loyal "colored servant" of a Confederate guerrilla leader. This man was made to row a small boat containing one careless Private Oscar Close of Company K, First Louisiana Cavalry (Union).

> He was in a small boat, with [Confederate guerrilla] Whitaker's negro to row for him. The boat disappeared very suddenly; could not have been gone more than ten minutes before it was missed, and yet a rigid search failed to discover it. Such was the intense darkness. It is my belief that Close fell asleep and the negro killed him or carried him off into some small bayou.[34]

The African American experience as soldier and freedmen does not end with the conclusion of the Civil War in 1865. The U.S. Government continued to rely heavily upon African Americans to fill its military ranks during Reconstruction, which lasted until 1877 in Louisiana. As early as 1863 in south Louisiana, many ex-slaves were given the opportunity to farm their own fields in an experimental, yet short-lived, program overseen by the Freedmen's Bureau. Most, however, ended up as contract laborers for revitalized plantations, often with new owners. Blacks were also afforded the civil rights of voting and public education for the first time. Demographically, large numbers of rural ex-slaves began migrating off the plantations and into the regional towns and cities, in a hope for a new start and better life.

In the final analysis, the African American experience in Louisiana's Lafourche region is significant not only to the Civil War as a whole, but to the larger study of black ethnic history. African Americans experienced a range of bondage and freedom over the span of the Civil War. They witnessed the war as both civilian and soldier. As civilian, they were often caught between the fires of two opposing armies and their respective ideologies toward blacks. As soldier, Louisiana blacks wore both the blue and gray uniform, and stand as the first official African American Union (if not Confederate) troops to organize and serve in a military campaign— not in the East, but in the Trans-Mississippi.

Notes

The original version of this paper was presented at the Southwestern Historical Association annual conference in Denver, Colorado, on April 10, 2009.

1. See http://www.imdb.com/title/tt0097441/ (accessed March 1, 2009).
2. Benjamin Quarles, *The Negro in the Civil War* (Boston: Little, Brown, and Co., 1953), 8.
3. See http://www.essays.cc/free_essays/e2/blc165.shtml (accessed March 1, 2009); A google.com search for the Fifty-fourth Massachusetts produced the following lead-in description to this social science Web site for kids: "The 54th Massachusetts was the first all-Black regiment to fight in the Civil War" http://www.socialstudiesforkids.com/articles/ushistory/54thmassachusetts.htm (accessed April 8, 2009).
4. Dudley Taylor Cornish, *The Sable Arm: Negro Troops in the Union Army, 1861–1865* (New York: Longmans, Green and Co., 1956), 86.
5. Herman Hattaway and Archer Jones, *How the North Won: A Military History of the Civil War* (Urbana: University of Illinois Press, 1983), 290–91.
6. See Lawrence L. Hewitt, *Port Hudson: Confederate Bastion on the Mississippi* (Baton Rouge: Louisiana State University Press, 1987); James G. Hollandsworth Jr., *The Louisiana Native Guards: The Black Military Experience during the Civil War* (Baton Rouge: Louisiana State University Press, 1995), 16–17; Cornish, *Sable Arm*, 78 (quote); http://www.nps.gov/hps/abpp/battles/sc007.htm.
7. See Stephen S. Michot, "Society at War: Sectionalism, Secession, and Civil War in Louisiana's Lafourche Region" (Ph.D. diss., Mississippi State University, 1994), 1–17.
8. Eighth U.S. Census Returns (1860); Michot, "Society at War," 20–46.
9. Michot, "Society at War," 103–19.
10. *Private and Official Correspondence of Gen. Benjamin F. Butler During the Period of the Civil War*, 5 vols. (Norwood, MA, 1917), 231–33.
11. Cornish, *Sable Arm*, 37, 59, 65; Hollandsworth, *Louisiana Native Guards*, 15.
12. *New Orleans Daily Picayune*, August 24, 1862; Cornish, *Sable Arm*, 67; Quarles, *The Negro in the Civil War*, 198–99; Hollandsworth in *Louisiana Native Guards*,

16–17, contends that black officers had approached Butler first about the idea of Union service, and that there were ex-slave contrabands among the initial recruits.
13. Cornish, *Sable Arm*, 66.
14. Ibid., 56–57, 66; Hollandsworth, *Louisiana Native Guards*, 13; *Battles and Leaders of the Civil War*, vol. 3, *Retreat from Gettysburg* (New York: Thomas Yoseloff, 1956), 553–83.
15. U.S. War Department, *The War of the Rebellion: A Compilation of the Official Records of the Union and Confederate Armies*, 128 parts in 70 vols. (Washington, D.C.: 1880–1901), series 1, part 1, 15:159; herein cited as the *Official Records*.
16. George N. Carpenter, *History of the Eighth Regiment Vermont Volunteers, 1861–1865* (Boston: Deland and Barta, 1886), 69–70.
17. *New Orleans Daily Delta*, November 7, 1862.
18. Carpenter, *Eighth* Vermont, 71–75; *Official Records*, 15:161.
19. Michot, "Society at War," 140–42.
20. Donald E. Evertt, "Demands of the New Orleans Free Colored Population for Political Equality, 1862–1865," *Louisiana Historical Quarterly* 38 (1955): 44; H. E. Sterkx, *The Free Negro in Ante-Bellum Louisiana* (Rutherford, N.J.: Fairleigh Dickerson University, 1972), 212–13; *New Orleans Daily Picayune*, March 10, 1862.
21. *Southern Claims Commission Records* (Washington, D.C.: National Archives, 1871–1880), Case #9906, *Mathurin Daigle v. United States*.
22. *French and American Claims Commission Records* (Washington, D.C.: National Archives, 1880–1884), Case #118, *Jean Merly v. United States*. See also Cases #117 and 425.
23. John M. Stanyan, *A History of the Eighth Regiment of New Hampshire Volunteers* (Concord, N.H.: Ira C. Evans, 1892), 147; John W. DeForest, *A Volunteer's Adventures: A Union Captain's Record of the Civil War* (New Haven, Conn.: Yale University Press, 1946), 74–76; *Helen Dupuy Diary* (Louisiana State University Archives), August 29, 1862.
24. DeForest, *A Volunteer's Adventures*, 56 (quote); Stanyan, *History of the Eighth*, 156; *New Orleans Daily Picayune*, April 28, 1962 (sec. 2, p. 4).
25. Charles P. Roland, *Louisiana Sugar Plantations during the American Civil War* (Leiden, The Netherlands: E. J. Brill, 1957), 99–100; George G. Smith, *Leaves from a Soldier's Diary: The Personal Record of Lieutenant George G. Smith, Co. C, 1st Louisiana Regiment Infantry Volunteers [White] During the War of the Rebellion* (Putnam, Conn.: George G. Smith, 1906), 34–35.
26. Edward Leslie Molineux Letters, January–March 1864 (Personal collection of William A. Molineux of Williamsburg, Virginia); See also, *Records of the Office of the Judge Advocate General (Army)*, Record Group 153.2.3 Court Marshall Case Files and Related Records.
27. See Michot, "In Relief of Port Hudson: Richard Taylor's 1863 Lafourche Offensive," *Military History of the West* 23 (Fall 1993): 103–34.
28. *Official Records*, 26:218.

29. *New Orleans Daily Picayune*, August 3, 1864; October 13, 1864; August 19, 1865; October 11, 1865; see also John C. Englesman, "The Freedmen's Bureau in Louisiana," *Louisiana Historical* Quarterly 32 (1949): 145–224.
30. Michot, "War Is Still Raging in This Part of the Country: Oath-Taking, Conscription, and Guerrilla War in Louisiana's Lafourche Region," *Louisiana History* 38 (1997): 157–84.
31. Carl A. Brasseaux, ed., "The Glory Days: E. T. King Recalls the Civil War Years," *Attakapas Gazette* 11 (1976): 25–27.
32. *Official Records*, 48:168–77.
33. *New Orleans Daily Picayune*, October 13, 1864.
34. *Official Records*, 48:175–76.

4. UNION SOLDIERS REACT TO SLAVES, SLAVERY, FREEDMEN, AND COLORED U.S. TROOPS DURING THE VICKSBURG CAMPAIGN

MICHAEL B. BALLARD

MANY HISTORIANS AGREE THAT BY THE END OF THE CIVIL WAR A large number of white Union soldiers had accepted freedom for slaves, and many had come to admire "colored" men as good combat soldiers. This generality is subject to debate, not because it lacks truth, but because it is difficult to know how widespread these attitudes were. Many federal soldiers viewed colored troops as laborers, freeing white soldiers from digging entrenchments and other physical tasks. Some rightly believed that freeing slaves weakened the South's ability to carry on agriculturally, thus hastening the economic breakdown of the Confederacy.

Union soldier attitudes certainly evolved, but with many nuances. When Abraham Lincoln's Emancipation Proclamation went into effect on January 1, 1863, large numbers of fighting men in blue were not happy with the idea of fighting for freedom of slaves, nor did they enthusiastically embrace the admission of blacks into the army. These men let it be known to their families, to each other, and to officers that they were fighting to save the Union, not to free slaves.

An examination of the reactions of white federal troops to slavery during the long Vicksburg campaign provides as microcosm of the varying soldiers' attitudes. Since the Vicksburg campaign ended in mid-July 1863, their attitudes may have indeed softened by the war's end. Still their comments are significant for no doubt many did not alter their views. Whatever the case, how these Union troops reacted is worth noting, for the variety of their observations says much about the early impact of freed slaves on the psyches of the men from the north, many of whom had never before seen slaves before the war brought them south.[1]

In the summer of 1862, U. S. Grant had been restored to command after Henry Halleck left for Washington to take over as commander of Union armies. Halleck had shelved Grant after Grant's army had been surprised by a Confederate attack at Shiloh on April 6. Reinforced Union forces salvaged the battle the next day. Halleck took command and ultimately occupied the important railroad town of Corinth, Mississippi, after his overwhelming numbers forced Confederates to retreat southward to Tupelo.

Grant now had the task of keeping the Mississippi-Tennessee border secure while being badgered by Halleck to send men to Tennessee to reinforce Don Carlos Buell. Grant both obeyed and resisted. He knew if he reduced his strength too much, he would be vulnerable to rebel counterattacks. He solved part of the problem by taking Iuka, Mississippi, a town east of Corinth on the Memphis and Charleston Railroad, on September 19. Grant's action, while not a decisive victory, meant Confederates would have difficulty sending reinforcements to Braxton Bragg, who was also in Tennessee with troops from Tupelo to attempt to counter Buell's activities.

Grant's army, commanded by William Rosecrans, also beat back two vicious attacks on Corinth by Earl Van Dorn's army. Grant now began harassing Halleck for more troops so he could begin operations against Vicksburg. He would begin by taking his army south into Mississippi down on either side of the Mississippi Central Railroad. Between the Corinth victory and the beginning of the north Mississippi operations, Grant spent much time trying to pull together as many troops as he could from scattered forces in the region. Union soldiers concentrating for upcoming operations in Mississippi had their first extended look at slaves.[2]

Around the countryside, Grant's men encountered runaway slaves. They also found slave owners who hid their slaves, both to prevent their escape and to keep federal troops from setting them free. Many of the Union troops became angry when they learned that slave owners had told slaves that federal troops shot all slaves they found running loose. Yet they laughed at the terrified black men, women, and children who expressed surprise that the Yankee soldiers did not have devilish features as they had been told by their owners.

Soldiers under the command of William T. Sherman, who commanded in Memphis, and who was hardly an abolitionist, became agitated when they saw hundreds of "blackbirds" walking into Memphis, filling the streets. The men cheered and applauded when they saw the freed slaves boarding boats that would take them north up the Mississippi River. Clearly these men did not like being in the proximity of slaves. They likely felt disdain for these black people whose life experiences could not be comprehended by northern soldiers who had not been long exposed to the institution of slavery. Doubtless these soldiers were struck negatively by the social characteristics, speech patterns, and general appearance. Having rarely, if ever, interacted with African Americans prior to the war, to midwesterners the contrasts between the slaves and whites had to be striking.[3]

Racism became clearly evident once the march into Mississippi began. The Confederate army continually retreated before Grant's army. This resulted in sporadic skirmishing, but no major battle. The soldiers in blue had time on their hands, and on occasion enjoyed watching slaves entertain. Sometimes they became agitated. One criticism was the "everlasting tum-tum of the Nigger's banjo." Yet many laughed heartily at the "niggerdance. It would make you laugh yourself blind almost if you could see a lot of 'ebonies' congregated by moonlight or candlelight, one fiddling, another patting' . . . and four or five dancing in their native style." These incidents and the soldiers' reactions were other examples of how Union soldiers found blacks representing another world from northern society. They looked upon these slaves as oddities and diversions rather than as people enslaved. The soldiers' bigotry and racism was evident, more so than they likely realized.

Others found these strange dark-skinned people very handy to carry knapsacks. Why the slaves so easily adapted to menial tasks apparently did not trouble Union soldiers. One bragged that he had "a nice Negro" to carry baggage one day, but the slave had disappeared by the next morning. Working for white men after being subjected to slavery by other white men did not appeal to many slaves. They obviously resented not being treated with respect by men they envisioned as saviors, as deliverers from bondage. Lincoln's election and abolitionist activities had no doubt raised expectations of freedom, but they were finding that dreams of unfettered freedom were illusionary.[4]

As Grant's columns moved deeper into Mississippi, they began to see aspects of slavery that sobered attitudes. The midwestern men had by a large majority joined the army to save the Union. Many gave little thought to slavery; slavery was not the issue. Yet the abuses suffered by enslaved people made deep impressions upon Union soldiers who witnessed brutal treatment, whether mental or physical. An Iowan wrote home about watching "some of the beauties" of slavery, a sarcastic observation, and said they "made an impression on my mind which can never be eraced [sic]." He detailed one such experience that occurred when his regiment was camped on the farm of "one of the Mississippi chivalry," Union soldiers terminology for wealthy white slave owners. Campfires were blazing when a young slave walked by, and the soldiers asked him questions about his owner and the treatment of slaves. They were told that the "master the day before had sent about thirty into the cane brakes to keep us from stealing them." Some of the Iowans immediately began a search and found "27 of the most wretched looking creatures I ever beheld, all women and children, half starved, filthy looking objects." They wore scant clothes in the cold weather. A soldier wrote that the scene produced "a thirst in my heart for vengeance when I looked upon the master." Feelings grew more intense when the Iowans learned that the owner chained the slaves in order to drive them into the swamp. The reactions were not filled with scorn as so often happened when federals encountered slaves.

The soldiers however had unrealistic views of solving freed slaves' dilemmas. They told the black people they were free, and they should encourage others to abandon plantations. Union military policy encouraged soldiers to take such actions, in the hope that taking away labor from southern agriculturalists would speed the destruction of the Confederate economic infrastructure. Though emancipation was allowable, such actions, while alleviating federal anger, did not take into account that freedom, without follow-up aid, often proved not to be an easy thing for slaves. Where would they find food, better clothing, and sustenance? These were questions that haunted freed slaves for months and years to come. Of course these soldiers reacted with anger to what they saw; they did not and could not envision the realities faced by freed slaves.[5]

While personal observations of slavery's cruelties had a lasting effect on the small percentage of Union soldiers who actually saw the evils of bondage with their own eyes, the surviving correspondence and diaries indicate most of Grant's men reacted very negatively when they learned of Abraham Lincoln's Emancipation Proclamation, effective January 1, 1863. Whatever ideas federal soldiers had about emancipation, they made clear to the folks at home and to each other that they were fighting for the Union, not to free slaves. Scores of these men were immigrants or came from immigrant families, and they saw their new homeland as too precious to be dismembered. Soldiers believed that placing emancipation on par with bringing the South back into the Union would only complicate the war and probably extend it.

An Iowan fussed about sending the "stinking niggers" north, a sharp departure from earlier cheers that accompanied freed slaves going north on the Mississippi. An Ohioan observed much unhappiness and heated political discussions, which he thought might lead to orders that the men must not talk politics under the penalty of death. Perhaps he was being hyperbolic, but if the situation seemed that bad to him, his words are an indication that discontent among soldiers must have been near the boiling point, at least among comrades he knew.

There is no way to be sure, since polls were not being conducted at the time, but rebellious feelings in varying degrees may have permeated large portions of the army. One soldier penned, "If I had thot [sic] that it was the idea to set the Negroes all free they would not have got me to act the part of a Soldier in this war." Yet he added, "I am for anything that will cause Union and peace." The slaves, however, seemed more an obstacle than a noble cause. The same soldier wrote home a short time later that he wished there would be a proclamation from Washington that allowed the army to kill slaves. Without slaves, there would be no need to keep fighting. Such extreme sentiments were not common, but other soldiers expressed similar bitterness. Men in the ranks wrote bitterly such things as, "I am union when union is our aim. But when It gets on the nigga [sic], I am not." This soldier went on to say, "I would now rather have the union divided and let slavery alone where it is than to have the union restored and [slavery] abolished." He further declared, "I don't think a white man was ever calculated to be shot at for the sake of a nigger." In the eyes of men in the ranks, abolitionists and northern politicians had so politicized slavery that the South would stand more firmly in their war effort. That meant more Union men would die.[6]

Such bitter sentiments did not prevail among all Grant's men. Considering the many thousands, no specific views could dominate. Those who had been deeply struck by the evil behavior of slave owners thought that destroying the peculiar institution would be worthwhile. They had seen older blacks left behind on plantations deserted by owners. The masters took young and able slaves with them. A soldier noted, "There was no money in these poor old worn out slaves and the cruel and barbarous master had abandoned them to their *fate*[.] As I looked at their worn out hands and fingers and bodies I thought of the long cruel years of bondage while under burning suns and in cold and heat they had labored for this *hellish* system of human slavery," so they had to find ways to survive. A not uncommon practice among slaveholders was the classing of their mixed-blood children as slaves, causing one soldier to proclaim, "*By G—d I'll fight till hell freezes over and then I'll cut the ice and fight on.*" The gratitude of slaves toward their perceived deliverers touched the hearts of a number of soldiers. They gave what gifts they could, offered their cooking skills, which were often considerable, and all sorts of free labor. Obviously these soldiers felt sympathy for the state of slaves, or did they merely wish to lash out at injustice? Did their anger indicate a change in racial attitudes? Perhaps in a few cases, but behavior overall indicated the army as a whole was not racially enlightened by these sorts of incidents.

In fact soldiers often found racially intoned situations humorous and a bit profound. One wrote, "They presented a very comical appearance. Some dressed in cast off [soldiers'] clothes[,] others in their plantation suits while the women were dressed in the coarsest fields suits to the gaudy silks[,] laces & velvets of their mistress." All had the countenance of human beings embracing freedom for the first time in their lives. Such experiences touched the hearts and minds of men in blue, but their racism is evident.

Union soldiers had mixed reactions to the enlistment of black regiments in the summer of 1862. Many men in Grant's army did not object to using the black soldiers to dig trenches; after all, that meant less work for whites. The sight of these men wearing the same uniforms Grant's veterans wore, however, caused negative feelings.

An Iowan complained, "The idea of arming and equipping Negro Regiments for the purpose of making them soldiers is, to my mind, worse than ridiculous nonsense. Niggers will *work if you make them do so.* I do not believe you could pick out one thousand Negroes out of 50,000 who would *fight* with *loaded* guns, or who would not run at the first appearance of danger.... We are all going to the devil." An Illinoisan reacted more practically. He had "no objection to Sambo's doing my fighting[;] if there is fight in Sambo lets [*sic*] have it." Others commented that it seemed only right for blacks to fight for their freedom. A Wisconsin soldier thought it good policy to allow black soldiers on battlefields. He believed the federal government could settle the war if "they arm the blacks and confiscate rebbel [*sic*] property, lay the towns in ashes, etc." In effect, Grant's soldiers did not mind blacks fighting on battlefronts, and they saw the advantage of freedmen wrecking rebel property. Why not work these black people, thereby reducing the number of white soldiers in harm's way and put the fear of God in southern whites who had constant fears of slave rebellions? These soldiers in blue might not care about black freedom one way or another, but they could see advantages in using freedmen in productive operations.

Anger at Lincoln's emancipation policy did contribute to desertion among Grant's troops, but the number is unknown and likely low since Grant never wrote about it being a problem. New recruits who found army life miserable deserted, too, though many, whatever their motives, were caught and punished. Getting up the Mississippi to potentially safe territory north of Union lines was not easy, but even veterans tired of sickness, death, swamps, and bad food tried to leave. Blaming all desertion on objections to emancipation would not be accurate.

Soldiers discussed what long-term impact emancipation might have on the war. Though not quite willing to go the desertion route, men continued to question why a war to restore the Union had to be focused on emancipation. An Illinoisan wrote his wife, "I am as far from being in favor of freeing the negro as any man tho [sic] I donte [sic] care what becomes of the negro if we can have peace." More important, what might become of freed slaves? An Iowan could not stand the thought of watching "stinking niggers" integrating his state.

Some of Grant's men logically feared that the question of emancipation could have a lasting negative impact on morale and attitudes. Soldiers who had been Democrats before the war often griped about the Lincoln party shifting war aims. An Ohioan noticed a "great deal of dissatisfaction and political clamor among Soldiers which portends that Something will have to be done shortly to put a Stop to this, or Something *else* will take place. I look for an *Order* to be issued prohibiting the discussing of politics among the Soldiers Subject to the penalty of death." The deep-seated racial comments underscored the main cause that led these soldiers to fight—saving the Union.

For the sake of peace, naysayers often agreed with an Iowan: "I am for anything that will cause Union and peace." Many blamed abolitionists and radical Republican politicians for fueling the continuation of the war with their continual assaults on slavery. There might be hope for peace if based only on bringing the Union back together. The emancipation issue had raised the stakes and made peace more difficult in the minds of quite a number of Grant's soldiers.[7]

White federal soldiers soon figured out, however, that emancipation would not have an immediate, profound impact on their attempts to take Vicksburg. For months into 1863, not all freedmen in the Vicksburg region had opportunities to enlist. Though freed by Lincoln's proclamation as of January 1, 1863, instead of liberty to do what they wanted, they found themselves picking cotton for Union officers in the Lake Providence area near the Mississippi north of Vicksburg. A few Union officers, more interested in making money than in freeing slaves, decided the freedmen would be more useful doing what they had experienced for most of their lives—working in cotton fields. Common white soldiers found the behavior of these officers disgusting, The officers, in effect, re-enslaved blacks to harvest cotton, which was illegally sold. Grant and his generals knew such things went on, but they found it difficult to monitor the large area over which the troops deployed in early 1863.[8]

Complicating the situation were slaves living in isolated areas of the Mississippi Delta, who may have rarely, if ever, seen Union soldiers for months as the Vicksburg campaign evolved. When Frederick Steele led his troops on an inland raid and reconnaissance from the river town of Greenville, many slaves stood shocked at the sudden appearance of the Yankees. Steele's operation was yet another Grant diversion intended to confuse Pemberton. Some slaves stepped forward to serve as guides, and they gave Steele accurate information about the area and told him that Confederates commanded by Samuel Ferguson had camped to the south to keep eyes out for Union forays. Slaves often were eager to help the Union cause when opportunities arose.

As Steele's men moved toward Ferguson's positions, Union soldiers found slave reaction humorous, and humor fueled their racist views. More and more blacks emerged from the plantations to watch Lincoln's troops pass by. One soldier wrote, "They seemed to be struck dumb, dazed, mouths wide open, staring in wonder and amazement, as we are the first Union troops that every trod this section." A black female slave brought laughter when she commented how surprised she was that these soldiers "haint got no hons." White southern propaganda, intended to frighten slaves, had preached that the invaders from the North had horns like the devil. Many Delta slaves believed the stories until they saw Steele's troops. Further evidence of slave isolation from war came when they scattered after Union batteries began sending shells south toward Ferguson's position. One soldier described the scene: "They strung out a distance of 150 to 200 yards, and I never saw such high stepping and tall running." Later when Steele marched his men back to Greenville, hundreds of slaves followed. Their fears did not overrule their desire for freedom. Steele's men were struck by how isolated these black families were from the world around them and no doubt impressed that, whatever strange experiences the war might bring to them, freedom was paramount.[9]

While Union soldiers found much to admire about slave hunger for freedom, that hunger did not soften their racism. After winning the Battle of Raymond, James McPherson's troops descended upon the town. The townspeople were disgusted when white men in McPherson's ranks paid undue attention to a mixed-blood young woman, many of whom were quite attractive, and how the troops stood by with pleasure as black women derided their now former owners. However, a significant event demonstrated just how complacent federal soldiers could be. When a young white boy shot one of the black women, other ex-slave women threatened to kill the boy if he did not call them "master." The boy did not back down, and since he was armed, the situation dissolved. No Union soldier came to the aid of the women.

White Raymond residents noted that the enemy soldiers had little use for most slaves other than finding ways to take advantage of them. Unlike the attitudes of slaves reacting to Steele's campaign, Raymond slaves, wrote one white resident, observed there was no jubilee for slaves aroused by McPherson's men. One resident recorded, "I pity the Negroes. They flocked in . . . expecting to experience freedom. Well, the women were put to washing for the hospital. They wash from daylight to dark." Locals may have intentionally written negative accounts about the conduct of federal soldiers, so they should be viewed a bit skeptically. Yet evidence indicates most of McPherson's men intimidated black women to work for free without providing living quarters. They did pass out rations, but the scant food, considering the scope of the work the women did, like making shirts, did not seem fair compensation.

Certainly the treatment of slaves by Union soldiers was no worse and likely not as bad as slave owners treated their "property." One Raymond woman concluded that McPherson's troops treated the "Negroes in the greatest detestation." She could have based her opinion on the fact that many blacks went back home to owners after the Union soldiers departed. Yet where else could they go? McPherson's corps was in the midst of campaigning and slaves, especially women and children, would be in harm's way. This portion of Grant's army had made their visit memorable, and whether the results had been positive or negative had been in the eye of the beholder. The undeniable fact was that blacks had tasted freedom, and, mistreatment or not, they would never be satisfied with their former condition.[10]

All through the course of the campaign, other examples of indifference to slaves by the Union army surfaced. One example was the destruction of slave cabins along the Mississippi. Occasionally, Confederate guerrillas fired at Union boats, which almost always resulted in detachments being sent ashore to burn everything in site as reprisal. The aggravation of snipers shooting at troop and supply vessels led Grant's men to embrace a scorched-earth policy, and they did not care who got in the way, whether southern slaves or southern civilians.[11]

At Milliken's Bend on the Louisiana side of the river, much more disturbing attitudes of Union soldier racism surfaced as a result of a little-known incident involving the punishment of a white soldier by Union colored troops. The background of what happened at Milliken's Bend was rooted in Frederick Steele's diversion at Greenville.

Isaac Shepard, colonel of the Third Missouri, participated in Steele's operation. Shepard, a Harvard graduate, editor of a Boston newspaper, and a member of the Massachusetts legislature, had come west when the Civil War started. A strong Unionist and abolitionist, he reached St. Louis where he became friends with Nathaniel Lyon, who shared Shepard's views. Shepard became a member of Lyon's staff, and after Lyon died at the Battle of Wilson's Creek, Shepard became lieutenant colonel of the Nineteenth Missouri, which was soon absorbed into the Third Missouri. Shepard commanded the regiment and performed well, especially during the Arkansas Post campaign early in 1863.[12]

Steele, likely familiar with Shepard's abolitionist views, asked Shepard to see to the welfare of freed men, women, and children who had followed Steele's division and were now crowded along the Mississippi River bank. About this same time Lorenzo Thomas, adjutant general of the U.S. Army, had come to the region to urge commanders to organize colored troops. Excited at the prospect of participating in implementation of the policy, Shepard appealed to his corps commander, William T. Sherman, to raise an "African Brigade" in Mississippi. Sherman responded positively, but Grant's inland campaign to take Vicksburg interrupted Shepard's plans. Steele's Division went to join Grant's army in the Vicksburg operations.

Slaves who had gathered at Greenville for river passage to freedom soon found themselves aboard boats traveling downriver to Milliken's Bend.

Shepard, due to illness, did not go with Steele's command and was recuperating at Milliken's Bend when Thomas arrived. On May 9, as Grant's army marched northeast into Mississippi from Port Gibson, where Union forces won a battle on May 1, Thomas authorized the First Mississippi Regiment of Colored troops, and the next day Shepard received orders to command an anticipated African brigade, to be recruited at Milliken's Bend.[13]

As Shepard began to organize potential black recruits, the reactions of white Union soldiers immediately became hostile. Shepard wrote that the mere presence of the blacks, including women and children, many of whom were ill, "excited ridicule and their helplessness aroused violence." Shepard described the conditions in which these freedmen lived as "squalid." They fell prey to Union soldiers who were "vicious and degraded," Shepard observed. An outbreak of smallpox made things worse. Shepard received some assistance, but all the while had to endure the "hatreds" and "perils" wrought by white soldiers who had no desire to be in such proximity to blacks. Seeing slaves and maybe even sympathizing with their plight did not cause soldiers in blue to want to embrace them as a free people.[14]

Within this milieu, an incident arose that led to Shepard's arrest and a court of inquiry, which in turn produced an exposé of widespread brutality and intolerance exhibited by white Union soldiers against the Milliken's Bend black community, including recruited U.S. colored soldiers. General Jeremiah C. Sullivan, a Virginia-born Indianan, and commanding officer at Milliken's Bend, ordered Shepard's arrest, for Sullivan was as appalled (and doubtless as bigoted) as white Union soldiers who found Shepard's actions an abomination. The court, requested by Shepard to clear his name, convened near Milliken's Bend on board the steamer *America*, on June 4, 1863, during the early stages of the siege of Vicksburg. Aside from being charged with having a white soldier whipped by black soldiers, Colonel Shepard also was accused of referring to himself as a brigadier general while ordering the punishment of a white soldier.[15]

Early in the court's proceedings, Shepard told the story of what had happened, and during the course of the hearing, several witnesses confirmed Shepard's version. The situation resulted from an alleged attack on a young black man by one John O'Brien, a private in Company A, Tenth

Illinois Cavalry. Two soldiers from Company A, both very drunk, one of them being O'Brien, came through the camp of the First Mississippi Colored troops late on a Saturday night. The two whites tied a black soldier to a tree; one of them kicked him several times, once viciously in the stomach. The two then went on to a "cotton shanty nearby" and assaulted two Negro women, "attacking one with a hatchet that was fortunately wrested from the brute and thrown away." Close by, a black boy thought to be about fourteen years old lay on the ground, no doubt trying not to be noticed. The two Illinois soldiers saw him, however, cursed and one took the hatchet and ran at the boy in a threatening manner. The other soldier stopped him, saying, in effect, that kicking the young man's "black brains out" would suffice. At that point, the aggressor, allegedly O'Brien, kicked the boy's cheek, causing "a severe gash," and then proceeded to grind the boot heel into the youngster's face, blinding his left eye. The attack continued until the victim seemed nearly unconscious. All the while, his fellow soldier cheered him on. An officer of the Fifty-seventh Ohio brought the attack to a halt when he arrested O'Brien, the latter proclaiming defiantly that he would kill all the blacks.

A white sergeant and a black guard escorted O'Brien, along with his victim, to Shepard's quarters. Shepard listened to reports of what had happened and noted that O'Brien refused to give the name of his accomplice. Shepard ordered the sergeant to take O'Brien to camp; Shepard felt that because of the severity of the wounds on the boy, and in light of other racist violence, it was time to set an example. Shepard said, "I told the sergeant under his direction to let four or five soldiers flagellate him and to tie him up." The whipping took place, but, according to all reliable accounts, amounted to very little. Shepard, perhaps having second thoughts, went to the camp himself and stopped the punishment after just a few strokes. Shepard remarked that "the whipping was slight, but the point I wish[ed] was gained, that the blacks ought to punish their own wrongs, and that was all I desired." Other witnesses described the "whips" used as "sugarberry bushes," common in Louisiana and having very lightweight limbs. So when the black troops struck O'Brien, the wood easily shattered, and, being drunk, he likely felt very little. He later claimed he was whipped with large tree branches that left him very bruised, but another witness said the bruises likely occurred when O'Brien, that same night, stumbled and fell backward against the hardwood tree to which he had been tied.[16]

Ultimately, Shepard was cleared of any wrongdoing, including the spurious charge of promoting himself to brigadier general, and restored to his command, but General Grant refused to allow the written record of the inquiry to be released to the newspapers. Shepard felt this should be done, for the initial story, before all the facts were in, had been published in northern newspapers, with some cartoons showing black soldiers beating a white soldier. Shepard knew that if all the facts came out, minds would be changed. Grant, however, understood that if the testimony was released, he would be embarrassed, President Lincoln would be furious, and the sordid details of what happened at Milliken's Bend would cause harsh reaction in the north at many levels.[17]

Those details should have been released, and a brief summary of them illustrates just how much suffering, humiliation, and injustice blacks had suffered from white Union troops before the O'Brian incident. Violent bigotry against blacks permeated the ranks of white Union troops. People who testified, both whites and blacks, cited specific criminal abuses of black troops and black civilians by white Union soldiers at Milliken's Bend that obviously were commonplace. That blacks were allowed to testify was a ray of hope, despite the circumstances.

Aside from O'Brien's denials and feeble attempts to defend him and attack Shepard by other white soldiers, the court of inquiry testimony revealed that black women often complained to white authorities that their daughters had been raped by white soldiers, the crimes being committed in front of the mothers. Grown black women also often fell victim to white rapists who obviously did not fear punishment. White soldiers randomly and at times viciously attacked black men, whether soldier or civilian, without cause. A white officer of the First Mississippi Colored Regiment testified that he once arrested five white soldiers for raping black women. The men did not deny what they had done, telling the officer, *"They are only niggers."* The officer turned the men over to the provost marshal, who released them the next day. Murder of blacks by whites was rare, but when such incidences occurred, perpetrators were not punished.

The O'Brien incident fueled white hatred of blacks, and Shepard was fortunate to escape being attacked or killed. One soldier, emboldened by liquor, remarked frankly, in front of an officer, "A bullet through Col. Shepard would settle it," and that he deserved no more consideration, probably less, than "the niggers in his camp." White officers, especially of the Tenth Illinois Cavalry, became more vigilant during the inquiry. They managed to prevent large-scale attacks on the black camp, but threats persisted. One drunken Illinoisan appealed to one of the officers, *"Can we have the privilege of cleaning out the d——d nigger camp?"* The officer said, "No, you can't do that!" with enough authority to convince the soldier to return to his camp. One black man, a blacksmith in the First Mississippi, told of one incident in which a white soldier terrorized a black family, including two children. During the course of his drunken assaults, he made a statement that must have summed up what many blacks at Milliken's Bend were beginning to believe: "You d——d niggers think you are free, and you are not as well off as you were with the Secesh!" This was not the only time blacks heard those sentiments during their tortuous stay at Milliken's Bend. Clearly the innate racism of northern whites portended future troubles for blacks who looked forward to total freedom if and when Union forces won the war.[18]

Though U. S. Grant did not want the transcript of the Shepard court made public, he did, on August 1, 1863, issue General Order No. 50: "Conduct disgraceful to the American name has been frequently reported to the Major General commanding, particularly on the part of portions of the cavalry. Hereafter, if the guilty parties can not be reached, the commanders of regiments and detachments will be held responsible, and those who prove themselves unequal to the task of preserving discipline in their commands will be promptly reported to the War Depart for 'muster.' Summary punishment will be inflicted upon all officers and soldiers apprehended in acts of violence or lawlessness."[19]

Ironically, the Battle of Milliken's Bend interrupted the proceedings of the Shepard inquiry, which was completed after the fight. Bravery of U.S. Colored troops in action during the battle on June 9 caught the attention of Union officers and men. Confederates in northeast Louisiana occasionally used diversions to irritate Grant during the Vicksburg siege. In the most notable of these operations, rebel troops commanded by John Walker attacked Milliken's Bend to drive away Union occupation forces. Colored troops were not the only Union troops on hand, but they fought and fought well, considering, as Grant wrote, they "had but little experience in the use of fire-arms." He went on to comment, "Their conduct is said, however, to have been most gallant, and I doubt not but with good officers they will make good troops."

One of the officers who led the black troops, Brigadier General Elias Dennis, wrote more pointedly than Grant. In his battle report Dennis placed the colored troops situation in greater perspective: "The African regiments being inexperienced in the use of arms, some of them having been drilled but a few days, and the guns being very inferior, the enemy succeeded in getting upon our works before more than one or two volleys were fired at them." Yet despite the handicaps, as in giving the colored troops inferior arms, because they were colored troops perhaps, the black soldiers stood their ground and got into "a most terrible hand-to-hand conflict of several minutes' duration, our men using the bayonet freely and clubbing their guns with fierce obstinacy, contesting every inch of ground." The Confederates flanked the Union troops and forced a retreat to the river and cover fire from two gunboats. Another attempted rebel flanking maneuver was stopped by the Eleventh Louisiana Infantry, of "African descent," which had been well placed to block an enemy flanking movement. The Eighth Louisiana also fought well. Eventually the hard fighting and gunboat fire led to the Confederates' retreat, ending the contest with a Union victory.

Dennis reported 652 total casualties out of 1,061 engaged, which included five colored regiments and one white Iowa regiment. He expected some missing colored soldiers, who panicked and ran when facing their first combat, to return and most did. Clearly, Grant's officers had not done enough to prepare the former slaves for battle, and inferior weapons made the situation worse. As time passed and Union officers and white troops came to respect increasingly the fighting abilities of black troops, attitudes changed, and colored troops would write a noble chapter of heroism during the rest of the war.[20]

In Vicksburg, freedmen not in uniform, and, no doubt, many who were, spent the remainder of the siege digging trenches and helping with supplies. Any duties Grant's white soldiers could avoid by substituting blacks meant the latter endured hard, hot work in the summer heat and humidity. One of Grant's staff, Adam Badeau, later wrote, "The labor in the trenches was performed either by men of the pioneer companies, by details from the line, or by negroes. Several of the pioneer companies had negroes attached to them, who had come within the national lines, and were paid according to law. These proved very efficient, when under good supervision." Badeau went on to say that labor performed by Grant's regulars was "light" when compared "with that done by the same number of pioneers or negroes; without the stimulus of danger, or pecuniary reward, troops of the line would not work so efficiently, especially at night, and after the novelty of the labor had worn off." These black men were technically not slaves anymore, but federal soldiers certainly enjoyed the fruits of their labor as their former white owners had.[21]

As the siege progressed toward ultimate federal victory, Grant's officers began digging mines, planting powder, and blowing huge holes in Confederate defenses. Such an explosion on July 1 gave James McPherson's troops an opportunity to meet a Confederate slave in a most unusual manner. Confederates, physically exhausted by long hours in the trenches and lack of food and water, forced male slaves, doubtless in poor condition themselves, to dig countermines in an attempt to stop federal operations. At 3 P.M. on July 1, Union miners exploded a large charge underneath the works of the Third Louisiana redan for the second time. All but one countermining slave died in the blast. The survivor flew high into the air and landed within Union lines. The story became legend among McPherson's soldiers. Some of them asked the shaken, but uninjured, slave how high he went up before coming down. He supposedly replied, "Dunno, massa, but t'ink about t'ree mile." Many federal soldiers told the story, all in ways to demonstrate the inferiority of this unfortunate black man who had almost lost his life. The humor was laced with racism.[22]

John Pemberton surrendered Vicksburg before any further explosions occurred. Pemberton initially made contact with Grant on July 3, but the official capitulation came the next day. The presence of the U.S. Colored troops in Grant's army gave the town its first look at black soldiers. Some sights were simply strange, while others ridiculed southern social structure.

White soldiers in both armies struck up friendly conversations. Union soldiers assisted disabled Confederates who could not stand after being crouched so many weeks in entrenchments. They also shared with Confederates much-needed food and water. Both armies seemed to ignore the colored regiments' presence. One incident did cheer the Confederates and illustrated the continuing racist attitudes among Union soldiers.

Colored troops, even those who had seen action, needed additional training, and that task was turned over to white federal instructors. The black soldiers did not always receive respect; indeed, their instructors seemed to enjoy giving them a hard time. During one drill, a Union instructor was armed with a large stick that he used to whip the black soldiers on their backsides when they did anything wrong. After such blows, instructors sometimes looked at a group of Pemberton's men who sat watching, and then winked, at which point the Confederates often erupted with a rebel yell.[23]

Federal soldiers, married or unmarried, had for several weeks had few opportunities to interact with females. Some broke through the icy demeanor of white Vicksburg women, though it was not an easy task. Other Union soldiers turned to black women, and interracial relationships convinced white Vicksburgians that they had been right all along about the barbarous Yankees. The men did not seem to care, even if their own comrades in arms objected. The sight of former slave women strolling the streets of the town holding hands with federal boyfriends became common, however repulsive it might have been to local civilians. No doubt there were federal soldiers equally offended. But the federal romantics apparently went about their courting peacefully. There was no violence as with the Illinois cavalrymen at Milliken's Bend. Interracial sexual activities had been going on for generations between white male slave owners and their female slaves, who had no choice but to yield. The many light-skinned blacks in the Vicksburg area and across the South said all that needed to be said about holier-than-thou southern white hypocrisy regarding mixing of racial blood.[24]

Beyond interracial socializing, Union officers had to deal with more significant racial issues once the city had been surrendered. Sherman knew more black men would be joining the army, and his personal racist views did not make such prospects pleasing. Though he would enforce emancipation because of his soldierly duty, he did not think slavery a necessarily evil institution. He did not believe blacks were fit to be soldiers, but he had no problem with them doing manual labor. The colored troops' performance at Milliken's Bend did not leave a lasting, positive impression on Sherman.[25]

Grant, however, saw potential for contributions of black soldiers. When writing about the fight at Milliken's Bend, he noted that the battle was the first significant combat the colored troops had experienced. He noted, "These men were very raw, having all been enlisted since the beginning of the siege, but they behaved well." Prior to the siege, Grant had ordered that "negro regiments now organizing in this department" should be treated equally when it came to receiving supplies, stores, and whatever else would be issued normally to white troops. Grant believed he must carry out the gist of Lincoln's wishes that everything be done that could be done to eliminate prejudice against the black soldiers. His goal proved to be hopeless. Yet Grant understand much more so than Sherman that the war to save the Union now would involve black participation, and the results, in increased numbers alone, favored the federal cause.[26]

James McPherson dealt with a different problem regarding the race issue. After the surrender, many of Pemberton's officers wanted to keep their slave body-servants. McPherson asked Grant if that was acceptable, and Grant said yes, but only if the former slaves were willing to go. McPherson knew that some of these officers were overtly or covertly threatening these freedmen if they did not agree to go. He grew frustrated when many former slaves came to his office insisting that they indeed wanted to go with their masters, or former masters. The situation was not that simple, and McPherson saw clearly what was happening. Angered, he canceled the policy, though he allowed a few exceptions. His experience clearly demonstrated that the nuances of emancipation would be complex.

African Americans learned eventually that interactions between federal soldiers and freedmen, as illustrated during the Vicksburg campaign, foretold that many of them would go from one type of slavery to another. Grant's army generally was racist, as were all federal forces, though they welcomed additional labor and applauded black soldiers who went into battle. Such attitudes were mostly for convenience and did not signal enlightened attitudes toward race. In the Union army, the Vicksburg campaign demonstrated that emancipation did not mean freedom. Racial divides during the war were strong enough and consistent enough to continue well into the future.[27]

Notes

1. For examples of historians' thoughts on Union soldiers' views of slavery as the war progressed, see James McPherson, *For Cause and Comrade: When Men Fought in the Civil War* (New York: Oxford University Press, 1997), 120–28; James I. Robertson, *Soldiers Blue and Gray* (Columbia: University of South Carolina Press, 1988), 31–36; Reid Mitchell, *Civil War Soldiers* (New York: Penguin, 1988), 27, 42, 126–27.

    The following study is drawn in large part from the author's book, *Vicksburg: The Campaign That Opened the Mississippi* (Chapel Hill: University of North Carolina Press, 2004; paperback, 2010).

2. The standard work on the Iuka and Corinth campaigns is Peter B. Cozzens's *The Darkest Days of the War: The Battles of Iuka and Corinth* (Chapel Hill: University of North Carolina Press, 1997). See also Michael B. Ballard's *The Civil War in Mississippi: Major Campaigns and Battles* (Jackson: University Press of Mississippi, 2011).
3. William Woodward to Wife [Louise], July 4, 15, 19, Woodward Papers, United States Army Military History Institute (USAMHI), Carlisle Barracks, PA; Daniel Dinsmore to brother, September 4, 1862, Jasper Barny to brother, October 1862, John C. Dinsmore Papers, Illinois State Historical Library (ISHL). The ISHL is now part of the Abraham Lincoln Presidential Library in Springfield, IL.
4. Sylvester W. Fairfield to Lizzie, December 1, 1862, Fairfield Papers, Charles F. Nelson Diary, November 28, 1862, Sylvester Bishop Diary, November 29, 1862, all in Indiana Historical Society (IHL), Indianapolis, IN; James Smith to Fair Friend Mattie, November 24, 1862, Smith Papers, ISHL; George P. Mertz Diary, November 26, 1862, Perkins Library, Duke University (DU); Henry H. Wright, *History of the Sixth Iowa Infantry* (Iowa City: State Historical Society of Iowa, 1923), 146–47.
5. Seneca B. Thrall to wife, December 3, 1863 [1862], Seneca Thrall Papers, University of Iowa (UI); Cyrus F. Boyd, *The Civil War Diary of Cyrus F. Boyd*, ed. Mildred Throne (1953; rpt., Millwood, N.Y.: Periodicals Service Co., 1977), 94; Adoniram J. Withrow to Lib, Cottoy, and Clara, December 8, 1862, Adoniram Judson Withrow Papers, Southern Historical Collection, University of North Carolina at Chapel Hill (UNCCH); Joseph Crider to Samuel Crider, November 29, 1862, and to Samuel Crider, January 30, 1862, Joseph Crider Papers, University of Missouri-Columbia Library; Edward Rolph letters in Laurence Lillibridge, ed., *Hard Marches, Hard Crackers, and Hard Bread: A Great Grandfather's Letters during the Civil War* (Prescott Valley, Az.: Lillibridge Publishing, 1993), 45.
6. McPherson, *Cause and Comrades*, 112–14; Mary Bobbitt Townsend, *Yankee Warhorse: A Biography of Major General Peter Osterhaus* (Columbia: University of Missouri Press, 2010), 21, 23–24; Townsend P. Heaton to John Heaton, February 11, 1863, Townsend Heaton Letters, Ohio Historical Society (OHS), Columbus; James N. Stewart to friend, February 14, 1863, in Helen F. Livingston, comp., "Sing the Jubilee: Compiled from the Letters, Diaries, and Papers of David James Palmer," Palmer Papers, UI.
7. Boyd, *Diary*, 120–21; Ephriam Brown to Drusilla Brown, January 25, 1863, Ephriam Brown Papers, OHS; Jerome Robbins Journal, Number 7, pp. 44–45, Jerome Robbins Journals, Bentley Library, University of Michigan (UM); James M. McPherson, *The Negro's Civil War: How American Negroes Felt and Acted During the War for the Union* (New York: Pantheon Books, 1965), 165; Thaddeus B. Packard Diary, February 9, 1863, and David Holmes to parents, February 24, 1863, David N. Holmes Papers, ISHL; Seneca Thrall to wife (Mollie), January 20, 1863, Thrall Papers, UI; Joel Norton to brother, February 5, 1863, Joel Norton Letters, Wisconsin Historical Society Archives (WHSA), Madison. For further context, see Ballard, *Vicksburg*, 162–64.

8. P. C. Bonner letter, March 3, 1863, excerpts from Winifred Keen Armstrong, ed., *The Civil War Letters of Pvt. P. C. Bonney*, Publications of the Lawrence County Historical Society, Lawrenceville, IL, 1963, in Thirty-first Illinois file, Regimental Files Subseries of the Vicksburg Campaign Series, Vicksburg National Military Park Archives.
9. Calvin Ainsworth Diary, 28–31, UM.
10. Lavinia to Emmie, [June ?, 1863], June 21, July 1, 1863, Crutcher-Shannon Papers, Mississippi Department of Archives and History.
11. John G. Jones to parents, March 23, 1863, Jones Papers, WHSA; Joseph F. McCarthy to Seth, January 14, 1863, McCarthy Papers, IHS; Byron MacCutcheon Autobiography, "Down the Mississippi to Vicksburg," n.p., John L. Matthews Papers, ISHL. See also Ballard, *Vicksburg*, 160.
12. Ezra J. Warner, *Generals in Blue: Lives of the Confederate Commanders* (Baton Rouge: Louisiana State University Press, 1986), 435–36.
13. Isaac F. Shepard Court of Inquiry Papers, typescript, Shepard Collection, University of California at Santa Barbara, 3–4. I am indebted to David H. Slay for loaning me a copy of the Court of Inquiry Papers, which he used in the researching and writing of his doctoral dissertation, "New Masters of the Mississippi: The United States Colored Troops of the Middle Mississippi Valley" (Texas Christian University, 2009). Dr. Slay is currently revising the dissertation for eventual publication.
14. Shepard Court, 4–5.
15. Ibid., 7–10, 13.
16. Ibid., 18–20.
17. Ibid., 82–84, iii, iv.
18. Ibid., 14, 17–19, 37–38, 40, 44, 51, 55–56.
19. Ibid., 84.
20. *The War of the Rebellion: A Compilation of the Official Records of the Union and Confederate Armies*, 128 vols. (Washington, D.C.: Government Printing Office, 1889–1901), Series 1, volume 24, part 2, 446–49, 453.
21. Adam Badeau, *Military History of Ulysses S. Grant, From April, 1861, to April, 1865*, 3 vols. (New York: D. Appleton, 1885), 1:337.
22. Ballard, *Vicksburg*, 369.
23. Ibid., 400.
24. Ibid., 419.
25. John F. Marszalek, *Sherman: A Soldier's Passion for Order* (New York: Free Press, 1993), 142, 192–93, 270–71.
26. Ulysses S. Grant, *Personal Memoirs of U. S. Grant*, 2 vols. (New York: Charles L. Webster & Co., 1885), 1:544–45; *Official Records*, 1–24–3, 220.
27. Ballard, *Vicksburg*, 403.

5. TOWN AND SWORD

Black Boxers at Columbus, New Mexico, 1916–1922

HORACE NASH

DURING THE POST–CIVIL WAR YEARS FROM RECONSTRUCTION TO THE turn of the twentieth century, the nation struggled with the proper place for newly freed black Americans. This concern was especially evident in the important debate on the African American role in the postwar U.S. Army. Shortly after the Civil War, primarily motivated by a need for manpower, Congress established six regular army regiments consisting of black enlisted men and white officers. Two of these units were cavalry regiments (Ninth and Tenth) and four were infantry regiments (Thirty-eighth, Thirty-ninth, Fortieth, and Forty-first). In 1869, Congress passed an army reorganization bill that consolidated the four black infantry regiments into two, the Twenty-fourth and Twenty-fifth Infantries, and kept the Ninth and Tenth Cavalry regiments intact. For some blacks the military became an appealing alternative to civilian life.[1]

For the next two decades, black regulars played prominent roles in settling the West, serving at diverse locations such as the Texas frontier, Indian Territory, New Mexico, Arizona, and the Dakota Territory. Indians called these men "buffalo soldiers" because their hair resembled the fur of the buffalo. Normally a term of respect, the name was first applied solely to members of the cavalry, but it soon referred to black infantrymen as well.[2]

During these years, the buffalo soldiers served honorably but were kept far from eastern population centers. Their location symbolized the country's surge toward segregation. In the 1890s the U.S. Supreme Court's decision in *Plessy v. Ferguson* (1896) sanctioned the strict segregation of the Jim Crow era, permitting laws and practices that discriminated against blacks especially in the South but to varying degrees elsewhere in the nation.[3]

The black regulars continued deployment in the West until the Spanish-American War. All four black regiments took part in that war, serving in Cuba, Puerto Rico, and later the Philippines. Many African Americans hoped that the participation of black regulars and volunteers would improve the social and legal plight of their race in the United States. With the increased racism in the post-frontier period, especially in the South where some of these units were stationed, tension between soldiers and local civilian communities heightened. When black soldiers refused to endure abuse from local whites and fought back, violent racial clashes often occurred.[4]

Between tours of duty in the Spanish-American War and newly acquired U.S. possessions in the Pacific, the buffalo soldiers returned to various stations in the United States, again mostly in the West. After service in the Mexican Punitive Expedition in 1916–1917 and along the U.S-Mexico border during the Mexican Revolution, these units were impacted by post–World War I military cutbacks. During and after service in World War II, they were either disbanded or merged into the integrated armed forces.[5]

The black soldiers symbolized pride and hope for black citizens of the period and beyond. In May 1994, General Colin Powell, an African American and former chairman of the Joint Chiefs of Staff, U.S. Armed Forces, made a commencement speech at Howard University in which he paid tribute to the proud record of the buffalo soldiers. Clearly, service in the military had produced a special place in the historical experience of African Americans.[6]

Since these black regulars spent most of their time in the West, their written history has primarily focused on the impact they had in that region. Historians of the black military experience during that period have examined not simply military operations but also camp and community life and the social, economic, and political aspects of the African American military experience. In recent decades, a number of studies have examined the interaction between black soldiers and white civilians in the West. The remainder of this chapter focuses on experiences of black soldiers in the West in a specific locale and how sports, most notably boxing, did much to overcome bigotry.[7]

On March 9, 1916, Mexican revolutionary Pancho Villa and a band of his followers attacked Columbus, New Mexico, a small isolated community in Luna County, three miles north of the Mexican border. Two buffalo soldier regiments, the Tenth Cavalry and the Twenty-fourth Infantry, joined General John J. Pershing's expedition into Mexico to punish Villa. After an unsuccessful effort, these forces returned to the United States on February 5, 1917. The white Twelfth Cavalry and the black Twenty-fourth Infantry were stationed at Columbus.[8]

By the end of March 1917, nearly 1,500 soldiers (1,170 black and 249 white) were stationed at Camp Furlong, just south of the railroad tracks in Columbus. Three years later, in March 1920, there were 4,109 enlisted men at the base, including 3,599 black and 510 white soldiers, and 75 officers (one black officer) present for duty. During the military buildup the civilian population of the town exploded, from almost 700 in 1916 to over 2,100 by 1920. At its height Columbus represented one of the single largest black military communities ever to reside in the West. A study of the Twenty-fourth Infantry's nearly seven years at Columbus provides insight into American racial attitudes of the early twentieth century and sheds important light on black military communities.[9]

A couple of months after the Punitive Expedition returned from Mexico, on April 6, 1917, the United States declared war on Germany. During the war both the Twenty-fourth Infantry and the Twelfth Cavalry were on duty at Columbus. The military duties of these units remained basically unchanged by the war. Their primary task was to protect the border. Many citizens had valid concerns about the spillover from the Mexican Revolution.[10]

In late July 1917, a battalion of the Twenty-fourth Infantry went to Camp Logan in Houston, Texas, to guard construction sites for new military camps. The other two battalions were sent on similar assignments to sites in New Mexico and Texas. The Camp Logan duty eventually turned into a disaster. In Houston, a race riot involving the Twenty-fourth Infantry occurred on August 23, 1917. Several soldiers, incensed at the unfair treatment of one of their comrades by Houston police, took to the streets in retaliation. The rioting soldiers subsequently were captured and arrested. Sixteen whites lay dead in the aftermath.[11]

The president of the Columbus Chamber of Commerce, John R. Blair, telegraphed the War Department that the Twenty-fourth Infantry was one of the best-disciplined units in the army. He stated that Columbus would be happy to have the soldiers returned to that city, together with any other black soldiers the government wished to send. The men from the Twenty-fourth were immediately returned to Columbus.[12]

Subsequent investigations led to 118 men being charged with mutiny, rioting, and murder. All but eight were found guilty of at least one of the charges. Seven were acquitted and one soldier, found to be mentally incompetent, did not stand trial. By the time all the court-martials had concluded, thirty-four death sentences had been handed down; eventually, ten of the death sentences were commuted to life. Twelve men were also initially sentenced to life.[13]

Local response to the Houston riot was mixed. Despite Columbus town officials seeming to be unconcerned, the Houston affair created an uneasy atmosphere in and around their town. Upon returning to Columbus after the incident, some black soldiers foolishly threatened local citizens. Thus, it is reasonable to assume that residents feared or came to fear the black soldiers. The situation may have inhibited white people from openly expressing opposition not only to the presence of the Twenty-fourth in Columbus, but also to a possible independent spirit in the town's emerging black community. Business and community leaders remained cautious about expressing disapproval of the black soldiers, fearing that if they were intimidated to step aside, other white citizens would be reluctant to step into the void. The soldiers, with the passage of time and a cooling-off period, likely gained the confidence of the community, but some local whites never overcame their fears.[14]

In the postwar period, changing community conditions heightened local white sensitivity to black behavior and became a major factor in the deterioration of relations between blacks and whites. After the war ended, the substantial increase in the number of black soldiers exacerbated local fears. More assertive black veterans who returned from duty in Europe and joined the regiment in mid-1919 caused the white community to view them as a "troublesome element." In early 1920, the removal of the all-white Twelfth Cavalry further intensified local fears.

At the same time, political division exacerbated racial tensions within the community. Prior to the 1920 fall election, Republican leaders courted the black vote. In contrast, Democratic leaders tried to get the Twenty-fourth Infantry out of Columbus before election time, arguing that the increase in crime justified the removal of the unit. Yet most business and community leaders followed the lead of Mayor Blair and countered efforts to get rid of the soldiers, whose presence not only assured some protection on the still uncertainties of frontier life but also contributed to the local economy. They were willing to have the black soldiers removed only if they were replaced by white ones, which they knew could not be guaranteed.[15]

New Mexico courts compounded potential racial tension by backing the state attorney general's decision to bar military members and their spouses from voting in the November elections. Since black soldiers did not claim Columbus as their residence, neither they nor their spouses were eligible to vote there. Subsequently, military investigators concluded that the crime problems in the town would not have been different had the soldiers been white, and that conditions at Columbus were probably no worse than those near other military installations. Complaints against black soldiers were, in effect, racially motivated, and other issues raised regarding their presence were nothing more than red herrings.[16]

Despite imperfections in the racial situation at Columbus, the community managed to develop relatively harmonious relations and avoided the conflicts that existed in so many other areas during this era. Black soldiers, their wives, children, and others routinely moved from post to post, and they formed the core around which a black community at Columbus evolved. They organized social gatherings, sporting events, religious activities, and other entertainment, seeking to improve the quality of their lives in the isolated western frontier environment. In the process, they created a vibrant community that operated with considerable independence.[17]

Although many social activities at Columbus were segregated, blacks and whites jointly attended some public events. As at many locations where black regulars had previously served, athletic and cultural interchange helped foster better race relations. The situation in Columbus proved to be similar. For example, the Twenty-fourth Infantry band and its musicians performed at numerous events, both as a military band and as a private orchestra.[18]

Sports events, especially boxing, became integral parts of local entertainment. The military emphasized sports to provide soldiers with "wholesome" recreation and to keep the soldiers in good physical shape. Ordinarily, each company fielded a baseball and a football team. Regimental teams in turn occasionally participated against teams from other military posts. On holidays a full day's schedule of sporting events usually took place. Thanksgiving Day, November 1917, was typical in Columbus. Athletic activities were scheduled, beginning at 8:00 A.M., with the public admitted free. In addition to track and field events such as the

220- and 440-yard races, high jump, and broad jump, team sports such as football were offered. In the football game a large crowd watched the Twenty-fourth Infantry's Machine Gun Company defeat the white Twelfth Cavalry's Third Squadron 6 to 0.[19]

Numerous boxing matches, more than football, provided a means for interracial contact more than any other activity. In contrast to societal norms, it was not uncommon for white soldiers to compete against black soldiers, one on one, in the boxing ring. In Mexico, during the Expedition, the black and white regiments had competed against each other often, and later at Columbus, the Twenty-fourth Infantry boxing teams competed against white ones from Fort Bliss located at nearby El Paso, Texas.[20]

Military boxing matches had taken place in town prior to Villa's raid, and the sport became a popular entertainment during the Punitive Expedition period. At that time the majority of the boxers had been white soldiers. After the Twenty-fourth Infantry became permanently settled at Camp Furlong, however, black boxers dominated the local boxing scene. Military personnel and civilians, both black and white, participated in these events as fighters, referees, promoters, and fans. Sometimes civilians from towns in the vicinity, like El Paso, attended.[21]

Despite the military's interest in sports, the initiative of members of the black community and local white civilians in Columbus contributed more to the town's enhanced boxing activity. Black businessman Henry Davis and white businessman Carter H. Johnson saw the business opportunities associated with the sport and formed an athletic club. These two men played dominant roles in sponsoring the fight game in the area. The matches were soon being reported in articles in the noted black newspaper, the *Chicago Defender*.[22]

Members of the military also became involved in all phases of boxing. In Mexico, soldiers from the Twenty-fourth Infantry had held boxing matches to overcome their boredom. Sergeant Joe Blackburn had been regimental boxing champion and later helped organize fights. When the unit returned to Columbus, he became a referee and trainer. Rufus Williams, who succeeded Blackburn as regimental champion, fought in Columbus and remained active as a fighter. He also served as a referee. A former officer in the Twenty-fourth Infantry recalled the regiment having several excellent boxers who then helped to develop new fighters in the different companies. Blackburn and Williams were leaders among these individuals.[23]

Within two weeks of the Twenty-fourth Infantry's return from Mexico in 1917, its athletic association held fights on Washington's birthday, and citizens in large numbers attended. Initially, most of the fights were held at the Crystal Theater, its 900-seat capacity the largest in town. Regularly scheduled monthly bouts then became a major form of entertainment for both black and white sports fans. Rufus Williams quickly became the top-rated soldier boxer.[24]

Besides Williams, other excellent boxers began to attract attention even beyond the Columbus and Camp Furlong community. In early April 1917 boxing promoters Henry Davis and Rufus Williams signed two Twenty-fourth soldiers, Thomas Hayden and Juan Cabell, to a ten-round bout to determine the regimental welterweight champion. Hayden knocked Cabell out in the sixth round. The local newspaper, the *Columbus Courier*, predicted that if Hayden continued to improve, he would soon command the attention of many outside promoters looking for boxers.[25]

A few days later, the United States entered the war against Germany. Because boxing was similar to bayonet fighting, military leaders during World War I increased their support of the sport. Also, the Twenty-fourth's commanders wholeheartedly approved of the more positive diversion that boxing offered since they were concerned about the off-duty pursuits of their soldiers. In May 1917, Rufus Williams defeated "Bull" Foster in ten rounds at the Crystal Theater, a repeat of Williams's victory the previous fall. This main event was accompanied by several preliminary bouts. In addition, a group from the Twenty-fourth Infantry Regimental Band provided music.[26]

As the sport's popularity increased, the crowds grew larger, especially the holiday bouts. The *Courier* touted the fights held on July 4, 1917, as the best ever in Columbus and noted further that attendance was larger than at any of the events the previous summer when there had been far more people in Columbus. Every seat in the theater was taken, and an estimated 200 people filled the standing-room area, forming a crowd of 1,100 onlookers.[27]

Henry Davis, anxious to promote his new find, Thomas Hayden, matched the boxer against a white soldier from Fort Bliss in late July 1917. Hayden scored a knockout, another impressive quick victory. The stage was now set for Hayden to meet Rufus Williams, the Twenty-fourth Infantry regimental champion, but the Twenty-fourth's reassignment to guard training camps prevented the fight from occurring and disrupted the entire fighting game at Columbus.[28]

The Houston affair and its aftermath was disturbing. Nonetheless, after the soldiers returned to Columbus, life there gradually returned to as normal as possible given the circumstances. Under the direction of fight promoters Davis and Johnson, the town's boxing matches resumed by late September 1917. On Thanksgiving Day the anticipated fight between Thomas Hayden, now nicknamed Speedball, and Rufus Williams took place. The *Courier* predicted that it would be one of the best matches ever staged in Columbus. Williams had not lost a bout in five years, and Hayden had won his last five fights by knockouts. Blacks from El Paso reserved a special railroad car to attend the fight. The highly touted fight lasted for eleven rounds, although Williams almost knocked Hayden through the ropes in the first round. Hayden came back, however, and clearly controlled the next ten rounds. In the twelfth round, referee Dick Monohan, an El Paso sports reporter, declared Hayden the winner when Williams was unable to continue. An estimated thousand people then attended a dance held after the fight.[29]

On Christmas Day, Hayden faced a white boxer, Johnny Sudenberg, of the Seventh Cavalry from Fort Bliss. Out-of-towners and local fans again poured into the Crystal Theater to watch Speedball easily defeat Sudenberg. Hayden was extremely popular and clearly the local boxing champion.[30]

Boxing benefited the entire region: the soldiers stationed at Camp Furlong and local civilians for miles around. Aside from entertainment, it provided a peaceable means of interracial contact. Referees were white and black, civilian and military, from Columbus and out of town. Matches attracted large audiences of soldiers and civilians and were routinely covered in newspapers as far away as El Paso. Prior involvement of individuals such as Blackburn and Williams helped make the sport successful in Columbus, but for the black soldiers, it was more than just a night's entertainment. There was a sense of racial pride in following the success of the local boxers, especially when they defeated white opponents. Knowing that blacks managed these activities also added to their feelings of accomplishment. Columbus matches occurred in the wake of black boxer Jack Johnson's decline at the national level, so the local boxers no doubt imagined themselves as taking his place. Some seemed to have the promise of doing so.[31]

Thomas "Speedball" Hayden had boxing experience before he entered the army. While on duty with the Twenty-fourth in Mexico, he came to the attention of the unit's officers as he was sparring with Rufus Williams, then the unit's champion. Hayden's growing reputation and Davis's promotional skill attracted boxers to Columbus. In February 1918, enticed by a challenge Davis placed in the *Chicago Defender*, a black boxer, Hock Bones, arrived from Memphis, Tennessee, to battle Hayden. Promoters arranged for the fight to be held in El Paso, but the Columbus fans protested so strongly that the event was rescheduled for Columbus. El Paso fans willingly made the trip. Considerable betting took place, and the fight was a sell-out. Even Colonel Wilson Chase, Camp Furlong's commanding officer, attended. Hayden dominated the fight, winning on points. The *Courier* reported that Bones had had his face "beaten to a jelly."[32]

"Speedball" Hayden provided the soldiers and local fans with a desired hero. Henry Davis became so excited over the young boxer's potential that he planned to devote his time exclusively to managing the boxer's fast-rising career. In May, Speedball defeated Rufus Williams in a rematch of the previous November fight.[33]

Hayden also drew large crowds when he fought in El Paso. In that city, on Memorial Day, he once more defeated Johnny Sudenberg in front of approximately 2,500 fans, winning ten out of the fifteen rounds. Throughout the summer the monthly fights continued. On August 27, 1918, a series of bouts was scheduled with some of the lesser-known boxers from the Twelfth Cavalry and Twenty-fourth Infantry pitted against each other. Prices were $1.10, $1.65, and $2.20 for General Admission, Reserved, and Ringside seats, respectively. In the main event a new boxer, Clarence "Kid" Ross, defeated Hock Bones, the latter's second loss at Columbus. The fight was decided by the three judges, two of whom were army officers. The third, Jack London, was a member of the village board of trustees.[34]

Increasingly the regimental athletic officer became more deeply involved in staging boxing events. The army's participation was part of an overall effort to improve recreational opportunity for soldiers. In military camps throughout the country, boxing was becoming part of the physical education routine, involving soldiers as spectators and participants.[35]

Military authorities at Camp Furlong provided a larger outdoor boxing arena. The increased number of soldiers recently assigned to the camp could not fit into the cramped theater and such tight quarters possibly led to tension. Ticket prices for fights in town had become expensive, so cheaper prices on post would enable more soldiers to attend the matches. On September 20, 1918, the authorities scheduled the first series of fights under the lights of the Twenty-fourth Infantry's athletic field. Lieutenant George W. Booth, the regiment's athletic officer, reduced admission prices to about half of the cost in town. A crowd estimated at 2,000 saw the fights, including a large number of army officers and their wives, many Columbus townspeople, as well as out-of-town visitors.[36]

A fearful influenza epidemic soon brought boxing and most other activities in Columbus to a halt. At the end of September, only one case had been reported in Columbus, but several were reported in camp. Columbus fight fans awaiting the rematch of Speedball Hayden and Clarence Ross had to wait. The entire camp was quarantined. On November 1, 1918, the *Courier* announced that, despite the influenza, the regimental football season would begin, and by mid-November the theater was open. Just a few weeks later, however, the Twenty-fourth was again quarantined. World War I ended with Columbus and Camp Furlong still suffering from the deadly worldwide influenza outbreak. One of the fatalities was local businessman, village board trustee, and occasional boxing referee Jack London.[37]

In January 1919, with the health threat presumably over, the Twenty-fourth Infantry regimental athletic board scheduled a boxing tournament to stimulate soldier participation, both as performers and as spectators. A series of minor bouts was held at the Crystal Theater in town, the admission price reduced to ensure a large attendance. Despite the military's increased involvement, the fights retained civilian participation, both black and white.[38]

On January 18, 1919, Speedball Hayden met Navy Rostan, a white boxing instructor from Camp Funston, Kansas, in a twenty-round bout. Hayden won by a knockout in the seventh round "with a straight right that landed squarely on the chin." Other matches followed. Some 2,500 fans attended these fights held at the arena erected in the Twenty-fourth Infantry camp. *El Paso Morning Times* reporter Hy Schneider noted that a $500 purse plus expenses went to the out-of-town fighter, while the *Columbus Courier* praised the efforts of Lieutenant Booth for staging the bouts.[39]

On February 12, Lieutenant James A. McCarthy of the Twenty-fourth Infantry took Speedball Hayden and a number of other fighters to put on an exhibition in nearby Deming, New Mexico, where Camp Furlong soldiers were on temporary duty salvaging building materials. Several Columbus boxers then regularly fought in Deming. At a bout on July 17 held at the Majestic Theater, a large crowd, including a considerable number of women, was in attendance. On April 1 in Silver City, New Mexico, Speedball Hayden lost his first fight, a decision to Eddie Johnson of Pueblo, Colorado. Columbus fans claimed that Hayden had been given a "rotten" deal, and several military officers agreed that Johnson should have been disqualified in the first part of the fight for repeated fouling. The *Courier* editor argued that a return match should be held in Columbus because of the Twenty-fourth's reputation for "giving a visitor a square deal."[40]

The Crystal Theater was now being torn down, and most fights were being held in the Twenty-fourth Infantry arena with its greater seating capacity. Efforts were still directed at making these popular events affordable. On May 9 the Twenty-fourth's athletic officer announced that a concert and boxing match would be held at the arena on Wednesday and Saturday evenings, and he invited the townspeople of Columbus to attend. Sufficient seating was available and no admission fees were charged. While these lesser fights occasionally furnished good entertainment, they were not equal to those between the regiment's better-known boxers.[41]

On June 20 Speedball Hayden fought his rematch against Johnson. Since most of the soldiers of the Twenty-fourth were in El Paso on military duty, the bout originally scheduled for Columbus was moved to Fort Bliss. An estimated 3,000 fans including a majority of the Twenty-fourth's officers and men saw Hayden win in a twenty-round decision over Johnson. Among those in attendance were the mayor of El Paso; General James B. Erwin, commander of the military district; Colonel G. Arthur Hadsell, commander of Camp Furlong and the Twenty-fourth Infantry; and Colonel Selah R. H. Tompkins, commander of the cavalry brigade at Fort Bliss.[42]

Not all Columbus fans were able to travel to the bout, so those who could not gathered at the local Western Union office, waiting for telegraph reports from El Paso. The wire brought news of Hayden's victory, causing much elation. According to Lieutenant Michael E. Halloran's telegram, "Johnson took a beating, but fought to the last round and showed great gameness." Hayden easily outpointed Johnson, overcoming his previous defeat at Silver City. He received approximately $990 as his share of gate receipts to his opponent's $750.57.[43]

Hayden's star had risen rapidly in local boxing circles, and on July 4 during a boxing tournament, which was part of the holiday program at Camp Furlong, he received special recognition. After the final bout,

Colonel G. Arthur Hadsell, commander of the Twenty-fourth Infantry and the New Mexico Sub-District, presented Hayden, on behalf of the officers' athletic board of the Twenty-fourth Infantry, with a beautiful belt of the national colors with a silver and gold buckle. Through his boxing feats, Hayden influenced the Columbus community more than any other black soldier at Camp Furlong.[44]

Other black boxers from Columbus also helped create good race relations in the community. On June 23, 1919, at Globe, Arizona, Rufus Williams, hoping for a comeback after his loss to Hayden, fought Johnny Sudenberg from Fort Bliss to a ten-round draw. The two boxers met in a rematch July 22, and Williams knocked Sudenberg out in the fifth round. Hy Schneider, the El Paso reporter, called Williams's victory "one of the most sensational comebacks in the history of the jolt and jab game in the southwest." Any hope Williams had for a sustained role as local boxer disappeared, however, when on November 7 in Phoenix, Arizona, Speedball Hayden severely punished him in a ten-round bout.[45]

Despite the fact that Columbus's top-rated boxers were sometimes fighting in other towns, an active fight game continued in the community. In early January 1920 the Twenty-fourth Infantry, always looking for new talent, had several boxers in training under Sergeant Joe Burton. The military continued its control over Columbus boxing until early 1920, when civilian promoters once more began scheduling bouts and holding them in town. According to the *Courier*, military promoters simply did not schedule enough matches, focusing primarily on intramural matches.[46]

In early January 1920 civilian promoter Carter Johnson erected "one of the best timbered rings in the country" with a seating capacity of 1,000. Newspaper stories predicted bright prospects for the venture: One reporter wrote, "That the club will prove a success goes without saying. Mr. Johnson's reputation assures good clean sport and he, as matchmaker and promoter, will be enabled to get top notchers here."[47]

The following month, Johnson scheduled "27 Rounds of Boxing" at his new outdoor arena, the main event being a fifteen-round bout between Fort Bliss's Eddie Hanlon and Jimmy "Hard-hitting" Wright, formerly of the Twenty-fourth. The gates to the club were opened at one o'clock and "a constant stream of soldiers and civilians streamed into the arena until it was filled." The Twenty-fourth Infantry band, "one of the finest musical organizations in the United States," said the *Courier*, paraded through the streets to the arena and between bouts entertained the fans. Blacks and whites mingled together freely. Gate receipts totaled $800. Of this sum Wright received $225 for winning in the main event, while the loser received $150. The opening was clearly a success for Johnson.[48]

On March 27, 1920, Speedball Hayden fought boxer Frankie Fowzer to a draw in ten rounds at the Columbus Athletic Club. Having left the military, Hayden was now generally fighting in other towns, so Columbus residents, who followed his fights closely, were glad to see him back in person again. In mid-May he was in Douglas, Arizona, to fight a well-known boxer in that region. The fight proved a disappointment to Hayden's supporters because he lost the fight by a decision. Later in the month, Henry Davis took Hayden and other boxers on a tour of the West Coast where they fought several bouts, Hayden winning all of his but one.[49]

The absence of these premier fighters did not kill Columbus's interest in boxing. It flourished as it always had, the El Paso-Columbus boxing connection remaining intact. Several boxers from Fort Bliss made trips to Columbus, and many of the Twenty-fourth Infantry boxers returned the favor. As usual, holidays were especially big days for boxing fans. On July 4, 1920, and shortly thereafter on Labor Day, for example, a series of major boxing matches was held. On Thanksgiving Day Speedball Hayden was declared a winner by disqualification in the fourth round when his opponent, "Gorilla" Jones, hit him in the groin. An estimated 300 women made up part of the crowd. A month later, in a rematch on Christmas Day, Jones knocked Hayden out in the ninth round of a scheduled twenty-round bout.[50]

For the remainder of the time the Twenty-fourth Infantry was at Columbus, boxing remained a chief source of local entertainment. In November 1921 at the rodeo in Deming, Speedball Hayden knocked out his opponent in the second round. In early 1922, however, the local favorite's skills were clearly fading; he was twice defeated. By July 1922 the decrease in soldiers assigned to Camp Furlong caused reduced attendance at boxing matches, and the sport quickly declined.[51]

Other sports at Camp Furlong were clearly secondary to boxing. The Twenty-fourth baseball team played teams from Fort Bliss as well as from Fort Bayard in New Mexico and Nogales, Arizona. Both blacks and whites, civilians and soldiers, attended these other events, but the crowds were not nearly as large as those at the boxing matches. In mid-January 1919, shortly after the influenza epidemic had subsided, the Twenty-fourth Infantry regimental football team traveled to Nogales to play the Twenty-fifth Infantry regimental team. The Twenty-fifth won by a score of 26–0 in front of an estimated crowd of 4,000. Several businesses in town even closed for the game. No crowd of that size ever watched a football game in Columbus.[52]

Ultimately reductions in the armed forces and peace along the international border led to the removal of black troops from Camp Furlong in late 1922, the army transferring the unit to Fort Benning, Georgia. The Twenty-fourth Infantry's presence in New Mexico was the continuation of a long and proud tradition of black military service in the West.[53]

At Columbus, local whites from the South, including Texans, who had hardened notions about proper relations between the races did not dominate community affairs, nor did they materially influence the local response to the soldiers. Importantly, few blacks had lived in the town prior to the Twenty-fourth's arrival. The absence of preexisting norms for black-white relations, together with a mix of individuals from various geographic locations, prevented hard-core racists from dominating the community. Therefore, other factors were simply more important in determining race relations.[54]

A much better relationship developed at Columbus than existed in many other areas of the nation. Self-interest was a dominant factor in shaping the white community's response to the black soldiers. During the Mexican Revolution, the town came to depend on the military for security and economic reasons. Black soldiers and their families sought to improve the quality of their lives by creating their own communities, while at the same time interacting with civilian blacks and even whites. Such activities and the economic benefits to the white community resulting from the presence of the black soldiers mitigated existing racism.[55]

Throughout the Twenty-fourth Infantry's stay at Columbus, sports events, especially boxing, became integral parts of the community's entertainment. More than any other activity the numerous boxing matches provided means for interracial contact and significantly promoted positive race relations. The experience of the black soldiers and athletes demonstrates some measure of racial cooperation and understanding through turbulent times. Moreover, the boxers were a source of inspiration and pride for civilian and military blacks, and helped create a more dynamic black community.[56]

For the black soldiers, though, their time at Columbus demonstrated that military service for them could never be a simple matter of just being a soldier because varying degrees of racial prejudice were always a dimension of that experience. Racial prejudice caused black soldiers to be treated differently than white ones, reflecting the black man's position in American society.

The Twenty-fourth Infantry's experience in New Mexico was more positive than earlier ones in Texas and the later one at Georgia. That truth is clearly demonstrated in the comments by an anonymous letter to the *Chicago Defender*, apparently written by a soldier complaining about the Twenty-fourth's experience at Fort Benning: "Everybody is disheartened and ready to leave. They used to kick on the border, but they certainly would like to be there now." As would happen in later years in the South, sports had built bridges across racial divides, bringing whites and blacks together in an unlikely place and during an unlikely time in American history.[57]

Notes

1. John Marszalek and Horace D. Nash, "African-Americans in the Military of the United States," chapter 11 in *The African-American Experience: An Historiographical and Bibliographical Guide*, ed. Arvarh E. Strickland and Robert E. Weems Jr. (Westport, Conn.: Greenwood Press, 2001), 237–38; William T. Bowers, William M. Hammond, and George L. MacGarrigle, *Black Soldier, White Army: The 24th Infantry Regiment in Korea* (Washington, D.C.: Center of Military History, United States Army, 1996), 5–8; William A. Dobak and Thomas D. Phillips, *The Black Regulars, 1866–1898* (Norman: University of Oklahoma Press, 1998), xi–xviii, 20.
2. Monroe L. Billington, *New Mexico's Buffalo Soldiers, 1866–1900* (Niwot: University Press of Colorado, 1991), xv–xvii; Frank N. Schubert, comp. and ed., *On the Trail of the Buffalo Soldier: Biographies of African-Americans in the U.S. Army, 1866–1917* (Wilmington, Del.: Scholarly Resources, 1995), xi–xv; Bernard C. Nalty, *Strength for the Fight: A History of Black Americans in the Military* (New York: Free Press, a Division of Macmillan Inc., 1986), 47–62; Ervin Normore Thompson, "The Negro Regiments of the U.S. Regular Army, 1866–1900" (Master's thesis, University of California, Davis, 1957), 11. See also, Morris J. MacGregor and Bernard C. Nalty, eds., *Blacks in the United States Armed Forces: Basic Documents, Volume III, Freedom and Jim Crow, 1865–1917* (Wilmington, Del.: Scholarly Resources, 1977), and Morris J. MacGregor and Bernard C. Nalty, eds., *Blacks in the United States Armed Forces: Basic Documents, Volume IV, Segregation Entrenched, 1917–1940* (Wilmington, Del.: Scholarly Resources, 1977). For a history of these units on the post–Civil War frontier, see Dobak and Phillips, *Black Regulars*; William H. Leckie, *The Buffalo Soldiers: A Narrative of the Negro Cavalry in the West* (Norman: University of Oklahoma Press, 1967); and Arlen L. Fowler, *The Black*

Infantry in the West, 1869-1891 (Westport, Conn.: Greenwood Press, 1971). Also see Jack D. Foner, *The United States Soldier between Two Wars: Army Life and Reforms, 1865-1898* (New York: Humanities Press, 1970), 127-48; Jack D. Foner, "The Socializing Role in the Military," in *The American Military on the Frontier: The Proceedings of the 7th Military History Symposium, United States Air Force Academy*, September 30-October 1, 1976, ed. James P. Tate (Washington, D.C.: Office of Air Force History, Headquarters USAF and United States Air Force Academy, 1978), 95; Quintard Taylor, *In Search of the Racial Frontier: African Americans in the American West, 1528-1990* (New York: W. W. Norton & Company, 1998), 165; James N. Leiker, *Racial Borders: Black Soldiers along the Rio Grande* (College Station: Texas A & M University Press, 2002), 3-4, 12. For recent historiographical essays on the black military experience, see Marszalek and Nash, "African Americans in the Military," 231-54, and Bruce A. Glasrud, "Western Black Soldiers since the Buffalo Soldiers: A Review of Literature," in *Buffalo Soldiers in the West: A Black Soldiers Anthology*, ed. Bruce A. Glasrud and Michael N. Searles (College Station: Texas A & M University Press, 2007), 5-30. For detailed discussion of the evolving use of the term buffalo soldiers, see Frank N. Schubert, *Voices of the Buffalo Soldier* (Albuquerque: University of New Mexico Press, 2003), 47-49, Billington, *New Mexico's Buffalo Soldiers*, xi; Garna L. Christian, *Black Soldiers in Jim Crow Texas, 1899-1917* (College Station: Texas A & M University Press, 1995), xiii-xiv; Dobak and Phillips, *Black Regulars*, xxvii and 287 n. 18; Leiker, *Racial Borders*, 13; and Glasrud "Western Black Soldiers," 5-6, 19.

3. Marszalek and Nash, "African Americans in the Military," 237-41; Glasrud, "Western Black Soldiers," 5-7, 18-19; John M. Carroll, ed., *The Black Military Experience in the American West* (New York: Liveright Publishing, 1971), 245-87, 375-81; Billington, *New Mexico's Buffalo Soldiers*, xi-xii, xv-xvii; "The Buffalo Soldiers," Time Machine, television series (Bill Armstrong Productions, and the Arts & Entertainment Network, 1992); Stephen Ambrose, "Blacks in the Army in Two World Wars," in *The Military and American Society*, ed. Stephen E. Ambrose and James A. Barber Jr. (New York: Free Press, 1972), 179-80; Foner, *United States Soldier*, 133-34; Foner, "Socializing Role in the Military," 95; Marvin E. Fletcher, *The Black Soldier and Officer in the United States Army, 1891-1917* (Columbia: University of Missouri Press, 1974), 1-31, 109-18; Edwin M. Coffman, *The Old Army: A Portrait of the American Army in Peacetime, 1784-1898* (New York: Oxford University Press, 1986), 370-71; Bowers, Hammond, and MacGarrigle, *Black Soldier, White Army*, 5-12; Taylor, *In Search of the Racial Frontier*, 165; Leiker, *Racial Borders*, 13; Christian, *Black Soldiers in Jim Crow Texas*, xii-xvi; Dobak and Phillips, *Black Regulars*, xvii-xviii; Monroe L. Billington, "Civilians and Black Soldiers in New Mexico Territory, 1866-1900: A Cross-Cultural Experience," *Military History of the Southwest* 19 (Spring 1989): 78-81; For discussion of the Jim Crow era, see C. Van Woodward, *The Strange Career of Jim* Crow, 3rd rev. ed. (New York: Oxford University Press, 1974).

4. Carroll, *Black Military Experience*, 375–81; Ambrose, "Blacks in the Army," 181; L. D. Reddick, "The Negro Policy of the United States Army, 1775–1945," *Journal of Negro History* 34 (January 1949): 16–20; Jack D. Foner, *Blacks and the Military in American History: A New Perspective* (New York: Praeger Publishers, 1974), 72–103; Ulysses Lee, *The Employment of Negro Troops* (Washington, D.C.: Office of the Chief of Military History, United States Army, 1966), 23–29; Billington, *New Mexico's Buffalo Soldiers*, xvi–xvii; Fletcher, *Black Soldier and Officer*, 1–31, 109–18, 157–59; Bowers, Hammond, and MacGarrigle, *Black Soldier, White Army*, 8–9; Taylor, *In Search of the Racial Frontier*, 164–91; Glasrud, "Western Black Soldiers," 5, 16–17, 19, 218.
5. Taylor, *In Search of the Racial Frontier*, 165–91; Foner, *Blacks and the Military*, 72–200; Lee, *The Employment of Negro Troops*, 23–29; Carroll, *Black Military Experience*, 380; E. L. N. Glass, ed., *The History of the Tenth Calvary, 1866–1921* (Tucson, Az.: Acme Printing Company, 1921; Ft. Collins, Colo.: Old Army Press, 1972); William G. Muller, comp. and ed., *The Twenty Fourth Infantry, Past and Present* (1923; reprint, Ft. Collins, Colo.: Old Army Press, 1972), pages unnumbered; L. Albert Scipio II, *Last of the Black Regulars: A History of the 24th Infantry Regiment (1869–1951)* (Silver Spring, Md.: Roman Publications, 1983), 42–49; John H. Nankivell, comp. and ed., *The History of the Twenty-Fifth Regiment, United States Infantry, 1869–1929* (Denver, Colo.: Smith Books Printing Company, 1927; Ft. Collins, Colo.: Old Army Press, 1972), 143–47; Monthly Returns, September 1912–December 1915, Returns from Ninth Cavalry, 1910–1916, Returns from Regular Army Cavalry Regiments, 1833–1916, National Archives Microcopy No. M744, Roll 94 (hereafter National Archives cited as NA); Frank N. Schubert, "The Black Regular Army Regiments in Wyoming, 1885–1912" (Master's thesis, University of Wyoming, 1970), 107–12; Leiker, *Racial Borders*, 13; For other studies, see Glasrud, "Western Black Soldiers," and Marszalek and Nash, "African Americans in the Military." For the best account of desegregation in the armed forces, see Richard M. Dalfiume, *Fighting on Two Fronts: Desegregation of the U.S. Armed Forces, 1939–1953* (Columbia: University of Missouri Press, 1969). See also Morris J. MacGregor Jr., *Integration of the Armed Forces, 1940–1965* (1981; reprint, Washington, D.C.: Center of Military History, United States Army, 1985); Ambrose, "Blacks in the Army," 177–92; Bowers, Hammond, and MacGarrigle, *Black Soldier, White Army*; and Lyle Rishell, *With a Black Platoon in Combat: A Year in Korea* (College Station: Texas A & M University Press, 1993).
6. Rayford Logan, *The Betrayal of the Negro from Rutherford B. Hayes to Woodrow Wilson* (Originally published as *The Negro in American Life and Thought: The Nadir, 1877–1901*, 1954; London: Collier Books, Collier-Macmillan Ltd., 1970), 335; Colin Powell, Commencement Address, May 14, 1994, Howard University (C-Span Network, 1994); Colin Powell, Speech at Buffalo Soldier Memorial, Fort Leavenworth, Kansas, July 25, 1992, in "The Buffalo Soldiers," Time Machine, television series; Colin Powell, *My American Journey* (New York: Random House,

1995); Leiker, *Racial Borders*, 3–4, 176; Ambrose, "Blacks in the Army," 179–80; Don Alberts, *Brandy Station to Manila Bay: A Biography of General Wesley Merritt* (Austin, Tex.: Presidial Press, 1980), 182 n. 19; Robert V. Haynes, *A Night of Violence: The Houston Riot of 1917* (Baton Rouge: Louisiana State University Press, 1976), 41; Taylor, *In Search of the Racial Frontier*, 190–91; Glasrud, "Western Black Soldiers," 5–6, 19; Fletcher, *Black Soldier and Officer*, 158–59. For a discussion of the meaning of these black military units to the larger black community, see Manning Marable, "The Military, Black People, and the Racist State: A History of Coercion," *The Black Scholar* 12 (January–February 1981), 6–17.

7. For recent studies dealing with interaction between civilians and black soldiers in the West, see the historiographical studies of Marszalek and Nash, "African Americans in the Military," 237–40, and Glasrud, "Western Black Soldiers," 5–30."

8. Horace D. Nash, "Community Building on the Border: The Role of the 24th Infantry Band at Columbus, New Mexico, 1916–1922," in Glasrud and Searles, *Buffalo Soldiers in the West*, 267–268; Clarence C. Clendenen, *Blood on the Border: The United States Army and the Mexican Irregulars* (London: Macmillan Company, Collier-Macmillan, 1969); Glass, *Tenth Calvary*, 67–81; Muller, *The Twenty Fourth Infantry*, pages unnumbered. For a detailed discussion of the African American experience along the U.S.-Mexican border during the Mexican Revolution, including the experiences of black military men, see Gerald Horne, *Black and Brown: African Americans and the Mexican Revolution, 1910–1920* (New York: New York University Press, 2005).

9. Horace D. Nash, "Town and Sword: Black Soldiers in Columbus, New Mexico, in the Early Twentieth Century" (Ph.D. diss., Mississippi State University, 1996), 81, 195; Nash, "Community Building," 267–68.

10. *Columbus Courier*, April 6, 1917.

11. *Columbus Courier*, July 27, August 31, 1917; *El Paso Herald*, August 25, 27, 28, 29, 1917. For a detailed study of the Houston riot, see Haynes, *A Night of Violence*.

12. Barnum to Adjutant General, War Department, telegram, August 25, 1917, File 8142-19, War College Division Files, RG 165, NA; Arthur E Barbeau and Florette Henri, *The Unknown Soldiers: Black American Troops in World War I* (Philadelphia: Temple University Press, 1974), 210 n. 30; *Albuquerque Journal*, September 4, 1917, quoted in *Columbus Courier*, August 31, 1917; Haynes, *A Night of Violence*, 62; *Santa Fe New Mexican*, August 25, 28, 1917; *El Paso Herald*, August 27, 1917.

13. *Columbus Courier*, August 31, November 30, 1917; 43; Nalty, *Strength for the Fight*, 104–5; Haynes, *A Night of Violence*, 1–7, 254–96; *Chicago Broad-Ax*, September 1, 8, 15, 1917, November 10, 1917, December 15, 1917; *El Paso Herald*, December 11, 1917; *El Paso Morning Times*, October 8, December 14, 1917, January 3, 9, 1918; *New York Times*, December 12, 1917; *New York Age*, December 22, 1917, January 5, February 9, 16, 23, March 2, September 14, 21, 28, 1918, June 7, 14, 1919; Thomas Richard Adams, "The Houston Riot of 1917" (Master's thesis, Texas A & M University, 1972), 101–5, 161, 167–81. See Garna L. Christian, "The Ordeal and the Prize: The 24th Infantry and Camp MacArthur," *Military Affairs* 50 (April 1986): 67, for an

account of racial conflict between a battalion of the Twenty-fourth Infantry and civilians in Waco, Texas. This incident occurred less than a month prior to the riot at Houston.

14. C. M. D. Ellis, "'Negro Subversion': The Investigation of Black Unrest and Radicalism by Agencies of the United States Government, 1917–1920" (Ph.D. diss., University of Aberdeen, United Kingdom, 1984), 179–80, 315; *Chicago Broad-Ax*, September 8, 1917; *El Paso Herald*, August 25, December 11, 1917; *El Paso Morning Times*, September 28, 29, October 8, 1917, January 9, 31, 1918; *San Antonio Express*, quoted in *El Paso Morning Times*, September 29, 1917; *Santa Fe New Mexican*, August 28, 29, 30, 1917; Nalty, *Strength for the Fight*, 104–5. Louis Burkhead, the local postmaster, opposed the presence of the soldiers and sought to have them removed. Wilson Chase to Commanding General, El Paso District, December 22, 1917, Box 34, DF 17216, EPD Correspondence, 1916–1918, RG 393, NA and Wilson Chase to Commanding General, Southern Department, February 28, 1918, Box 168, File 250.1, SDHQ General Correspondence, RG 393, NA; Muller, *The Twenty Fourth Infantry*, pages unnumbered.

15. *Deming Headlight*, November 5, 1920; *Deming Graphic*, November 9, 16, 30, 1920; J. A. Baer to Inspector General of the Army, "Report of Investigations of Conditions on the Mexican Border at Stations Garrisoned by Negro Troops," April 17, 1920, Box 1373, File: 319.1 Mexican Border to 341.3 Mexican Border, Central Decimal Files, Project Files, 1917–1925, Mexico, Records of the Adjutant General's Office, Record Group 407, NA (hereafter cited as Baer Report, CDF Project Files, Mexico, RG 407, NA; hereafter Record Group cited as RG); E. G. Beuret, "Report of Investigation Concerning Complaints of Conditions as to Vice and Crime at Columbus, New Mexico," January 19, 1921, Box 39, File 330.14: Criticisms, VIII Corps Area, Office of Inspector General, Decimal Correspondence File, 1922–1940, Records of United States Army Continental Commands, 1920–1942, RG 394, Washington National Records Center, Suitland, Maryland (hereafter cited as Beuret Report, VIII Corps Area, OIG Correspondence, RG 394, WNRC); W. V. Morris, "Report of Investigation of Conditions at Columbus, New Mexicio," May 11, 1921, Box No. 607, File 333.9: Columbus, New Mexico (2), General Correspondence, 1917–1934, Records of the Office of the Inspector General, RG 159, WNRC (hereafter cited as Morris Report, OIG General Correspondence, RG 159, WNRC).

16. *Deming Graphic*, October 5, 26, November 9, 16, 30, December 14, 1920; *Deming Headlight*, November 5, 1920, March 11, 18, 1921; *El Paso Times*, March 9, 12, 1921; File: "Investigation, 24th Infantry," Governor Merritt C. Mechem Papers, January 1, 1921–December 31, 1922, New Mexico State Records Center and Archives, Santa Fe, New Mexico; Baer Report, CDF Project Files, Mexico, RG 407, NA; Beuret Report, VIII Corps Area, OIG Correspondence, RG 394, WNRC; Morris Report, OIG General Correspondence, RG 159, WNRC.

17. Glasrud, "Western Black Soldiers," 11–12, 217–20, and Marszalek and Nash, "African Americans in the Military," 240–41; Fletcher, *Black Soldier and Officer*, 97–108;

Nash, "Community Building," 267–76; *Columbus Courier*, February 2, 9, 16, 23, March 2, 23, April 20, June 8, August 31, October 5, 1917; Officer Questionnaires, Research Notes, Fletcher Collection, Archives, United States Army Military History Institute (USAMHI), Carlisle Barracks, Pennsylvania; V. P Franklin, *Black Self-Determination: A Cultural History of African-American Resistance* (Brooklyn, N.Y.: Lawrence Hill Books, 1992), 8–9; Fred Davis Baldwin, "The American Enlisted Man in World War I" (Ph.D. diss., Princeton University, 1964), 132–33. Mobile military communities have long been a part of the military experience, and camp followers of all sorts were part of that community, for good or bad. For discussions of mobile military communities at other places and times, see Fred Anderson, *A People's Army: Massachusetts Soldiers and Society in the Seven Years' War* (Chapel Hill: University of North Carolina Press, 1984; New York: W. W. Norton and Company, Norton Paperback, 1985), 88, 118–19, 127–30, 191; Holly Ann Mayer, *Belonging to the Army: Camp Followers and Community during the American Revolution* (Columbia: University of South Carolina Press, 1996); Walter Hart Blumenthal, *Women Camp Followers of the American Revolution* (Philadelphia: George S. McManus, 1952; Salem, N.H.: Ayer Company, 1994); Miller J. Stewart, "Army Laundresses: Ladies of the 'Soap Suds Row,'" *Nebraska History* 61 (Winter 1980): 421–36; Coffman, *The Old Army*, 104–36, 287–327; Anne M. Butler, *Daughters of Joy, Sisters of Misery: Prostitutes in the American West, 1865–90* (Urbana: University of Illinois Press, 1985), 122–49; Anne M. Butler, "Military Myopia: Prostitution on the Frontier," *Prologue* 13 (Winter 1981): 232–50; Darlis Miller, "Foragers, Army Women, and Prostitutes," in *New Mexico Women: Intercultural Perspectives*, ed. Joan M. Jensen and Darlis A. Miller (Albuquerque: University of New Mexico Press, 1986), 141–68; Sandra L. Myres, "Frontier Historians, Women, and the 'New' Military History," *Military History of the Southwest* 19 (Spring 1989): 27–37, Billington, *New Mexico's Buffalo Soldiers*, 166–68; Patricia Stallard, *Glittering Misery: Dependents of the Indian Fighting Army* (Norman: University of Oklahoma Press, 1978); Michael J. Clark, "A History of the Twenty-Fourth United States Infantry Regiment in Utah, 1896–1900" (Ph.D. diss., University of Utah, 1979), 53–54, 63–64; Tom D. Phillips, "The Black Regulars: Negro Soldiers in the United States Army, 1866–1891" (Ph.D. diss., University of Wisconsin, 1970), 576–77, 789–808; Schubert, *Buffalo Soldiers*, 45–68, 143–44, 154, 157–58, 169–74; Robert Bruce Johnson, "The Punitive Expedition: A Military, Diplomatic, and Political History of Pershing's Chase after Pancho Villa, 1916–1917" (Ph.D. diss., University of Southern California, 1964), 700–708, 751–64, 821–31; and Billington, "Civilians and Black Soldiers," 82.

18. Glasrud, "Western Black Soldiers," 11, 217–20, and Marszalek and Nash, "African Americans in the Military," 240–41; Nash, "Community Building," 267–76; Fletcher, *Black Soldier and Officer*, 100; Dobak and Phillips, *The Black Regulars*, 150–59.

19. *Chicago Defender*, April 7, October 13, December 1, 8, 22, 29, 1917, February 2, 16, 23, March 2, 1918, July 5, 1919; *El Paso Morning Times*, November 11, 1917, July 2, August 23, October 3, 1918, June 18, August 2, 1919, July 29, 1920; *El Paso Herald*,

July 5, 1917, June 19, 1919; *Columbus Courier*, July 13, November 23, 30, December 21, 1917, February 1, 22, May 10, 31, September 6, 20, 27, 1918, February 6, March 5, 1920; Baldwin, "The American Enlisted Man," 125–33; Dobak and Phillips, *The Black Regulars*, 148–50.

20. *Chicago Defender*, January 6, April 7, 1917; *Columbus Courier*, February 23, October 26, November 3, 23, 30, 1917; Officer Questionnaires, Research Notes, Fletcher Collection, USAMHI; Johnson, "The Punitive Expedition," 765–67.

21. *Columbus Courier*, March 27, July 31, November 27, 1914, December 17, 24, 1915, May 12, June 9, September 8, 15, 22, 29, October 27, November 24, December 1, 8, 1916, March 2, July 13, October 26, November 23, 30, December 21, 1917, February 22, July 5, 19, 1918, August 27, September 3, 10, October 15, November 12, December 24, 1920; *Columbus Daily Courier*, May 17, 19, 22, 1920; *Chicago Defender*, April 7, 1917, February 2, March 2, April 27, 1918; *El Paso Morning Times*, November 11, 22, 24, 1917, July 20, February 2, August 23, 1918, August 2, 1919, May 16, 1920; *El Paso Times*, May 3, July 8, June 18, 1921, January 6, April 18, 1922; *El Paso Herald*, June 19, 1919; *Deming Headlight*, May 17, June 17, 1921; *Deming Graphic*, February 13, 1919.

22. *Columbus Courier*, March 2, 9, April 6, July 13, October 5, November 23, 30, December 21, 1917, February 1, 22, March 22, May 10, 31, July 5, August 23, 30, September 6, 20, 27, 1918, February 7, 1919, February 6, March 5, September 3, November 12, 1920; *Columbus Daily Courier*, May 17, 19, 22, 1920; *El Paso Morning Times*, August 23, 1918, June 18, August 2, 1919; *El Paso Times*, May 3, July 8, 1921; U.S. Department of Commerce, Bureau of Census, Fourteenth Census of the United States, 1920, Luna County, New Mexico, Population Schedules, NA, Microcopy No. T625, Roll 1076; *Santa Fe New Mexican*, July 26, 1916; *Chicago Defender*, March 24, April 7, July 28, October 13, December 29, 1917, January 24, February 2, 16, 23, March 2, 9, 16, 23, April 27, May 11, June 3, 1918, July 5, 1919; *Deming Headlight*, June 17, 1921.

23. *Chicago Defender*, January 27, February 3, March 24, April 7, October 13, December 8, 1917; Johnson, "The Punitive Expedition," 765–67; *Columbus Courier*, May 30, 1919, January 9, 16, 23, 30, February 13, 27, 1920; *Columbus Daily Courier*, May 1, 12, 17, 1920; *El Paso Morning Times*, November 17, 1917, June 18, August 2, 1919; *El Paso Times*, January 1, 1922; *Deming Headlight*, October 19, 1917; Officer Questionnaires, Research Notes, Fletcher Collection, USAMHI; Fourteenth Census of the United States, 1920, Luna County, New Mexico, Population Schedules, NA, Microcopy No. T625, Roll 1076.

24. *Columbus Courier*, January 26, February 23, March 9, 1917; *Chicago Defender*, January 27, February 3, March 24, April 7, October 13, December 1, 8, 29, 1917; *Deming Headlight*, October 19, 1917.

25. *Columbus Courier*, April 6, 1917.

26. *Columbus Courier*, January 27, April 6, May 4, 18, 1917, August 22, 1919; *El Paso Herald*, July 5, 1917, June 14–15 (Weekend Edition), 1919; *El Paso Morning Times*, July 2, October 3, 1918; *Indianapolis Freeman*, September 21, 1918; *New York Age*, April 6, 1918; *Army and Navy Journal*, September 1, 1917; *The War Department U.S.*

Commission on Training Camp Activities (Washington, D.C.: n.d.), 12–13; *Annual Reports, War Department Fiscal Year Ended June 30, 1918. Report of Chairman on Training Camp Activities to the Secretary of War* (Washington, D.C.: n.d.), 3–7; *Report of Chairman on Training Camp Activities to the Secretary of War, 1918* (Washington, D.C.: Government Printing Office, 1918), 8–10; "Tobacco and Pugilism in the Army," *Literary Digest* 58, no. 6 (August 10, 1918): 32; Thomas Foster, "Why Our Soldiers Learn to Box," *Outing* 72 (May 1918): 114–16; John L. Griffith, "The Value of Athletics as Part of Military Training," *American Physical Education Review* 25 (April 1919): 191–95; F. L. Kleeburger and Earl H. Wight, "War Sports Embracing Grenade Throwing, Boxing, and Athletic Drills, Arranged in Accord with Military Procedure," *American Physical Education Review* 23 (June 1918): 383–98; "The Problem of Athletics in Colleges and Schools under Present War Conditions," *American Physical Education Review* 22 (October 1917): 447–48; Johnson, "The Punitive Expedition," 765–67; Bernice Larson Webb, *The Basketball Man: James Naismith* (Lawrence: University Press of Kansas, 1973), 186–89; Baldwin, "The American Enlisted Man," 125–33.

27. *Chicago Defender*, July 28, 1917; *Columbus Courier*, July 6, 1917.
28. *Chicago Defender*, July 28, October 13, 1917; *Columbus Courier*, July 13, 1917.
29. *Chicago Defender*, December 1, 8, 1917; *El Paso Morning Times*, November 17, 22, 24, 1917; *Columbus Courier*, September 21, October 5, 19, November 9, 16, 23, 1917.
30. *Columbus Courier*, December 7, 21, 1917; *El Paso Times*, December 23, 26, 1917; *Chicago Defender*, December 22, 29, 1917.
31. *Chicago Defender*, October 13, December 1, 22, 1917, February 2, 16, 23, March 2, 1918, June 12, 1920; *Columbus Courier*, March 2, July 13, October 26, November 23, 1917, February 22, August 23, 30, 1918, March 5, November 12, 1920; *Columbus Daily Courier*, May 1, 17, 19, 22, 1920; *Deming Headlight*, October 19, 1917, January 11, 1918; *El Paso Morning Times*, November 11, 1917, February 23, July 20, August 23, 28, September 21, 1918, June 18, July 5, August 2, 1919. For more information on the role of sports in the lives of soldiers and in enhancing race relations, see Marvin E. Fletcher, "The Black Soldier Athlete in the United States Army, 1890–1916," *Canadian Journal of History of Sport and Physical Education* 3 (December 1972): 16–26; Billington, *New Mexico's Buffalo Soldiers*, 116–20; Billington, "Civilians and Black Soldiers," 82; Fletcher, *Black Soldier and Officer*, 101–4; Schubert, *Buffalo Soldiers*, 177; Clark, "Twenty-fourth Infantry Regiment in Utah," 104, 113; Michael J. Clark, "Improbable Ambassadors: Black Soldiers at Fort Douglas, 1896–1899," *Utah History Quarterly* 46 (Summer 1978): 291; Ronald G. Coleman, "The Buffalo Soldiers: Guardians of the Utah Frontier, 1886–1901," *Utah Historical Quarterly* 47 (Fall 1979): 435–36; Phillips, "The Black Regulars," 576–77, 615–26; Garna L. Christian, "Adding on Fort Bliss to Black Military Historiography," *West Texas Historical Association Year Book* 54 (1978): 53; Mary Ellen Rowe, "The History of Fort George Wright: Black Infantrymen and Theodore Roosevelt in Spokane," *Pacific Northwest Quarterly* 80 (July 1989): 94; Mary Ellen Rowe, "Fort George Wright, Washington, 1894–1912: A Case Study in Civilian-Military Relations before the

First World War" (Master's thesis, University of Washington, 1980), 62–63, 66, 71–72. For a detailed discussion on the reaction to boxer Jack Johnson, see Tony Al Gilmore, *Bad Nigger! The National Impact of Jack Johnson* (Port Washington, N.Y.: Kennikat Press, 1975). For discussion of Johnson's impact on the black citizens of Georgia, see John Dittmer, *Black Georgia in the Progressive Era, 1900–1920* (Blacks in the New World. Urbana: University of Illinois Press, 1977; Illini Books Edition, 1980), 68–71. In early 1911 at Spokane, Washington, a civilian theater planned to show a film of Jack Johnson's recent victory over a white boxer at Reno, Nevada; however, blacks were barred from attending this particular theater. The city council, concerned about the explosive possibilities with black soldiers stationed at nearby Fort George Wright, prohibited the showing. The soldiers sought to obtain the film and show it on post, barring whites. Military officials refused to allow the films on post since they had been prohibited in the city. This incident left soldiers resentful and may have contributed to the deteriorating race relations between the black soldiers and local citizens. Rowe, "Fort George Wright, Washington," 71–72. See also Horne, *African Americans and the Mexican Revolution*, 25–45, and David K. Wiggins, "The African American Athletic Experience," chapter 11 in *The African-American Experience* by Strickland and Weems Jr., 260. For more on the history of black boxers of this period, see Nathaniel S. Fleischer, *Black Dynamite: The Story of the Negro in the Prize Ring from 1798 to 1938; with Numerous Illustrations*, 5 vols. (New York: C. J. O'Brien, 1938 to 1947).

32. *El Paso Morning Times*, February 23, 1918, June 18, 1919, September 6, 1920; *El Paso Herald*, June 19, 1919; *Deming Graphic*, February 13, 1919; *Chicago Defender*, March 10, July 21, October 13, 1917, February 2, 16, 23, March 2, 9, 23, April 27, June 3, 1918; *Columbus Courier*, January 22, February 1, 22, August 23, 30, 1918, February 6, 1920; *Columbus Daily Courier*, May 1, 1920; Fourteenth Census of the United States, 1920, Luna County, New Mexico, Population Schedules, NA, Microcopy No. T625, Roll 1076.

33. *Indianapolis Freeman*, May 18, 1918; *Chicago Defender*, April 27, May 11, June 3, 1918; *Columbus Courier*, February 22, May 10, 1918; *Columbus Daily Courier*, May 14, 1920; *El Paso Morning Times*, December 4, 1918; *El Paso Herald*, June 19, 20, 1919.

34. *Chicago Defender*, June 3, 1918; *Columbus Courier*, May 31, August 23, 30, 1918; *El Paso Morning Times*, August 23, 28, 1918.

35. *Columbus Courier*, May 10, July 5, September 6, 20, 27, 1918; *El Paso Morning Times*, September 28, 1918; *Indianapolis Freeman*, September 21, 1918; *Twelfth Cavalry Standard*, November 9, 1918; Nancy Kathleen Bristow, "Creating Crusaders: The Commission on Training Camp Activities and the Pursuit of the Progressive Social Vision During World War One" (Ph.D. diss., University of California, Berkeley, 1989), 136; Baldwin, "The American Enlisted Man," 31–45, 125–33. For a brief summary of the Commission on Training Camp Activities (CTCA) efforts in sports work, see *Annual Reports, War Department, Fiscal Year Ended June 30, 1918. Report of Chairman on Training Camp Activities to the Secretary of War*

(Washington, D.C.: n.d.), 3–7; *The War Department, U.S. Commission on Training Camp Activities*, 12–13; *Report of Chairman on Training Camp Activities to the Secretary of War*, 1918, 8–10.

36. *Columbus Courier*, September 6, 20, 27, 1918; *El Paso Morning Times*, September 21, 1918; *Indianapolis Freeman*, September 28, 1918.
37. *Columbus Courier*, September 27, October 18, November 1, 8, 15, 22, 29, December 7, 13, 20, 1918, August 22, 1919; *El Paso Herald*, June 14–15 (Weekend Edition), 1919; G. Keyes to Commanding General, Southern Department, "Camp Welfare at Columbus, and Hachita, New Mexico," May 6, 1919, Box 167, File 250.1, Southern Department Headquarters Decimal File, General Correspondence, 1916–1920, RG 393, NA (hereafter cited as Keyes Report, SDHQ General Correspondence, RG 393, NA); Chaplain's Monthly Reports, Alexander W. Thomas, November 1918–January 1919, Box 7, and Chaplain's Monthly Reports, Paul T. Thompson, October 1918–January 1919, RG 247, WNRC.
38. *Columbus Courier*, January 3, 10, 17, June 27, 1919; *El Paso Morning Times*, January 12, 1919.
39. *Columbus Courier*, January 17, 24, 1919; *El Paso Morning Times*, January 18, 19, 22, 1919.
40. *Deming Graphic*, January 21, 28, February 18, March 4, November 11, 1919; *Deming Graphic*, quoted in the *Columbus Courier*, November 7, 1919; *Columbus Courier*, February 14, April 4, May 9, 16, July 18, 1919; *Deming Headlight*, March 7, April 4, July 11, August 1, 8, September 5, October 23, November 7, 14, 1919; *El Paso Morning Times*, December 4, 1918, November 4, 1919.
41. *Columbus Courier*, May 9, 16, 30, 1919.
42. *Columbus Courier*, June 20, 27, 1919; *El Paso Morning Times*, June 19, 21, 1919; *El Paso Herald*, June 4, 14–15 (Weekend Edition), 17, 18, 19, 20, 21–22 (Weekend Edition), 1919.
43. *Columbus Courier*, June 27, 1919.
44. *Columbus Courier*, July 4, 11, 1919; *Columbus Daily Courier*, May 1, 1920; *El Paso Morning Times*, July 5, November 5, 1919. While Hayden was receiving his award from the Twenty-fourth Infantry, his promoter and manager, Henry Davis, had been sent to Toledo, Ohio, to attend the Dempsey-Willard bout and report on the fight for the *El Paso Morning Times*. *Chicago Defender*, July 5, 1919.
45. *Columbus Courier*, July 25, September 19, November 14, 21, 1919; *El Paso Morning Times*, June 24, 26, July 24, November 5, 8, 1919; *El Paso Herald*, June 4, 1919.
46. *Columbus Courier*, December 19, 1919, January 2, 9, 16, 23, 30, February 6, April 2, November 12, 1920; *El Paso Morning Times*, November 28, December 10, 26, 1919, January 24, 1920.
47. *El Paso Times*, January 24, 1920; *Columbus Courier*, January 30, February 6, 20, 1920.
48. *Columbus Courier*, February 13, 20, 27, March 5, 1920.
49. *Columbus Daily Courier*, April 20, 23, May 1, 8, 13, 14, 17, 19, 22, 27, June 2, July 2, 6, 26, 1920; *Columbus Courier*, March 26, April 2, August 6, 27, September 17, No-

vember 5, 12, December 10, 1920; *El Paso Morning Times*, May 16, July 4, 9, 11, 18, 19, 25, 29, 30, 1920. By early 1920, some of the Twenty-fourth Infantry boxers had left the military, continuing their boxing careers as civilians but remaining closely associated with the Twenty-fourth Infantry and the town of Columbus.

50. *Columbus Courier*, October 18, 1918, August 6, 27, September 3, 10, October 15, 22, 29, November 5, 12, 19, 26, December 3, 10, 17, 24, 31, 1920; *Columbus Daily Courier*, May 12, 15, 17, 18, 21, June 17, 23, 29, July 6, 9, 10, 16, 20, 23, 1920; *El Paso Morning Times*, July 19, August 30, 31, September 3, 5, 10, November 5, 20, 26, December 9, 11, 26, 27, 1920; *El Paso Times*, May 24, June 15, 17, July 10, 1921; *Chicago Defender*, April 2, 23, June 18, 25, July 16, 1921.

51. *Columbus Mirror*, May 17, 31, June 14, 21, 1921; *Deming Headlight*, April 1, May 27, June 17, 24, October 14, November 18, 1921, July 7, November 3, 1922; *Deming Graphic*, June 21, 1921; *El Paso Morning Times*, December 26, 1920; *El Paso Times*, May 3, 24, 30, June 1, 7, 8, 9, 12, 15, 16, 17, 18, July 8, 10, November 12, December 31, 1921, January 1–6, March 31, April 16, 18, 1922.

52. Richard Johnson, "My Life in the U.S. Army, 1899 to 1922," Unpublished Memoirs, July 1952, Revised September 1960, 168–80, Manuscript Collections, (USAMHI); *Indianapolis Freeman*, April 27, 1918; *Columbus Courier*, July 5, 19, 26, August 2, 9, September 6, 1918, January 17, 24, February 21, May 16, 30, June 13, 20, 27, July 4, 11, 25, November 14, 21, 28, 1919, January 2, February 6, March 5, April 2, December 31, 1920; *Columbus Daily Courier*, April 16, 17, 29, May 1, 4, 5, 6, 8, 10, 18, 22, 24, 25, June 1, 16, 17, 18, 19, 26, July 1, 2, 17, 19, 20, 1920; *El Paso Morning Times*, July 4, 14, 19, August 19, 1918, January 15, May 12, June 21, 1919, May 17, 21, 22, 23, 24, June 8, 12, 16, 19, 20, 21, 1920; *El Paso Times*, June 8, 18, 20, 22, 1922; *El Paso Herald*, June 14–15 (Weekend Edition), 17, 20, 21–22 (Weekend Edition), 1919; *Silver City Enterprise* quoted in *Columbus Courier*, July 25, 1919; *Twelfth Cavalry Standard* quoted in *Columbus Courier*, June 13, 1919.

53. Nash, "Community Building," 267–76; Muller, *The Twenty Fourth Infantry*, pages unnumbered; Bowers, Hammond, and MacGarrigle, *Black Soldier, White Army*, 17–18.

54. Marszalek and Nash, "African Americans in the Military," 240–41; Nash, "Town and Sword," 361–67.

55. Marszalek and Nash, "African Americans in the Military," 240–41; Nash, "Town and Sword," 363–64; Nash, "Community Building," 267–76. For a discussion of athletic and cultural exchanges between temporary black military communities and local civilians, see Glasrud, "Western Black Soldiers," 217–20; Billington, *New Mexico's Buffalo Soldiers*, xvii, 201.

56. Marszalek and Nash, "African Americans in the Military," 240–41; Nash, "Town and Sword," 363–64; Nash, "Community Building," 267–76.

57. *Chicago Defender*, October 28, 1922; Bowers, Hammond, and MacGarrigle, *Black Soldier, White Army*, 17–18. See also, Horne, *African Americans and the Mexican Revolution*, 56–57. Historians Marvin E. Fletcher and L. D. Reddick had referred to the post–Civil War period of the black regular service as the "golden age,"

Reddick arguing that it ended about the time of the Spanish-American War and Fletcher maintaining that it had ended by 1917. Fletcher, *Black Soldier and Officer*, 160; L. D. Reddick, "The Negro Policy of the United States Army, 1775–1945," *Journal of Negro History* 34 (January 1949): 18–19.

6. BLACK SOLDIERS AND THE CCC AT SHILOH NATIONAL MILITARY PARK

TIMOTHY B. SMITH

THE CIVILIAN CONSERVATION CORPS (CCC) CAMP AT SHILOH NATIONAL Military Park in Tennessee looked the same as any other camp of the era. The living quarters were neatly arranged. There were latrines, cooking areas, parking areas for wheeled vehicles, commissary, quartermaster, and medical facilities. The men milled around, going about their business under watchful supervision of the officers. Above it all flew the United States flag. Nothing was out of the ordinary except the men themselves. This camp, situated near Pittsburg Landing on the battlefield of Shiloh, was for African American veterans.[1]

The year was 1934, and the federal government had just sent more than four hundred black World War I veterans to Shiloh to work in two CCC camps.[2] Over the course of eight years, the men improved the park and aided in the battlefield restoration that the park founders had so dearly desired. These black veterans who had risked their lives for their country in the Great War now worked to preserve a battlefield of an earlier generation.

Shiloh had special meaning for these men: The Civil War battlefield played a major role in the Union's eventual victory over the Confederacy. Sadly, even as they restored one of the very spots where their freedom had been partially won, they faced Jim Crow segregation and other forms of racism.[3] Their story is one of many such paradoxes, of honorable work that benefited the nation, and of prejudicial treatment in the national parks. It offers valuable insight into the nature of race relations, government New Deal work, and the management of cultural resources in the United States during the Great Depression.

Shiloh and the Civilian Conservation Corps

Among the chief beneficiaries of the New Deal's job creation programs were Shiloh and other national parks, to which thousands of laborers were sent to construct, rehabilitate, and restore. In the case of Shiloh, the Civil Works Administration (CWA) employed several hundred local men from Hardin and McNairy counties on erosion control projects, road maintenance, and excavations at Shiloh's Indian mounds. The Public Works Administration (PWA) also provided money for new visitor, employee, and administrative facilities and funded several writers who studied and wrote about Shiloh's history. The Bureau of Public Roads surveyed the park and funded road modernization projects. By far, however, the CCC was the dominant New Deal program at Shiloh.[4]

Normally, the CCC employed young men between the ages of eighteen and twenty-five.[5] Although World War I veterans were much older, they were allowed to work in the CCC because of the efforts of the "Bonus Army." Wanting to cash in their congressionally appropriated service bonuses, the unemployed veterans marched on Washington, D.C., in the summer of 1932 to demand their money. What they received instead was a rough handling by Douglas McArthur and the army, along with an offer to join the CCC. Some 200,000 World War I veterans ultimately joined the CCC, 30,000 of them black veterans.[6]

Daily Life at the Shiloh Camps

The first of the two black CCC camps at Shiloh, Tennessee, Camp MP-3 (Camp Young), was established on July 15, 1933.[7] Made up of men from Company No. 2425, Camp Young was situated at the southwestern corner of the park. The earliest enrollees lived in tents "deep in the shade of the large white oaks," as one eyewitness described it, while they built permanent quarters on the other side of Shiloh Branch.[8] Ultimately, the camp boasted eighteen buildings, with the four barracks aligned in two rows with a "beautiful green carpet of grass" in between, a mess hall and recreation hall on opposite ends of the green, large oaks, and numerous flowerbeds. The camp had an initial enrollment of approximately two hundred men from across the South.[9]

The second camp, Tennessee Camp MP-7 (Camp Corinth), was established nearly a year later on June 14, 1934, approximately twenty-two miles southwest of the park.[10] Enrollment at Camp Corinth fluctuated more than at Shiloh, with numbers ranging between one hundred and fifty and two hundred enrollees, most coming from the South also.[11]

The two camps had similar organizational structures. White military officers on detail oversaw the camps: An army captain or navy lieutenant normally served as camp commander, and a junior officer served as second in command. A camp surgeon was similarly detailed from the military. Each camp also had a corps of white technical officers who led the work groups and advised on engineering, forestry, and other technical matters. Camp foremen who served as clerks, mechanics, historical assistants, and landscape personnel came and went. Enrollees with specialized skills were detailed as foremen, drivers, clerks, storekeepers, or cooks and were given supervisory responsibilities over other enrollees. All worked closely with the Shiloh National Military Park superintendent, who developed the work programs.[12]

The camps also resembled each other in their physical arrangement. Originally, Camp Young consisted of two office buildings (one with an engineer's room), several tool storage areas, a mess hall, and a recreation center. Four large bunkhouses eventually replaced the original tents. By 1941, the camp had eighteen permanent and six portable buildings heated by coal stoves and a modern, enclosed latrine and septic system. The enrollees burned their refuse daily, hauled away other garbage, and initially drew water from a nearby spring on Shiloh Branch. Like Camp Young, Camp Corinth had an ample latrine and septic system. The camp drew water from a 134-foot deep well that furnished "ample water which is potable without chlorination."[13]

Upon entering service at the Shiloh camps, the enrollees were given a medical examination and inoculations and were issued uniforms. Most brought personal items from home: a nice suit for going to town, a musical instrument. An "Oath of Enrollment" was also required, with the men promising to remain in the camp for at least six months and obey the orders of their superiors. Some enrollees were sent to conditioning camps to develop the health and fitness required to perform the work. The men were paid $30 a month, $25 of which was sent home to their families. Enrollees who moved up in the ranks over time received higher wages.

This introduction to the CCC was similar to the experience of thousands of other whites and blacks in camps across the nation.[14]

To make sure the enrollees at the Shiloh camps remained in good physical health, the camp surgeon visited them daily and examined the men for venereal diseases once a month (kitchen personnel were examined more frequently). The buildings were also inspected monthly, and a camp safety program required weekly meetings, safety posters, fire drills, and proper work safety precautions. The state board of health approved all of the health measures.[15] Laundry was thoroughly checked for "bed bugs or other vermin" and sent to the cleaners weekly.[16]

The daily routine in the two CCC camps resembled those at other camps, white or black. Reveille sounded at 6:00 A.M., followed by calisthenics and breakfast at 6:45 A.M. The men worked from 8:00 A.M. until noon. After lunch, they returned to their job sites and worked until 4:00 P.M. They had an hour to themselves before reporting in dress uniform for supper at 5:30 P.M. Lights went out at 10:00 P.M., with taps played fifteen minutes later. Saturdays were a time of leisure or field trips, unless work had been missed during the week due to bad weather. Sundays and holidays were days of rest and, if the men so chose, worship.[17]

The Camp Corinth enrollees worked on the seventeen miles of the Shiloh-Corinth Highway connected to the park. Their two major duties were road improvement and telephone line construction. They maintained the highway and the rights-of-way and adjoining areas, graded the sides of the road, planted grass and laid sod, planted trees and shrubs, and collaborated on transplanting projects. Where drainage and erosion were problems because of years of excess pasturing and over-cultivation, they built check dams and riprap or improved or sloped banks. By example, they encouraged the local farmers to adopt similar conservation measures on their farms, which resulted in terracing and better methods of farming. The enrollees also placed pipelines and conduits along the road and removed tree stumps, the ultimate goal being the "general beautification of [the] highway."[18]

Camp Young enrollees performed a variety of jobs in the park, including roadwork, erosion control, landscaping, forestry management, and fire prevention. The workers streamlined drainage in the park and the national cemetery, building small dams at strategic locations to prevent erosion. At the Confederate general Albert Sidney Johnston death site, they built ninety-six dams. They also filled in and beautified an eroded area called "Dead Man's Gravel Pit," which was so named because of a rockslide that had killed three workers in 1899. They created a test area in Rea Field on Shiloh Branch for experimenting with new methods of erosion control and new types of wood and stone dams.[19]

Most of the Camp Young enrollees worked on road cleanup and the general beautification of the park, and several features they built still exist, including the guardrails along the tour route, a bridge near the mouth of Dill Branch, and seven parking areas within the park. They also built foot trails, leaf pits, a fire tower, a brick restroom at the headquarters area, picnic areas, and a 50-foot protection wall to keep a road from being undercut. At the campsites, they built several buildings, razed others, installed a camp phone system, laid approximately 450 feet of water pipe, and removed several non-historic roads. They also gathered firewood and performed other odd jobs.[20]

When not working, camp life revolved around recreation opportunities and education programs for which the CCC was well known. At Corinth, the camp had the benefit of "ample class-rooms, libraries, blackboards and textbooks, and especially a sympathetic co-operation of the Commanding Officer." Yet in 1935, only about 30 percent of the enrollees took advantage of the classes. One inspector noted that "it has not been an easy matter to get any major percentage of their number interested in any form of education training." The average educational level of the men was fourth grade, and twenty-four men had no schooling at all.[21]

The apathy changed when Captain Toliver T. Thompson, African American military officer and former coordinator of Tuskegee Institute, became both camps' educational director. It was said he "injected a new spirit into the educational and recreational work here." Thompson implemented many new programs, as well as scientific films and lectures on topics such as the battle at Shiloh, tree pruning, and explosives. The educational staff kept the training at an elementary level, teaching evening courses in arithmetic, reading, spelling, history, writing, English, and citizenship. These educational activities were important to a generation of Americans who did not have much formal education, and especially to the black enrollees who had even less because of segregation.[22]

The vast majority of enrollees were interested in vocational training, and the corps shifted its focus accordingly. The men were taught woodworking, blacksmithing, carpentry, auto repair, and other trades, including "rabbit production." Some of their efforts resulted in a profit, which the company commander placed in a bank account at the Farmers and Merchants Bank in Corinth.[23]

The camps did well in monthly and annual inspections. Camp numbers fluctuated depending on discharges, new recruits, sickness, and an occasional absence without leave. Camp Young won the title of best in its district for 1935, earning a tremendous compliment from the army inspector: "It is with great pleasure that I select Co. 2425, MP-3, as the outstanding company in my entire district. The appearance of the camp is excellent. The morale is high, and the conduct of the members is highly commendable. I do not believe that I have seen a better camp in my two years of contact with the CCC." The Corinth camp won the award for 1936.[24]

Segregated Camps at Shiloh

The major differences between white and black camps in the CCC were the segregation and other forms of racism that pervaded camp life and the local opposition that the black camps encountered. It appears that, at first, Tennessee state officials were uncertain how even to manage the public reaction to such camps. The state commissioner of agriculture, O. E. Van Cleve, mentioned to Tennessee governor Hill McAlister that "should you be called upon to designate a particular project for colored camps you might suggest the National Parks." Federal officials agreed, directing "complete segregation of white and colored enrollees" and establishing the black camps at Shiloh and other "military reservations."[25]

Despite the precautions, area residents complained about having black camps nearby. United States senator Kenneth McKellar of Tennessee told Governor McAlister, who had chosen the camp locations, that the "colored camps are problems, and the only way they can be managed is to take them up with the local authorities before making a recommendation." Likewise, the governor felt that "it [is] far better for the colored race not to have these camps in our State if they must be established where race hostility will immediately develop." McNairy County was particularly vocal in its objection to black camps, with citizens issuing a statement in the *McNairy County Appeal* that "[voiced] the sentiment of our entire population." "We do not want them here," the statement read, "as ours is not a negro community, and we do not know how to handle them." The locals raised such a furor that the projected camp at nearby Adamsville was changed from a black to a white camp.[26]

In 1937, a resident of Corinth wrote to President Roosevelt himself:

> The Negro CCC camp is near here and the houses are rented to these Negros [sic] and family while the land is rented to the Government. A poor farmer is unable to pay big rent for a house and has to have land to work so they are left out here. While the Negros [sic] feed families and relatives from the camp. Aren't these barracks built for them. Please look into this.[27]

The men themselves seemed to be highly motivated and satisfied, although some complained about unfair treatment. At Camp Young, the enrollees and their foremen were separated from the white officers in the mess halls and served food of lesser quality. "The Army officers have steaks, salads, desserts and all this was and is paraded before our eyes," one man reported, and he also complained that they were forced to use a bathhouse located several hundred feet away from their quarters because the one in their quarters was reserved for the army officers. "What is good enough for one is good enough for the others," wrote one of the foremen.[28] An enrollee at Camp Corinth, writing under a pseudonym, complained to the Veterans Administration about "this commander that won't proper feed us," and accused the camp commander of diverting money allotted for food to buy paint for his own quarters. "We feel we should have a fair deal such as is due," he protested, "Please let someone come."[29]

In response, the Veterans Administration sent a special investigator who, upon discovering that the signature (I. E. Smart) was fictitious, concluded that the letter was written in reaction to the camp's strict discipline. The investigator told the enrollees that "they should be appreciative of what the Government is doing for them." Although the men said they were well fed, they expressed their desire for simpler food such as cornbread and buttermilk—something more akin to what they were used to at home. The investigator explained that they needed certain calorie levels so they could perform their work but recommended that the camp commander look into broadening the menu.[30]

Segregation was the norm. Although the enrollees had built picnic areas at the Indian mounds and Rea Springs, they were not allowed to use them because the areas were reserved for whites only (they had to build their own picnic area adjacent to their camp on Shiloh Branch). When family and friends visited, the enrollees had to remain in designated areas. Such face-to-face encounters with segregation and other forms of racism at Shiloh remained in the minds of the black veterans who had served their country twice on battlefields: first in combat and later in conservation.[31]

Conditions were such that some of the enrollees complained to the National Association for the Advancement of Colored People (NAACP) in the fall of 1937 about the treatment of blacks at Shiloh. "We are advised," the NAACP leadership informed the CCC, "that a gang of outsiders working around the camp steal the clothing and shoes of the enrollees for which the enrollees have to pay; that no serious effort is made by the officers to patrol the camp so that the property of the enrollees can be protected; that there is a further complaint about food." The letter prompted another investigation by CCC leaders.[32]

The forms of racism practiced or tolerated at Shiloh were nothing out of the ordinary for the time. Rather, they were indicative of the racism that existed in the CCC and many other New Deal agencies. Housing segregation in the Tennessee Valley Authority and Federal Housing Authority occurred frequently. Blacks were often paid less than whites in many New Deal programs. Racial discrimination and segregation ran rampant particularly in the South, where federal government officials deferred to local laws and practices.[33]

Long-Term Impact of the Shiloh CCC Camps

Camps Young and Corinth continued to function independently until October 31, 1941, when the two were joined into NP-9, and enrollees worked on both the park and the roadway. Some of the men were assigned to a short-term "side camp" at Lookout Mountain in Chattanooga, Tennessee; others worked at nearby Pickwick Dam. The outbreak of World War II marked the beginning of the end for the CCC camps, with the extra manpower and labor redirected toward the war effort. Shiloh's combined CCC camp, reduced in status to a side camp, was disbanded on April 15, 1942.[34]

The contributions of the CCC and other New Deal programs to the development and management of the national parks are comparable to those of the National Park Service's Mission 66 program.[35] The long list of projects at Shiloh alone illustrates the enormity of that legacy and the importance of understanding the diversity of the CCC experience in evaluating the resources where CCC activities took place.[36] More difficult to quantify but of tremendous significance was the impact that the CCC camps had on their enrollees. The 30,000 black World War I veterans were a small but important part of the New Deal effort. In many national and state parks, they performed good, solid work and made substantive and lasting contributions to the nation.

However, their CCC experience was a double-edged sword: The vocational, financial, and educational opportunities the CCC provided lay under the mantle of segregation and other forms of racism that affected African Americans nationwide. While work and camp life were supposed to be regulated uniformly across all camps, black enrollees had to endure prejudicial treatment that white enrollees never faced, much of it codified by the federal government. Sadly, African American veterans were denied full equality in the CCC camps, even on a hallowed battlefield where their very freedom and citizenship had been partially gained.

At the same time, the New Deal's relief and recovery programs also helped African Americans on a fundamental level by providing work, food, housing, and educational opportunities to those in need of assistance. Although segregation had permeated New Deal programs, the New Deal marked an important point in the steady march toward equality for African Americans that led to the desegregation of the United States military in 1947 and the civil rights movement of the 1950s and 1960s.[37]

Of all the benefits accrued from the New Deal, perhaps the most profound was the renewed sense of purpose the CCC experience instilled in the enrollees and, in the case of the Shiloh camps specifically, in the middle-aged men whose service in World War I had been too quickly forgotten. They became actively engaged in the important work of improving a national park for the benefit of present and future generations. One camp inspector said it best when summing up the results of the educational and work programs in 1939: "Results as yet Intangible Mentally and Spiritually as affecting rehabilitation of vets, but indicated from present participation percentage of 98.96."[38]

Notes

This article originally appeared in *CRM: The Journal of Heritage Stewardship* 3, no. 2 (Summer 2006): 73–84.

1. The treatment of black soldiers in Civil War history is much debated. Most of the attention focuses on northern recruitment of black regiments and their wartime service. More recent research examines the possibility of black soldiers in the Confederate army. Yet, the story of Shiloh does not usually include African American soldiers on either side. Coming early in the Civil War before the Lincoln administration had made any decisions about the fate of former slaves, Shiloh had no United States Colored Troops (USCT) regiments and few individual black men among the masses of soldiers that fought on April 6–7, 1862. Even so, the history of Shiloh does have hundreds of black soldiers in it. For African American soldiers in the Union army, see Dudley Taylor Cornish, *The Sable Arm: Black Troops in the Union Army, 1861–1865* (New York: Longmans, Green and Company, 1956), and Joseph T. Glatthaar, *Forged in Battle: The Civil War Alliance of Black Soldiers and White Officers* (New York: Free Press, 1990). For African Americans in the Confederate army, see Richard Rollins, ed., *Black Southerners in Gray: Essays on Afro-Americans in Confederate Armies* (Murfreesboro, Tenn.: Southern Heritage Press, 1994).
2. Established in 1894 under the War Department, Shiloh National Military Park entered the National Park System in August 1933, when it and other military parks and national cemeteries were transferred to the National Park Service. The preservation of Civil War battlefields as national parks was (and still is) widely considered to be an appropriate way of commemorating the men whose bravery and sacrifice during the Civil War changed the course of American history. For Shiloh, see Timothy B. Smith, *This Great Battlefield of Shiloh: History, Memory, and the Establishment of a Civil War National Military Park* (Knoxville: University of Tennessee Press, 2004).
3. Jim Crow segregation grew out of the sectional reconciliation that had begun in the 1870s but had deteriorated by the 1890s, allowing segregation to dominate race relations. Segregation received official sanction in the 1892 *Plessy v. Ferguson* Supreme Court decision, and it was the norm in the 1930s when the federal government created the CCC. See James M. McPherson, *Ordeal by Fire: The Civil War and Reconstruction* (New York: Knopf, 1982); Eric Foner, *Reconstruction: America's Unfinished Revolution, 1863–1877* (New York: HarperCollins, 1989); for race and segregation, see David Blight, *Race and Reunion: The Civil War in Memory and Reunion* (Cambridge, Mass.: Harvard University Press, 2001), and C. Vann Woodward, *The Strange Career of Jim Crow*, 3rd ed. (New York: Oxford University Press, 1989).
4. Charles E. Shedd, *A History of Shiloh National Military Park, Tennessee* (Washington, D.C.: Government Printing Office, 1954), 45–46; "Research Studies Made

During the CWA Period, Shiloh National Military Park," in *Historical Reports: Research Reports on Army Units in the Army of Tennessee*, Vertical File, Shiloh National Military Park.
5. Franklin D. Roosevelt proposed the idea of a civilian conservation corps during his 1932 presidential campaign. He signed the CCC into law in March 1933—not long after his presidential win.
6. "Dedication of THC Marker for CCC Co. 2425, MP-3, Shiloh National Military Park, July 14, 1990," in Dedication Remarks for Placement of CCC Marker, July 14, 1990, Vertical File, Shiloh National Military Park; John C. Paige, *The Civilian Conservation Corps and the National Park Service, 1933–1942: An Administrative History* (Washington, D.C.: National Park Service, 1985), 97. For African Americans in the CCC, see Olen Cole, *The African-American Experience in the Civilian Conservation Corps* (Tallahassee: University Press of Florida, 1999).
7. The camp was originally organized in June at Fort Oglethorpe in Georgia.
8. The permanent quarters were completed in November 1933.
9. "ECW Monthly Progress and Cost Report," February 1937, RG 79, E75, Box 7, National Archives and Records Administration, hereafter cited as NARA; "Dedication of THC Marker for CCC Co. 2425, MP-3, Shiloh National Military Park, July 14, 1990," in Dedication Remarks for Placement of CCC Marker, July 14, 1990, Vertical File, Shiloh National Military Park; "Camp Inspection Report," October 3, 1938, RG 35, E 115, Box 199, NARA; "2425th Company, MP-3, Pittsburg Landing, Tennessee," Official Annual Civilian Conservation Corps "C" District, Fourth Corps Area—1937, Patsy Weiler Collection, Albert Gore Research Center, Middle Tennessee State University, hereafter cited as MTSU. The Official Annual is also in the CCC in Tennessee Collection, Tennessee State Library and Archives, hereafter cited as TSLA. See also Civilian Conservation Corps, RG 93, TSLA, for Tennessee camps. The enrollees came from Alabama, Mississippi, Florida, Georgia, North Carolina, Louisiana, Tennessee, and South Carolina.
10. Like MP-3, MP-7 had begun operation elsewhere, at Fort McPherson, Alabama, in July 1933, and then moved to Glencoe, Alabama, near Gadsden. Camp MP-7 was called Corinth because of its proximity to the Mississippi border town bearing that name.
11. Smith, *This Great Battlefield of Shiloh*, 123; "2423rd Company, MP-7, Corinth, Mississippi," Official Annual Civilian Conservation Corps "C" District, Fourth Corps Area—1937, Patsy Weiler Collection, Albert Gore Research Center, MTSU; "Tennessee Camp MP-7," May 25, 1937; "Emergency Conservation Work Camp Report," November 29, 1935, RG 35, E 115, Box 199, NARA; "Camp Report," July 8, 1934; "Camp Report," May 25, 1937; Toliver T. Thompson to J. S. Billups, November 29, 1935, RG 35, E 115, Box 199, NARA; Jean Hager Memo, May 25, 1937, RG 35, E 115, Box 199, NARA; Shedd, *A History of Shiloh*, 46. Enrollees came from Alabama, Mississippi, Georgia, Tennessee, and Florida. Later, men from New York, New Jersey, and West Virginia also joined the camp.

12. "Rated Members," November 27, 1936, RG 35, E 115, Box 199, NARA; "Camp Report," July 8, 1936, RG 35, E 115, Box 199, NARA; "Forestry Personnel," November 27, 1936, RG 35, E 115, Box 199, NARA; "Army Personnel," November 27, 1936, RG 35, E 115, Box 199, NARA; "Camp Report," November 29, 1935, RG 35, E 115, Box 199, NARA; "Fourth Enrollment Period Report, Tennessee Camp MP-3," March 31, 1935, Shiloh National Military Park Archives, hereafter cited as SNMP; Paige, *An Administrative History*, 66. For more information on District C, Fourth Corps Area, see the CCC in Tennessee Collection, TSLA.
13. Later, a pump house was built, with iron piping to all the buildings.
14. Paige, *An Administrative History*, 74–76.
15. T. J. McVey Report, June 18, 1934, and "Camp Report," November 6, 1937, both in RG 35, E 115, Box 199, NARA; "Camp Inspection Report," October 3, 1938, May 15, 1940, and May 1, 1941, RG 35, E 115, Box 199, NARA.
16. "Camp Report," November 29, 1935, November 27, 1936, RG 35, E 115, Box 199, NARA; T. J. McVey Supplementary Report, November 27, 1936, RG 35, E 115, Box 199, NARA.
17. Paige, *An Administrative History*, 79–82.
18. Camp Report, July 8, 1936, November 27, 1936, May 25, 1937, RG 35, E 115, Box 199, NARA; T. J. McVey Construction Report, November 27, 1936; RG 35, E 115, Box 199, NARA; Narrative Report of Tennessee Camp MP-7, March 31, 1935, RG 79, E 42, Box 28, NARA.
19. Erosion Control Memo, March 11, 1935, Series 2, Box 9, Folder 168, SNMP; Alex Bradford to R. A. Livingston, March 31, 1935; RG 79, E 42, Box 27, NARA; Smith, *This Great Battlefield of Shiloh*, 99. For a detailed look at a particular project, see "Final Construction Report, Shiloh National Military Park, Eastern Corinth, Hamburg-Crump, and Peabody Monuments Roads, project 4A1," Series 1, Box 76, Folder 1126, SNMP. Included are maps, paperwork, and bids for the project.
20. The company also responded to a major flood on the Tennessee River, for which it received letters of commendation from the corps area commander and the Red Cross. See T. J. McVey Report, June 18, 1934; "Camp Inspection Report," May 31, 1939, "Work Project Report Supplemental to Form 11," April 30, 1941, "ECW Monthly Progress and Cost Report," February 1937, RG 35, E 115, Box 199, NARA; Alex Bradford to R. A. Livingston, March 31, 1935; RG 79, E 42, Box 27, NARA; "2425th Company, MP-3, Pittsburg Landing, Tennessee," Official Annual Civilian Conservation Corps "C" District, Fourth Corps Area—1937, Patsy Weiler Collection, Albert Gore Research Center, MTSU.
21. "Report of Education Program," November 29, 1935, "Monthly Camp Education Report," June 1936, "Camp Educational Program," November 27, 1936, RG 35, E 115, Box 199, NARA; Fourth Enrollment Period Report, March 31, 1935, SNMP; "CCC Camp Educational Report," May 31, 1939, RG 35, E 115, NARA; Paige, *An Administrative History*, 86. Educational classes were standard in the early years of these camps.

22. "Report of Education Program," November 29, 1935, "Monthly Camp Education Report," June 1936, "Camp Educational Program," November 27, 1936, RG 35, E 115, Box 199, NARA.
23. "Report of Education Program," November 29, 1935, "Monthly Camp Education Report," June 1936, "CCC Camp Educational Report, May 31, 1939, "Camp Educational Program," November 27, 1936, "Monthly Camp Educational Report," April 1937, "Supplementary Report," May 31, 1939, "Work Project Report Supplemental to Form 11," April 30, 1941, RG 35, E 115, Box 199, NARA; "CCC Camp Educational Report," May 31, 1939, RG 35, E 115, NARA.
24. "Camp Report," November 29, 1935, and undated, both in RG 35, E 115, Box 199, NARA; "2423rd Company, MP-7, Corinth, Mississippi," Official Annual Civilian Conservation Corps "C" District, Fourth Corps Area—1937, Patsy Weiler Collection, Albert Gore Research Center, MTSU; Fourth Enrollment Period Report, March 31, 1935, SNMP.
25. O. E. Van Cleve to Governor Hill McAlister, July 19, 1935, and Secretary of War to Senator Kenneth McKellar, July 15, 1935, both in Hill McAlister Papers, Box 77, Folder 8, TSLA; John A. Salmond, *The Civilian Conservation Corps, 1933–1942: A New Deal Case Study* (Durham, N.C.: Duke University Press, 1967). The black CCC companies at Shiloh were but 2 of the nearly 150 such companies at camps nationwide.
26. Kenneth McKellar to Governor Hill McAlister, August 27, 1935; Governor Hill McAlister to Kenneth McKellar, August 30, 1935; John W. Hamilton to Governor Hill McAlister, August 14, 1935; and Ralph Perry to John W. Hamilton, August 15, 1935, all in Hill McAlister Papers, Box 77, Folder 8, TSLA. Further research may reveal the extent to which public resistance to the presence of black CCC camps pushed the activity of the CCC to national parks.
27. "A Corinth Citizen" to President Roosevelt, June 30, 1937, RG35, E 115, Box 199, NARA.
28. Unknown to James C. Reddoch, January 24, 1936, RG 35, E 115, Box 199, NARA.
29. I. E. Smart to "Officers of the Veterans Administration at Washington DC," April 13, 1936, RG 35, E 115, Box 199, NARA.
30. J. S. Billups to J. J. McEntee, July 13, 1936, RG 35, E 115, Box 199, NARA.
31. Chief National Park System Planning Section to Acting Superintendent, July 27, 1939, Series 2, Box 12, Folders 225, SNMP.
32. Charles H. Taylor to Adjutant General, October 5, 1937, RG 35, E 115, Box 199, NARA. Although the CCC investigated the matter further, its results are not documented.
33. John Hope Franklin, *From Slavery to Freedom: A History of Negro Americans*, 3rd ed. (New York: Vintage Books, 1969), 534–36; Leslie H. Fishel Jr. and Benjamin Quarles, *The Negro American: A Documentary History* (1967; Glenview, Ill.: Scott, Foreman and Company, 1976), 448, 455, 463; James Oliver Horton and Lois E. Horton, *Hard Road to Freedom: The Story of African America* (New Brunswick, N.J.: Rutgers University Press, 2001), 265–67; Paige, *An Administrative History*, 94.

34. "Camp Inspection Report," May 15, 1940, RG 35, E 115, Box 199, NARA; Michael A. Capps, "Shiloh National Military Park: An Administrative History" (Shiloh National Military Park, 1993), 43–45. For more information on the side camp, see Series 2, Box 7, Folders 112–13, SNMP. The side camp workers built the Ochs Museum at Point Park.
35. See Timothy M. Davis, "Mission 66 Initiative," *CRM: The Journal of Heritage Stewardship* 1, no. 1 (Fall 2003): 97–101, for more information on Mission 66.
36. Shiloh was one of many national and state parks that benefited from CCC labor.
37. Franklin, *From Slavery to Freedom*, 523–25, 534, 538; Paige, *An Administrative History*, 97.
38. "CCC Camp Educational Report," May 31, 1939, RG 35, E 115, Box 199, NARA.

7. CHALLENGING THE DUNNING ORTHODOXY

The Reconstruction Revisionism of Francis Butler Simkins and Robert Hilliard Woody

JAMES SCOTT HUMPHREYS

"I AM DELIGHTED TO KNOW THAT YOU ARE WORKING WITH SO MUCH interest and pleasure in a new book," the Brazilian scholar Gilberto Freyre wrote to Francis Butler Simkins in August 1927. The "new book" was a projected study of the Reconstruction era in South Carolina, a project Simkins had been researching since the previous summer. Officials at Farmville State Teacher's College granted him a year's leave of absence for the 1929–1930 academic year, and he and coauthor Robert Woody also received a Research Fellowship from the Social Science Research Council to help fund their work. The two scholars had embarked on a project that would reap academic and professional rewards for them and one that would alter the course of Reconstruction historiography.[1]

In the early twentieth century, the prevailing theory of Reconstruction was known as the "Dunning School," named after Columbia University professor William Archibald Dunning. Simkins had taken several of Dunning's classes at New York City's Columbia University while pursuing his doctoral degree, but he was no Dunningite. Still, Dunning exerted a profound influence on Reconstruction historiography.[2]

As Wendell Holmes Stephenson pointed out in a 1948 article, in their writings, William Dunning and his students usually sided with conservative whites. The Dunning scholars' portrayal of Reconstruction as a time of endless troubles for southern whites, who were victimized by the policies of Radical Republicans, became the general consensus among historians and laymen in the early twentieth century.[3] D. W. Griffith's controversial *The Birth of a Nation*, a motion picture portraying blacks in negative stereotypes, embedded further these prejudices in the popular mind.[4] This anti-Radical view eventually constituted "the orthodox story of southern Reconstruction," to use the historian Vernon Wharton's phrase.[5]

All orthodoxies, however, produce opponents, and a challenge to this view of Reconstruction quietly began to emerge in the early decades of the 1900s, black intellectuals being among the first dissenters.[6] In a 1909 address titled "Reconstruction and Its Benefits," the black scholar William Edward Burghardt Du Bois, speaking before a crowd at the American Historical Association, explained what he considered to be the impressive gains made after blacks received the right to vote in the postbellum period.[7] According to Du Bois, the popular notion that black suffrage led to disastrous results in the South during Reconstruction was mistaken. In reality, black suffrage proved instrumental in the development of a public school system in the South and in the writing of new, progressive constitutions. Furthermore, Du Bois found no link between black suffrage and many of the alleged afflictions of the Reconstruction period—economic disruption, social dislocation, and moral decay. Giving the black man the right to vote was a progressive measure of inestimable value to southerners, freedmen, and whites alike, he argued. Du Bois's address to the AHA was unique, to say the least. As David Levering Lewis has written, "To suggest that there had been benefits to Reconstruction was equivalent to descrying benefits in the aftermath of the plague." Although "Reconstruction and Its Benefits" appeared in the July 1910 edition of the *American Historical Review*, it did not affect Reconstruction historiography, which continued to remain firmly grounded in the Dunning interpretation.[8]

In 1924, officials of Carter Woodson's *Association for the Study of Negro Life and History* published Alrutheus A. Taylor's *The Negro in South Carolina During the Reconstruction*.[9] Holding an M.A. in history from Harvard University, Taylor was employed by Woodson as a researcher or what ASNLH's officials termed an "Associate Investigator," having previously also worked for the Urban League and the YMCA.[10]

Like W. E. B. Du Bois, Taylor saw the Dunning school as inadequate to explain the role of blacks during the Reconstruction period. Postbellum South Carolina, a microcosm of Reconstruction in the South, it was often thought, seemed the most fertile ground on which to build a new theory. In his book, Taylor included chapters on political and nonpolitical events affecting South Carolina blacks, placing the Dunning school under withering fire. According to Taylor, the passage of the black codes had prompted the rise of Radical rule in the South. Taylor also argued, like Du Bois, that white leaders bore more of the blame for the corruption in South Carolina's Reconstruction government than did black politicians. After all, the spoils ended up in white hands.[11]

Simkins was familiar with both Du Bois's article and Taylor's book, both writings providing insights into Reconstruction crucial to his work.[12] Furthermore, any fair-minded scholar researching the history of Reconstruction South Carolina could not have dismissed such iconoclastic writings, but many white historians were not fair-minded in dealing with the period. Still, Simkins saw that there was a need to do more than Du Bois and Taylor had done, and to do it better.

A native of Edgefield, South Carolinia, Simkins knew intimately the state that served as the subject of his and Woody's book. Reminders of the Reconstruction period—the stately home of Martin Gary, the august courthouse in Edgefield Village, the colossal image of Ben Tillman—were the scenes of his youth. His proximity to his subject made Simkins, in the words of the historian James Welch Patton, "an heir to the Reconstruction tradition," although Patton neglected to clarify whether he meant the tradition of Dunning or that of Du Bois and Taylor.[13]

Robert Woody's background also played a significant role in shaping his attitudes toward the South, blacks, and Reconstruction. Born in 1903, Woody spent his early years in North Carolina's Haywood County, located in the Great Smoky Mountains.[14] He rarely, if ever, saw an African American before he reached the age of thirteen or fourteen, and this lack of contact made black life intriguing to him. A former student described this "lifelong fascination with black people" as a "detached, wanting to know type thing." The former student explained further that Woody's curiosity was "important for that book on South Carolina during Reconstruction. He really didn't bring any race prejudices to it."[15]

Woody admitted that he and Simkins knew little about Reconstruction in any state beside South Carolina. "We were probably neither for nor against the Dunning school," explained Woody, "just ignorant." If this contention was true, then the two historians may have had only a passing knowledge of the Reconstruction monographs of Dunning's students. In an ironic way, their ignorance may have been a blessing. Knowing little about the Dunning school meant that they avoided being shackled to a harsh conception of Reconstruction. Possibly, Simkins and Woody could see an old story in a new light.[16]

Many years later James Patton described Simkins's and Woody's project as "an ambitious undertaking," because the lack of a broad study of postbellum South Carolina created a void in Reconstruction studies that needed to be filled. Other scholars agreed. J. Rion McKissick, the dean of the School of Journalism at the University of South Carolina, writing in 1930, declared "that a comprehensive, impartial history of Reconstruction is keenly needed. All that we have now is fragmentary." University of South Carolina history professor Yates Snowden pointed out that several books already existed on the subject. The studies, he declared, seemed "all good *in their way.*" But a gap remained. Snowden explained that "a history of that period in this State is still a great desideratum, and so no one would welcome the publication of the Simkins-Woody studies more than I would." Orin Faison Crow of the University of South Carolina's education department also supported the two historians' work. "No writers, especially southern writers," wrote Crow, "have yet adequately handled certain phases of reconstruction in South Carolina."[17] Simkins and Woody had clearly uncovered a topic pregnant with possibility for the historical record and their own reputations.

The book the two scholars produced, *South Carolina During Reconstruction*, contained twenty chapters spanning 563 pages and a twenty-one-page bibliography. The chapters were written separately with little collaboration between the authors. A close comparison of Woody's dissertation with chapters in *South Carolina During Reconstruction* reveals that Woody wrote the chapters dealing with economics and politics and that, except for minor changes, most of the material in these chapters came verbatim from his Duke University dissertation. Meanwhile, Simkins wrote the sections about provisional and congressional Reconstruction. Chapters dealing with social matters, such as education, also belonged to Simkins, according to his coauthor. A comparison with previous Simkins articles corroborates his authorship.[18]

Simkins and Woody wrote that although the Reconstruction of South Carolina contained sordid aspects, it had another side, aspects "less showy and of a more constructive nature." "For this reason," they declared, "we forgo the temptation of following in the footsteps of historians who have interpreted the period as only a glamorous but tragic melodrama of political intrigue." Their portrayal of Reconstruction, Simkins and Woody averred, would take into account neglected aspects of life in the state during the period. Agriculture, commerce, transportation, public finance, religion, issues related to free labor, and many other topics beyond the purely political all deserved attention. In their book, Simkins and Woody hoped "to recreate the life of a people during a short span of years." No period in the history of the Palmetto state, according to the authors, exerted greater influence over South Carolina than did the Reconstruction years.[19]

The chapters dealing with provisional and congressional Reconstruction came from Simkins's pen. Simkins argued that the Black Codes passed by the South Carolina legislature in September 1865 marred Governor James L. Orr's otherwise successful administration. He described them accurately as "a series of restrictions [which] attempted to assign colored persons to the position of inferior caste." The codes, he explained, helped neither whites nor blacks, because they appeared to be a step toward the building of a system similar to slavery. Whites overreacted in placing such elaborate and impractical regulations on blacks, codes that Simkins believed, nonetheless, were necessary for the maintenance of white supremacy.[20]

Simkins traced developments in South Carolina from the beginning of military Reconstruction in 1867 to the approval of a constitutional convention by the state's voters in 1868. Blacks, who played a major role in the referendum on a constitutional convention, fell under the domination of elements from outside South Carolina such as the Union League, which extolled the virtues of the Republican party in order to attract the votes of the freedmen. But, Simkins argued, blacks knew little about the processes of democracy or the meaning of the vote. They knew enough, however, to go to the polls with alacrity, while many white voters stayed home in protest. The referendum for holding a constitutional convention passed.[21]

Simkins examined the convention and the document it produced. Blacks, some of whom had been recently enslaved, comprised a majority of the members of the body, many of them comporting themselves with great dignity. A majority of the white delegates came from other states.[22] Although the final document received criticism from many white native South Carolinians, "the best legal principles of the age," Simkins posited, formed the basis of the 1868 constitution. Simkins enumerated a litany of progressive measures included in the document: universal manhood suffrage, elimination of property qualifications for voting and holding office, and free public education. South Carolina voters who went to the polls overwhelmingly approved the work of the convention. The constitution remained in effect until 1895, when Conservative leaders sought change in state government. Even then, the document written in 1868 served as a basis for the Conservatives' constitution.[23]

Robert Woody then examined the rise of the carpetbaggers, scalawags, and blacks who dominated South Carolina politics from 1868 to 1877. Blacks made up a majority of the lower house for two years, and they also filled other important posts such as secretary of state and county auditor. Many black South Carolina politicians had little education and no training in government. Some, however, had worked hard to improve skills vital to public life. Woody cited black politicians who showed impressive ability as orators and lawyers, but also demonstrated that more than a few politicians, black and white, practiced corruption. The positive efforts of black leaders notwithstanding, the Radical government in South Carolina achieved little, Woody said. Ultimately, its survival depended on the willingness of the Union army to protect it. In 1877, Radical rule ended after federal troops left the state.[24]

Simkins's and Woody's goal of writing something more than a political study of Reconstruction South Carolina came to fruition in chapters 6 through 16. Here, the authors dealt at length with economic and social developments. Four chapters, written by Woody, dealt with such economic matters as railroads, public debt, and commerce. Simkins's chapters focused on matters concerning agriculture, education, and religion.

Revealing his Dunningite tendencies, Robert Woody argued that the South Carolina economy stagnated during the Reconstruction period due to the incompetence and dishonesty of many Radical political leaders, especially Governor Robert K. Scott and a number of state legislators. According to Woody, public debt and burdensome taxation did not become serious problems until northerners, scalawags, and blacks seized control of the reins of state government. Graft, especially related to the railroads, abounded. Governor Daniel Chamberlain attempted but failed to institute reforms, finding little support in the legislature. Attempts to industrialize the state resulted in few economic gains; capital seemed always to be in short supply.[25] These ills would bedevil South Carolina for many years to come, a point Woody neglected to mention.

An explanation of the few economic gains of Reconstruction tempered Woody's dismal view of the inefficient workings of state government. The resurrection of the cotton industry, the rebuilding of towns, and other advances boded well for the future, many of the state's residents believed.

Although economic progress was slight, Woody explained, these improvements offered reason for hope.[26]

When Simkins wrote his chapters on social matters, a number of significant points emerged. Simkins, for example, found achievements in the Radical program for the South, pointing out that educational progress, which began when the war ended, continued after the Radicals assumed power in the late 1860s. Even the integration of the public schools ranked high on the agenda of some of the northern reformers, a possible development southern whites detested and a goal that collapsed during Reconstruction.[27] The Radicals' "principle of schools open to all," that is, universal education, Simkins explained, revealed a commitment to democratic education, a commitment that exerted a long-lasting impact on South Carolina. The Bourbons carried on many of the radical reforms, but, as Simkins pointed out, "the financial support given Negro schools immediately became less than that given white schools, and as the years passed this disparity became greater." With this blunt statement, Simkins made it clear that blacks suffered inequity in education funding. He registered tacit disapproval, but that is all.[28]

Simkins compared the lives of blacks during slavery to their lives as freedmen, thereby revealing his views of the institution of human chattel and his conception of the nature of blacks. Materially, blacks may have been better off as slaves, said Simkins, because they had better food and acceptable work clothes. After slavery's demise, they lived in crude and dank homes possibly in worse condition than their former slave cabins. Simkins called the ramshackle condition of their homes their "most obvious failing." Blacks also suffered in numerous physical and mental ways after the war. For example, as freedmen, Simkins argued, their physical health declined. The death rate among the freedmen increased, and mental illness emerged after the war as a serious affliction. In many ways, Simkins explained, the lives of the freedmen after slavery were dismal.[29] Surely blacks suffered from mental illnesses during slavery, but whites probably failed to notice. Simkins did not point this out, demonstrating his lack of understanding of blacks under slavery. Thus, he showed the limits on his objectivity in analyzing the life of slaves.

In the postbellum period, black attitudes toward life's most pressing demands showed little sense of responsibility, Simkins insisted. Marital fidelity meant little to many blacks, and cohabitation was rampant among the freedmen. Simkins partially blamed the slave system for fostering these attitudes. During slavery, small living quarters, which forced black men and women to live close to each other, heightened "the natural sensuality of the African." The coming of freedom gave even more rein to such sensuality. Because black men proved inept as husbands and fathers after the war, many families were led by females. Simkins believed the image of the emotionally strong and sexually liberated black woman was not an exaggeration. Black children, nevertheless, were treated with extreme cruelty by their parents, and what today would be called "black on black" violence occurred often. However, handling money unwisely, rather than black on black violence, ranked as "the worst crime which the Negro committed against himself." According to Simkins, frivolous and unnecessary traveling, which became a passion for blacks, absorbed much of their money.[30]

Having earlier cast black life in depressing terms, Simkins now probed its hopeful sides, illuminated by his own desire to understand the motivations of blacks during Reconstruction.[31] Simkins recognized that aspects of black behavior sprang from their humanity. "The tendency of the Negro to work less and frolic more had its compensations," he wrote. "Perhaps," conjectured Simkins, the black man "was fulfilling the legitimate craving of every free man for recreation; perhaps his wife deserted field work because she was busy with the tasks of setting up a home. To censure the Negro to a great degree for moral delinquencies involves the creation of arbitrary standards." In other words, in their basic desires, blacks were no different from whites and should be judged no differently.[32]

While previously Simkins accused blacks, especially black men, of failing to fulfill obligations to their family, he also argued that family life held an attraction for blacks. Being married was a source of pride to many of them, and maintaining their families often became a priority for black women, who, because of their family responsibilities, had less time for fieldwork. Black families, wrote Simkins, gained greater independence by establishing homes in a dispersed fashion, rather than living close to one another as they had done during slavery, a point more recent scholars have verified.[33] Extraordinarily gifted at living on what the fields, forests, and rivers yielded, blacks were "happy-go-lucky," he concluded.[34]

Simkins had also previously expressed disdain for the crude houses of blacks, but he now found redeeming qualities in the simple homes. He felt blacks were unsuited for better housing, because they were not "fully civilized." Possessing little modesty or aesthetic feeling, the freedmen had constructed houses reflecting their simple psychological makeup, which was focused more on visceral pleasures than on building an impressive place to live. "They hunted and fished, shouted in church and made love to the 'sisters' on the way home, wore old finery and bright calicoes, and ate molasses and the products of their farms."[35] Blacks, he failed to see, were forced to focus on subsistence and not luxury.

Simkins wrote at length about black religion during the Reconstruction era, something historians of that era had largely ignored. White-controlled churches witnessed a sharp decline in black membership in the postbellum era, a movement Simkins saw as "an inevitable consequence of the coming of freedom." Blacks, refusing to continue the inferior status foisted upon them in the antebellum churches, set up congregations of their own. During Reconstruction, whites generally welcomed religious separation, and, in the early twentieth century, argued Simkins, whites and blacks remained "rigidly separated" in their respective churches, the South's most segregated institutions. Referring to such freedom of religion as "perhaps the most momentous social change of Reconstruction," Simkins believed few legacies of the era were as lasting. Most aspects of the Radical program for the South had collapsed by the early twentieth century and the Republican leaders who held office during Reconstruction had been discredited in the eyes of most southern whites. The doctrine of religious segregation stood out as the "principal religious accomplishment" of Reconstruction. "No one at present ever dreams of challenging its existence," he wrote. Throughout his life, Simkins never abandoned the notion that religious separation came at the behest of blacks, not whites, and was a positive development for the freedmen and the blacks who came after them.[36]

Emotionalism remained the ethos of black and white religious worship after the war. Simkins, the staid Episcopalian, took the energetic form of black worship seriously, offering readers a vivid, non-condescending description of black religious gatherings, which included loud singing and dancing. According to Simkins, "if it [energetic worship] was more strenuous than that of the white man, it was because the Negro was a more genuine type of early American, more darkened by the shadows of backwoods ignorance."[37] Simkins believed that blacks resembled whites when white culture was less developed. Although he probably did not realize it, Simkins was arguing that "the Negro was a more genuine type of early American" since his cultural development mirrored that of whites. But, of course, to Simkins, white culture provided the best definition of Americanism.

Throughout *South Carolina During Reconstruction* and in other writings as well, Simkins expressed such ambivalence toward the plight of blacks in South Carolina, seemingly measuring his words lest he offend. He pointed out inequities and abuses, but he neither defended nor denounced them. In the final chapter to *South Carolina During Reconstruction*, however, he wrote eloquently and forcefully about the bitter legacy Reconstruction bequeathed to blacks. The chapter stands out as the most definitive statement he had ever written about black oppression.[38] In almost every way, wrote Simkins, the end of Reconstruction stalled or destroyed the progress of South Carolina blacks. The Republican party, which had represented their interests, reached a moribund state after the rise to power of the Bourbons. Black political participation received a coup de grâce in 1895, with the coming of constitutional disenfranchisement. Stripping blacks of the right to vote was unnecessary, Simkins said, because blacks had already been intimidated to the point that they dared not vote. This fear remained unabated in the early twentieth century. Explained Simkins, "everyone familiar with conditions in the rural counties knows that the possibility of violence is the principal reason why there are not more Negro voters." Whites, he added, were determined to defend the political status quo, haunted by the supposed horror of black rule during Reconstruction.[39]

As Reconstruction ended, blacks once again found themselves second-class citizens, members of a "colored caste." A spate of Jim Crow laws then solidified their social and legal inferiority.[40] Simkins minced no words in enumerating the unfair treatment the laws imposed on black South Carolinians. "These and other laws in which the issue of race is not mentioned have usually been applied so as to discriminate against the Negro," he declared. Continued Simkins:

> The assumption of equality of all men before the law has usually been flaunted whenever the issue of white supremacy has been involved. Juries have, in almost all cases, consisted exclusively of whites, and they have seldom turned a Negro free for an alleged crime against a white person and they have seldom convicted a white person for an alleged crime against a Negro. White public opinion has not always been content to let the law take its course in dealing with Negro culprits; since Reconstruction white mobs have lynched several scores of Negroes, and no one has been punished for these lawless acts.[41]

Having made this strong statement about the law, Simkins turned to the question of segregation in public education. He had addressed the issue of inequality in funding for white and black schools earlier, but this time he went further, writing, "The law against the mixing of races in schools has meant that Negro schools are very much inferior to those provided for the whites." However, Simkins did not call for the desegregation of the public schools, a policy virtually no white southerner, liberal or conservative, favored in the early 1930s.[42]

Several decades after Reconstruction, he continued, blacks still struggled, not only against discriminatory laws, but also against demeaning social customs meant to reinforce white supremacy. The heritage of Reconstruction offered blacks little hope for the future. For the first time, Simkins excoriated the social system that kept blacks in bondage.[43] The final chapter of this landmark study was a remarkable piece of social commentary and the clearest statement of Simkins's views on race and the status of blacks in South Carolina society.

In the early 1930s, when Simkins wrote these words, the American past had rarely been written about with such breadth and in such depth. Simkins and Woody had captured the nuances of an era too often portrayed negatively by historians and popular writers, who lacked a sense of careful discrimination and exacting fairness. But even Simkins and Woody, two excellent historians, were not always fair; their writing revealed hints of the Dunning school of thought toward Reconstruction. Simkins demonstrated his willingness to challenge historical orthodoxy but at the same time demonstrated the hold the same orthodoxy had on him. That Simkins could patronize the freedmen as simple-minded and less developed culturally than whites, yet write with compassion concerning the grinding discrimination blacks faced in the early twentieth century, underscored his inner conflict over race issues. From the middle of two worlds, those of Dunning and Du Bois, Simkins seemed to be groping for a way to reconcile southern tradition and social justice. *South Carolina During Reconstruction* illuminated the multifaceted nature of his mind. Still in manuscript form at this point, the work of Simkins and his coauthor was more of a transitional study on the continuum of Reconstruction historiography than a revisionist one.

When they finished the draft, the authors chose to send it to the University of North Carolina Press, founded just ten years earlier. They could have sought a publisher outside the South, perhaps Columbia

University Press. Perhaps they knew *South Carolina During Reconstruction*, both provocative and controversial, was the type book the UNC Press editor desired to publish. William Terry Couch, a southern liberal, took risks few publishers were willing to take in the early twentieth century, by publishing works designed to question prevailing social, economic, and political conditions in Dixie. The same year Couch published Simkins's and Woody's study, for example, he also published Virginius Dabney's *Liberalism in the South*. The next year the Press released Arthur F. Raper's *The Tragedy of Lynching*, and later in the 1930s, Couch accepted for publication Herman Clarence Nixon's *Forty Acres and Steel Mules*.[44]

Couch first saw Simkins's and Woody's manuscript sometime in the fall of 1930, because, at that time, he wrote letters to several scholars asking for a confidential reading and evaluation of their work. As mentioned earlier, Rion McKissick, Orin F. Crow, and Yates Snowden expressed a desire to see the manuscript published.[45] Snowden also offered telling commentary on his ex-student:

> I know Simkins well; he is self assertive; has a passion for novelty, and in his desire to free himself from parochialism and "Southern prejudice" he sometimes, especially in his studies [?] of the Negro, "out-Herod's Herod." Some of his conclusions would meet the warm approval of Oswald Garrison Villard! But surely, that characteristic would not hurt him at Chapel Hill, judging by several notable books bearing the imprimatur of "the U. of N.C. Press!"[46]

Soon after the UNC Press published the book in the spring of 1932, positive reviews of *South Carolina During Reconstruction* began to appear in magazines, journals, and newspapers. One of the reviewers was Charles W. Ramsdell, a student of William Dunning and the author of a monograph dealing with Reconstruction in Texas. Ramsdell wrote approvingly of the Simkins and Woody study in a short review for the *American Political Science Review*. "The chief contribution of the book," he declared, "is the account of the economic and social revolution which resulted from the change to free labor and the destruction of the old agricultural system."[47]

In the *New Republic*, Henry Steele Commager lauded the book as "a triumph for the spirit of scientific inquiry," praising the authors for resisting the tendency common among southern historians to write about Reconstruction from a partisan viewpoint. Like Ramsdell, Commager viewed the authors' emphasis on economic and social issues of greater significance than the attention they gave to political matters. Commager explained that Simkins and Woody presented black politicians and South Carolina's Radical government in an objective light by pointing out their positive qualities. The authors, wrote Commager, had also shown that much continuity, particularly white supremacy, existed between antebellum and postbellum South Carolina.[48]

Commager also argued that *South Carolina During Reconstruction* revealed tendencies that seemed to be increasingly more important to Reconstruction studies. Historians, for instance, showed a heightened interest in analyzing more fairly the controversial aspects of Reconstruction, such as the black codes, and social and economic aspects of Reconstruction also seemed to be receiving greater scrutiny. These themes may have grown more important to historians because of what Commager termed "recent experience," referring to the devastating impact of the Great Depression.[49]

Howard K. Beale, writing in the *American Historical Review*, praised the authors for "remarkable objectivity," while criticizing them for basing their work on "an underlying philosophy of the propertied white." The authors seemed to accept without question that blacks should not have been granted social equality, Beale declared. He accused Simkins and Woody of refusing to acknowledge the point of view from which they wrote, meaning, of course, white supremacy.[50]

From the ranks of black scholars, who, in the early twentieth century, often felt dismissed and discriminated against, Simkins and Woody had won respect. Writing in the *Journal of Negro History*, Rayford W. Logan described *South Carolina During Reconstruction* as an "attractive and scholarly tome" and "a definitive study," one "indispensable" to scholars.[51] "Not that the conclusions are revolutionary—practically all of them have been stated before," wrote Logan, in a bow to Du Bois and Taylor. "A new era has been reached, however," Logan wrote, "when two professors in two different Southern schools find a Southern university press willing to publish in an artistic volume that will hardly yield any profit a common-sense, objective view of the most controversial period in American history." Logan also complimented Simkins and Woody for the fair manner in which they portrayed the behavior and motivation of blacks. The authors, he wrote, demonstrated that blacks and whites acted similarly during Reconstruction, and that blacks should thus not be judged overly harshly. Quipped Logan, "there is none of Nancy Astor's hysteria that alcohol makes Negroes five times worse than it does white men." Both blacks and whites were human, and the quality of their actions stemmed from considerations unrelated to race. This stood out as a stunning remark for the early 1930s, but Logan did not elaborate further. According to Logan, "although the authors doubt the wisdom of a small-farm economy, many readers will conclude that, after all, the great tragedy of Reconstruction was the failure to give the Negroes forty acres and a mule." While he overstated the authors' views on this point, Logan nevertheless penned a highly complimentary review.[52]

Although the generally positive reviews of *South Carolina During Reconstruction* attested to its success and the reaction of black scholars was heartening, other developments enhanced the book's reputation even further. Simkins and Woody received the American Historical Association's John H. Dunning Prize in 1932, their work winning out over several other books that had been submitted for consideration to AHA officials.[53]

The book failed to bring great commercial success. The UNC Press sold a total of 905 copies. The authors' willingness to pay the partial costs of publication, however, reaped academic and professional rewards for the two southern historians. More important, the publication of their book cast new light on an old story. That light served to drive out some of the prejudices and half-truths that too often characterized the study of Reconstruction in the early twentieth century.[54] In truth, though, it also entrenched some others.

Some aspects of the importance of *South Carolina During Reconstruction* continue to call for further investigation. As the historian David Levering Lewis has pointed out, W. E. B. Du Bois's *Black Reconstruction*, a Marxist interpretation of the period and a major work in Reconstruction historiography, reflected the influence of Simkins and Woody. For example, in a chapter titled "The Black Proletariat in South Carolina," Du Bois explained that *South Carolina During Reconstruction* was one of the three sources that provided "the main facts in this chapter." He cited the book seventeen times in that chapter alone and a number of times in other chapters. Simkins, nevertheless, viewed Du Bois's work negatively. Du Bois's book, filled with long quotations, was to Simkins a tedious read. He also argued that Du Bois had not adequately supported a number of his assertions. He failed to mention that many manuscript departments were closed to black scholars, complicating Du Bois's research. Du Bois's

Marxist approach to Reconstruction also frustrated Simkins. It had no more relevance to the study of southern history, he said, than "the dialectics of St. Augustine or Thomas Aquinas." Despite Simkins's harsh review, *Black Reconstruction* won great acclaim as a seminal work.[55]

Standing in the shadow of Simkins and Du Bois was Robert Woody. The chapters he wrote in *South Carolina During Reconstruction* were excellent, but the book proved to be his only major publication. He published *The Papers and Addresses of William Preston Few* in 1951, and he wrote numerous articles and book reviews.[56] Duke University officials tapped Woody to head the university library's George Washington Flowers Memorial Collection of Southern Americana, a task he began in 1937. Woody made his greatest contribution to southern history as a teacher. Thirty-two graduate students wrote dissertations under his direction, addressing a wide range of topics from southern literature to slavery, from the American Revolution to church history.[57]

Simkins's writings, not his teaching, comprised his legacy. Out of the seven books he would publish during his career, *South Carolina During Reconstruction* was his most important. The impact the book exerted on the study of one of the United States's most misunderstood eras lifted a relatively unknown historian out of professional obscurity while promoting his image as a racial liberal. In addition to a plethora of favorable reviews, Simkins's and Woody's tome was judged exemplary by officials of the American Historical Association. *South Carolina During Reconstruction* lifted Simkins and Woody to the forefront of progressive Reconstruction scholars.

Notes

1. Gilberto Freyre to Francis Butler Simkins, August 15, 1927, "Correspondence E-J" Box, in Francis B. Simkins Papers, Special Collections, Longwood Library, Longwood University, Farmville, Virginia. Hereafter cited as FBS Papers, Farmville, Virginia; "Simkins-Chandler," *Farmville Herald*, August 22, 1930, 5; *Fellows of the Social Science Research Council 1925–1951* (New York: Social Science Research Council, 1951), 369–70.
2. James S. Humphreys, "South Carolina Rustic: Historian Francis Butler Simkins, A Life" (Ph.D. diss., Mississippi State University, 2005), 102, 123, 266–67.
3. Wendell Holmes Stephenson, "A Half Century of Southern Historical Scholarship," *Journal of Southern History* (February 1945): 3–32.

4. John Hope Franklin, "Silent Cinema as Historical Mythmaker," in *Myth America: A Historical Anthology*, ed. Patrick Gerster and Nicholas Cords, vol. 2 (St. James, N.Y.: Brandywine Press, 1997), 110–17.
5. Vernon L. Wharton, "Reconstruction," in *Writing Southern History: Essays in Honor of Fletcher M. Green*, ed. Arthur S. Link and Rembert W. Patrick (Baton Rouge: Louisiana State University Press, 1967), 307.
6. Stephen Gilroy Hall, "'Research as Opportunity': Alrutheus Ambush Taylor, Black Intellectualism, and the Remaking of Reconstruction Historiography, 1893–1954," *UCLA Historical Journal* 16 (1996): 43–49, 54.
7. David Levering Lewis, *W. E. B. Du Bois: Biography of a Race 1868–1919* (New York: Henry Holt and Company, 1993), 383–85; William Edward Burghardt Du Bois, "Reconstruction and Its Benefits," *American Historical Review* 15 (July 1910): 781–99.
8. Du Bois, "Reconstruction and Its Benefit," 781–99; Lewis, *W. E. B. Du Bois*, 384–85.
9. Hall, "'Research as Opportunity,'" 39; Alrutheus Ambush Taylor, *The Negro in South Carolina During the Reconstruction* (Washington, D.C.: The Association for the Study of Negro Life and History, 1924).
10. Hall, "'Research as Opportunity,'" 40–45; For Taylor's title in the ASNLH, see Taylor, *The Negro in South Carolina*, title page.
11. Taylor, *The Negro in South Carolina*, 45–48, 49–53, 289, 310–11.
12. Both Du Bois's article and Taylor's book appear in FBS's and Robert Hilliard Woody's bibliography in *South Carolina During Reconstruction*. See "Bibliography" in FBS and Woody, *South Carolina During Reconstruction* (Chapel Hill: University of North Carolina Press, 1932), 574, 586.
13. James Welch Patton, "The Historian," in *Francis Butler Simkins 1897–1966: Historian of the South, A Pamphlet Published By His Family In Memory Of The Edgefield Native Who Spent His Teaching Career At Longwood College In Farmville, Virginia* (Columbia: State Printing Company, n.d.), 29.
14. Interview: E. Stanly Godbold (February 29, 2000); [E. Stanly Godbold], "Robert Hilliard Woody: An Appreciation," *South Atlantic Quarterly* (Winter 1974): 4.
15. Interview: E. Stanly Godbold.
16. [Godbold], "Robert Hilliard Woody," 6–7.
17. Patton, "The Historian," 29; Rion McKissick to William T. Couch, October 3, 1930, Yates Snowden to William T. Couch, October 3, 1930, Orin F. Crow to William T. Couch, October 5, 1930, in the University of North Carolina Press Records, Sub-Group 4: Author/Title Publication Records, in the University Archives, Wilson Library, The University of North Carolina at Chapel Hill. Hereafter cited as UNC Press Records.
18. [Godbold], "Robert Hilliard Woody," 7.
19. FBS and Robert Hilliard Woody, *South Carolina During Reconstruction*, vii–viii.
20. Ibid., 43–48, 50–52, 48 (quote).
21. Ibid., 64–89.
22. Ibid., 91–94.

23. Ibid., 90–111, 93–94 (quote).
24. Ibid., 122–46.
25. Ibid., 112–223, 288–311.
26. Ibid., 266–87.
27. Ibid., 416–43.
28. Ibid., 442–43.
29. Ibid., 329–37, 329 (quote).
30. Ibid., 330–37, 331 (quote), 334 (quote).
31. For positive aspects of black life during Reconstruction, see Simkins's chapter titled "Brighter Phases of Social Life," in FBS and Woody, *South Carolina During Reconstruction*, 338–72.
32. Ibid., 338.
33. Ibid., 358–62; See, for example, Charles S. Aiken, *The Cotton Plantation South Since the Civil War* (Baltimore, Md.: Johns Hopkins University Press, 1998).
34. FBS and Woody, *South Carolina During Reconstruction*, 360.
35. Ibid., 360–61.
36. Ibid., 387–88, 393–95.
37. Ibid., 399–402, 409, 410–15, 409 (quote).
38. See "The Heritage Of Reconstruction," in FBS and Woody, *South Carolina During Reconstruction*," 542–63.
39. FBS and Woody, *South Carolina During Reconstruction*, 547–52, 551 (quote).
40. Ibid., 552–53.
41. Ibid., 553.
42. Ibid., 553.
43. Ibid., 553–55.
44. See "The Critical Temperament Unleashed: William Terry Couch and Southern Publishing," in Daniel Joseph Singal, *The War Within: From Victorian to Modernist Thought in the South, 1919–1945* (Chapel Hill: University of North Carolina Press, 1982), 267–68, 270–73, 275–78.
45. The UNC Press to J. Milton Ariail, October 1, 1930; Rion McKissick to William T. Couch, October 3, 1930; Yates Snowden to William T. Couch, October 3, 1930, in UNC Press Records.
46. Yates Snowden to William T. Couch, October 3, 1930, in UNC Press Records.
47. "*South Carolina During Reconstruction*, Review Copies Sent Out," in UNC Press Records; Charles W. Ramsdell, Review of *South Carolina During Reconstruction*, by FBS and Robert Hilliard Woody, *American Political Science Review* 26 (August 1932): 757.
48. Henry Steele Commager, "Reconstruction Reconstructed," Review of *South Carolina During Reconstruction*, by FBS and Robert Hilliard Woody, *New Republic: A Journal of Opinion* 135 (July 27, 1932): 295–96.
49. Ibid., 295–96.
50. Howard K. Beale, Review of *South Carolina During Reconstruction*, by FBS and Robert Hilliard Woody, *American Historical Review* 38 (January 1933): 345–47.

51. Rayford W. Logan, Review of *South Carolina During Reconstruction*, by FBS and Robert Hilliard Woody, *Journal of Negro History* 17 (October 1932): 497–99.
52. Ibid.
53. "Historical News," *North Carolina Historical Review* 9 (April 1932): 220; Robert Hilliard to William T. Couch, February 24, 1932, in UNC Press Records.
54. Peter Cowles, Assistant Director of the UNC Press to FBS, February 5, 1959; Peter Cowles to FBS, February 2, 1961, in UNC Press Records.
55. David Levering Lewis, *W. E. B. Du Bois: The Fight for Equality and the American Century 1919–1963* (New York: Henry Holt and Company, 2000), 361, 363, 367–68, 373; W. E. Burghardt Du Bois, *Black Reconstruction: An Essay Toward a History of the Part which Black Folk Played in the Attempt to Reconstruct Democracy in America, 1860–1880* (New York: Harcourt and Brace, 1935), 181, 236, 429–30; Francis Butler Simkins, Review of *Black Reconstruction*, by W. E. Burghardt Du Bois, *Journal of Southern History* 1 (November 1935): 530–32.
56. [Godbold], "Robert Hilliard Woody," 4–6; Robert Hilliard Woody, ed., *The Papers and Addresses of William Preston Few* (Durham, NC: Duke University Press, 1951).
57. [Godbold], "Robert Hilliard Woody," 3–4, 6.

8. CONFRONTING RACE IN AMERICAN HISTORY

EDNA GREENE MEDFORD

IN THE ACCLAIMED 1903 COLLECTION OF ESSAYS, *THE SOULS OF BLACK Folk*, the eminent African American scholar W. E. B. Du Bois suggested that "the problem of the twentieth century is the problem of the color line."[1] The pronouncement should have surprised no one; it was not as if some new condition had befallen black people. Du Bois was simply acknowledging an immutable fact: the influence of race in American history. The "problem" was a long-standing one; it predated the nation's founding and grew in complexity with shifting economic and political currents.

As Du Bois recognized, the great challenge of America was (and still is) its struggle to reconcile the promise of its founding principles with the seemingly irreconcilable realities of race. Of course, even in a homogeneous society, certain groups experience exclusion and discrimination (as in the case of the Harijan or Dalit population—the so-called untouchables—in India or the Hmong people in Vietnam and other parts of Southeast Asia). While the United States has avoided such caste-based distinctions, racial differences have been an especially vexing problem for the nation. It was so almost from the very beginning of European settlement. Race surfaced as a central factor in America's history as a consequence of the presence of three supposedly distinct racial groups on the North American continent. Although the white majority was ethnically diverse, a population of primarily English origin was able to impose its cultural and institutional will on the rest. European economic interests and racial/cultural biases precluded a similar assimilation of minorities of color. An unrelenting quest for Native Americans' lands, and the decision to exploit African labor to cultivate it, encouraged the creation of a national identity founded on whiteness.[2]

In order to achieve a homogeneous society, nonwhites were excluded from the body politic.[3] In the case of Native peoples, the task was fairly easily accomplished. They were declared members of "sovereign" nations, treaties advantageous to Europeans were signed, and disagreements that could not be resolved through negotiation were settled through wars. The outcome of such conflicts generally involved the Native peoples ceding their valuable lands. Eventually, confinement on reservations physically removed them to the periphery of American society while making them wards of the federal government.

The African presence created a different, thornier problem. Indispensable as laborers, they necessitated a system that would keep them subordinate without compromising American ideals. Slavery offered a powerful and seemingly sustainable solution. It ensured that most Africans and their descendants would be perpetually "bound to service." By classifying black men and women as property, white Americans were able to deny them legal standing in the society and prevent them from enjoying the rights and privileges most Americans took for granted. The free born and the freed would be treated similarly. African Americans, even free blacks, were seen as "a species apart" and possessing, in the words of Chief Justice Roger B. Taney in the United States Supreme Court decision *Scott v. Sandford*, "no rights which white men were bound to respect."[4] Legislation circumscribed many aspects of their lives; in its absence, custom kept black people segregated, impoverished, socially ostracized, and politically impotent.

When conflict over the expansion of slavery divided the nation and erupted into war in 1861, black men stood at the ready to preserve national union and win their freedom. Congress and President Lincoln declined their offer, insisting that this was a white man's war. But as the conflict dragged on, the president realized the necessity of emancipating the Confederacy's enslaved population and arming it. For the rest of the war, black men served honorably, despite disparate treatment and concerns that they would be unable to confront white men on the battlefield.[5]

For a fleeting moment after emancipation and Union victory, black men and women looked forward to the promise of a new beginning in which the Declaration of Independence and the Constitution would apply equally to them. The Reconstruction amendments granted them citizenship and the right to vote. Through self-help, philanthropy, and federal government assistance (in the form of the Freedmen's Bureau),

African Americans seized the opportunity to educate themselves and their children. They acquired land for farming by pooling their modest resources, and when they had no money to pool, they rented land through the system of sharecropping. This season of relative black progress ended abruptly as federal troops were removed from the South. What followed was disfranchisement, economic dependence, and the denial of social justice. Disillusioned by their inability to advance in the former Confederacy, some elected to establish new lives in the West. Before the century ended, African American fortunes had suffered a devastating blow as discrimination, intimidation, and violence dashed their hopes for full-fledged membership in the American family. Nothing was more injurious to their quest for progress than the 1896 decision *Plessy v. Ferguson*, which legally sanctioned the separation of the races, already a reality in custom.

The African American condition changed slowly over the next several decades. The new century opened with race riots that crisscrossed the nation: Statesboro, Georgia, and Springfield, Ohio (1904); Atlanta, Georgia, and Brownsville, Texas (1906); Springfield, Illinois (1908). Tensions escalated as blacks left the South in pursuit of economic opportunity and civil rights. It did not take long for them to discover that racism crossed state boundaries and regions. In 1919, during the notorious "Red Summer," rioting disrupted life in more than twenty-five cities across the country. The worst occurred in Chicago where over the course of nearly two weeks thirty-eight people (including twenty-three blacks and fifteen whites) lost their lives.[6]

The 1919 riots had followed closely behind the First World War. In justifying war with the Germans, Woodrow Wilson had declared that the "world must be made safe for democracy."[7] Ironically, African Americans, who eagerly volunteered for military service, were denied democracy at home. Initially rejected as volunteers, they were later inducted in disproportion to their numbers in the population. Those who served in Europe did so primarily in service units. Others fought alongside the French combat forces, where they earned decorations for valor. To ensure that no black would be eligible for promotion to general officer, the government retired Colonel Charles Young, the highest ranking black officer at the time of the war, on the spurious allegation that he suffered from hypertension and was unfit for duty. Young attempted to establish his fitness by traveling from Ohio to Washington on horseback, but the decorated West Point graduate and veteran of the 1916 Punitive Expedition into Mexico failed to convince the military to reconsider its decision. Even more egregious, black men who ran afoul of the law in certain southern towns were lynched while still in the uniform of their country.[8]

By the 1920s, a new militancy had taken hold in the African American community. Blacks fought back (sometimes with the assistance of sympathetic whites) through protest organizations that had been formed in the midst of increasing racial oppression. Those who had relocated to the North during the Great Migration took advantage of their access to the ballot and their newfound strength in numbers to seek change through the political process. In the meantime, a cultural renaissance that incorporated protest as an important element of expression inspired black men and women to press on. When the Great Depression upended the economy, African Americans demanded relief and launched a "Don't Buy Where You Cannot Work" campaign. Politically, northern black voters switched allegiance (from the Republicans to the Democrats) when the "party of Lincoln" ignored their interests.[9]

As World War II replaced the Depression as a source of concern for the nation, African Americans again entered military service, this time in pursuit of a double victory—against the Axis Powers and racism at home. They were quickly reminded that such service did not shelter them from the racist customs of the day. Discrimination and ill treatment became a constant reminder of their perceived inferiority. In certain southern cities, black soldiers were treated with greater disdain than German prisoners-of-war, who were allowed access to public facilities such as restaurants and swimming pools while African American men were turned away.

But the war years saw significant breakthroughs in civil rights as well. A threatened march on Washington by labor leader A. Philip Randolph in 1941, precipitated the formation of the Fair Employment Practices Commission, whose stated aim was to ensure equal access to defense industries. In the area of politics, legal challenges to white primaries began the movement toward reversing African American disfranchisement. Also in the postwar era, the assault on discrimination intensified. Even the military experienced change. In 1948, President Truman desegregated the armed services, the same year that the Supreme Court ruled against restrictive housing covenants. The grassroots civil rights movement of the mid-1950s and the 1960s—from the Montgomery Bus Boycott to the Memphis Sanitation Strike—facilitated the advance of civil rights, one protest at a time.

At the center of this long struggle were men and women who met attacks upon their humanity with dignity and a determination to persevere. Until recently, their story was all but excluded from the nation's recorded memory. In those instances when they occupied the pages of a history text, they appeared more as caricatures than as historical beings worthy of study. African American scholars and a smattering of others attempted to counter the simplicity of such characterizations and to address the omission of their history, but often their efforts were ignored or dismissed. In the last forty years, however, the nation has witnessed a sustained challenge to this conspiracy of exclusion and misrepresentation as scholars have pursued a more balanced and comprehensive interpretation of the past. The essays contained in this volume—a fitting tribute to an astute interpreter of the role of race in American history—remind us both of just how far historiography has progressed in this regard and how many questions still remain unasked and unanswered. Focused primarily on the antebellum, Civil War, and postwar years, they provide insight into how race has shaped the American character and our past.

Slavery, the topic of the first chapter, has commanded special attention since Ulrich B. Phillips proclaimed in the early twentieth century that the southern plantation had been "a school constantly training and controlling pupils who were in a backward state of civilization." He also suggested that slavery was not very profitable and likely would have declined had the war not occurred.[10] As Mark R. Cheathem's study suggests, slavery was a business whose success depended on the "financial acumen" of the planter. His subject, Andrew Jackson Donelson, apparently had little. Nor did it help that he lacked the will to live within his means. History tells us that he was in good company on this score.

Cheathem tells us that, like many of his fellow planters, Donelson defended his exploitation of black men and women as humane and beneficial to his laborers (since Africans, he concluded, were inferior beings who were in need of civilization) and as necessary to ensure that white men could enjoy liberty. Yet, even Donelson could not escape the consequences of the enslavement of one man by another. It was impossible for him to ignore the dissatisfaction of the enslaved person with his plight. Apologists for the institution expended considerable energy in an attempt to convince themselves and the nation that black people concurred in their own bondage because they did not overtly resist with any frequency. But as Donelson's experiences indicate, enslaved people resisted in ways both clandestine and overt. Running away, slowing the pace of work, feigning illness, even physically attacking an overseer were but a few of the ways in which black people pushed back against efforts to strip them of the basic rights of humankind. If Donelson found that having enough to eat and proper attire did not ensure contentment, how much truer then for those who had neither? Enslaved people saw themselves as more than laborers whose stirrings for freedom could be quieted by adequate amounts of food and clothing; they were individuals with personal agendas; members of communities with a shared belief system; human beings determined to assert their humanity and to get as much out of life as possible. Planters and other owners of enslaved labor may have convinced themselves that their business in chattel was a natural, even a divinely sanctioned enterprise. Enslaved people were not likely to share their delusion.

The Civil War forced even deluded slave owners to question long-held assumptions. Wartime exigencies altered relationships, created new alliances, and established a new reality for all concerned. The three Civil War chapters included here illuminate our understanding of how these changes affected the various populations within the Confederacy.

Thomas Cockrell's study of Mississippi Unionists reveals that the motivations to remain loyal to the North were as varied as the reasons for Confederate support—economic self-interest, adherence to political principles, personal grudges, to name a few. He shows that Unionists were not a monolithic group; neither were they all as pro-North as one would expect. A slightly stronger dislike for the Confederacy than the Yankees sometimes provided enough incentive to propel a man into the Union camp. A desire to remain outside of Confederate control made some reluctant southerners less pro-Union than antiwar. Black Unionists may have been variously motivated as well, but their premier incentive for loyalty was the promise of freedom. It steeled them in their willingness to risk their lives and in their determination to prevail on the battlefield. Their success in combat vindicated Lincoln in his decision to emancipate the slaves and establish black military units.

Stephen Michot argues for the need to focus more intensely on the Trans-Mississippi theater, especially on the experiences of black soldiers and civilians in the Lafourche region of Louisiana. His essay expresses particular interest in the Native Guards of New Orleans, who, out of self-interest (they were free blacks, some of whom had substantial property), offered their services to the Confederacy, and when the Union forces occupied the area, became a part of the Northern army. Michot finds as well that black men who joined the Union ranks suffered abuse at the hands of white officers and enlisted men, while civilians were similarly reviled by their "liberators."

The irony of black men offering their services to the Confederacy and of enslaved people being mistreated by federal soldiers has generated a great deal of attention, especially as we begin the sesquicentennial commemoration of the Civil War and the Emancipation Proclamation. The paradox gives those who are inclined to reject slavery as the reason for the conflict opportunity and cause to question northern motivations and racial attitudes. Certainly, such skepticism is appropriate in historical inquiry. But the subject has become so controversial because of its implications; both sides are heavily invested in interpreting this seeming black loyalty to the Confederate cause.

Before one embraces the notion that contented slaves shunned freedom or that free blacks rushed to defend the Confederacy because they accepted a subordinate position in society and rejected northern "meddling" with southern domestic institutions, it would be appropriate to consider the motivations of these supposed black Confederates and the circumstances under which they came to support the rebellion. Students of Civil War history generally acknowledge the support rendered by those black men who, perhaps out of loyalty to their particular states or to their owners, believed that their future rested with the white men with whom they were most familiar.[11] Black support for the Confederacy did not happen in a vacuum. Free blacks and enslaved people had heard the charge against the North—that Union forces cared nothing about black people, and if given the chance, they would sell African Americans to Cuba. The expectations and fears resulting from such charges were often confirmed by interaction with northern soldiers. As Michot indicates, northern attitudes about African Americans (whether enslaved or free) reflected the prevailing prejudices in both the South *and* the North. Union soldiers, especially those recently arrived immigrants who had not yet fully assimilated into American society but had already absorbed its racist ideology, were but a microcosm of the societies from which they hailed. They abused black people at will, often with the concurrence of commanding officers. Under such circumstances, perhaps it was not so unusual that some black men elected to close ranks with the enemy that they knew.

Nor was it remarkable that free black men would agree to serve the Confederacy out of fear that to do otherwise would bring unwanted suspicion of Union sympathy. Men who had acquired property were inclined to protect what little they had; they could not simply abandon it and leave the South. The Native Guards and other men who chose to offer their services to the Confederacy doubtless were motivated by economic self-interest and personal survival. They could not predict who would ultimately prevail. Hence, their allegiances shifted with the changing fortunes of either side. The bold increased their survivability by serving both, sometimes volunteering outwardly to assist the Confederacy while clandestinely helping the Union forces.[12]

And, of course, there is the matter of impressments as military laborers. Free black men and enslaved laborers had no choice but to serve when ordered to do so by the Confederate government. As they had done for the southern economy before and during the war, black people provided the coerced noncombatant labor that facilitated military operations. They threw up the fortifications, worked in the armaments factories, served as teamsters and orderlies, and performed whatever services required of them. They did the same for the Union forces, sometimes voluntarily, and at other times as a result of some degree of coercion. What can be reasonably surmised is that neither side honored or valued the right of black people to choose.

The same can be deduced in the matter of sexual encounters between African American women and Union soldiers. That such activity transpired is not open for debate. Why and under what circumstances it occurred, however, needs closer attention. Much of the early historiography on slavery condemned African American women as jezebels, promiscuous in their sexuality and largely responsible for the licentiousness of white men. While such assumptions have been discredited, like certain other interpretations, this one is hard to die. It is possible (even likely) that some women (black as well as white) used whatever tools were at their disposal to their advantage. Some may have been flirtatious, even willing sexual partners of white men. We have limited sources that can shed light on such connections.[13] What we do know from those sources, however, is that black women would have experienced the omnipotence of southern white men long before northern soldiers arrived at their doors. To what extent they had the right to refuse sexual advances (or thought they could) is an important topic that needs to be explored before we can reach any conclusions about how black women did or did not use their sexuality.

The attitude of white Union soldiers to enslaved African Americans, freedpeople, and black soldiers is also the focus of Michael Ballard's essay. Covering the six months between January 1, 1863, when President Lincoln announced emancipation in Confederate-held territory, and the Vicksburg campaign of that year, he finds that the generally negative attitude Union soldiers had of black people, whether emancipated civilians or soldiers, did not change as a consequence of the proclamation of freedom. Indeed, as he indicates, many federal soldiers resented having to fight a war to end slavery; it was simply not why they supported the Union. Yet, we know that Lincoln would not have won a second term had he failed to secure the vote of the Union soldiers.[14] They supported his reelection in overwhelming numbers, even though he refused to retract the emancipating decree. But this was November 1864. While it does not mean that the soldiers had come to embrace black people as worthy of liberating, it speaks to their faith in Lincoln's overall plan for the nation. Ballard acknowledges that the six months between emancipation and Vicksburg may not have been enough time to fully evaluate the proclamation's impact on long-term attitudes about black freedom. However, it certainly seemed long enough for Lincoln. By August 1863, he was already beginning to acknowledge what his white troops may have been as yet unwilling to accept—the debt the nation owed to black men. In response to a letter from Illinois Republicans inviting the president to travel to Springfield for a political event, Lincoln justified his reasons for not retracting the proclamation. "You say that you will not fight to free negroes," he writes.

> Some of them seem willing to fight for you . . . But negroes, like other people, act upon motives. Why should they do any thing for us, if we will do nothing for them? If they stake their lives for us, they must be prompted by the strongest motive—even the promise of freedom. And the promise being made, must be kept.[15]

Despite their experiences during the war, in the postwar years and beyond, black men continued to pursue employment as soldiers. Deliberately removed from the large population centers of the East, they kept peace between the white settlers and Indians on the frontier and engaged in military operations along the U.S.-Mexican border. Horace Nash's study is concerned with the role of these buffalo soldiers who as ambassadors of sorts helped to minimize racial tensions and improved race relations through their participation in boxing. It is hard to determine to what extent the interaction of blacks and whites in a sports arena impacted daily encounters between the two races. Presumably, individual boxers may have earned a degree of respect from both groups, but appreciation for athletic prowess rarely (if ever) trumps long-held beliefs about race. Essential questions to ask would include how segregated the venue was (was seating assigned along racial lines, for instance) and how might it have changed over time? How were the "positive race relations" that Nash noted manifested in the non-athletic arena? To what extent were African Americans, soldiers or civilians, welcomed in other public places as a consequence of these matches?

Timothy Smith finds no such interaction between the races in his essay on black veterans of World War I, who had been assigned to the Civilian Conservation Corps to restore the Shiloh battlefield in Tennessee. Smith sees it as paradoxical that these men met racism and discrimination at the camp, "one of the very spots where their freedom had been partially won." The CCC had been established during the Great Depression to provide employment primarily to young men, but veterans also found jobs with the agency. The two black camps at Shiloh were segregated, the civilian equivalent to the experiences of African Americans during the most recent war and reflected the experiences of black soldiers before them. One is struck by the extent to which those experiences from two eras converge. Work at Shiloh afforded black men certain opportunities that they valued—vocational training, education of a more general sort, and a chance to earn a living at a difficult time in the nation's economic history. The Civil War offered some of the same incentives. Given the status of black people in both instances, the disparate treatment was, unfortunately, an expected and (from the perspective of many whites) acceptable characteristic of race relations.

James Scott Humphreys reviews Francis Butler Simkins and Robert Woody's challenge to the Dunning School of Reconstruction's southern perspective on the post-Civil War years. Humphreys finds that even in their revisionist approach, Simkins and Woody were limited in their understanding of the African American experience, and in some instances revealed their own racial and cultural biases. His study shows that even when historians attempt a balanced interpretation of the past, the legacies of race often get the best of them.

As historians, we bring our own baggage to the study of the past—personal biases, unique worldviews, hidden (and not so hidden) agendas; it is what makes historical interpretation so interesting and valuable on the one hand and potentially harmful and irresponsible on the other. Issues of race become skewed according to *who* is narrating the story and *why* they find it necessary to tell it.

As Humphreys indicates, black scholars were the first to challenge the pro-South interpretation of race in history. They, too, had an agenda. Believing that attitudes about African Americans' roles in American history shaped perceptions in their own time, these scholars set out to chronicle the contributions, achievements, and trials of their people. Their scholarship was motivated as well by the desire to inform African Americans themselves of the nature of their presence in history. Carter G. Woodson best expresses the need to educate the masses of black people in the following statement, which although lengthy, merits quoting:

> The teaching of history in the Negro area has its political significance. Starting out after the Civil War, the opponents of freedom and social justice decided to work out a program which would enslave the Negroes' mind, in as much as the freedom of his body had to be conceded. It was well understood that if by the teaching of history the white man could be further assured of his superiority and the Negro could be made to feel that he has always been a failure and that the subjection of his will to some other race is necessary, the freedman, then, would still be a slave. If you can control what a man's thinking you do not have to worry about his action ... If you make a man feel that he is inferior, you do not have to compel him to accept an inferior status, for he will seek it himself. If you make a man think that he is an outcast, you do not have to order him to the back door. He will go without being told; and if there is no back door, his very nature will demand one.[16]

The seven essays contained herein collectively confirm the complexity of race as a central factor in our history. The essayists remind us that racial assumptions often defy logical thought; these assumptions presume things that are not even remotely accurate while ignoring or denying the painfully obvious. Assumptions are the stuff from which stereotypes are born:

all African Americans are musically inclined; black men are especially good at sports; black people are more aggressive than other racial groups; black children are unable to excel academically unless the lesson can be delivered with hip-hop rhyme and rhythm. Such simplistic assumptions rest on traditions and attitudes that were born not in our own time but in an earlier era when it was acceptable to exclude an entire race from society's advantages while another race ensured its own privileged place in it.

Is it any wonder that as a nation we have such difficultly discussing issues of race? President Clinton attempted to start a national dialogue on the subject when in 1998 he established a commission under the leadership of the noted historian John Hope Franklin. The commission traveled around the country, where it provided a forum for supposedly candid discussion. What resulted, despite Dr. Franklin's efforts, was less than a breakthrough in racial understanding. The dialogue never caught on with most Americans.

More recently, President Obama discovered just how sensitive the nation is to suggestions that race colors (no pun intended) our interactions with each other. When Harvard professor Henry Louis Gates was arrested after exchanging words with a policeman who mistakenly thought he was breaking into his own home, the president rose to the defense of his friend, Professor Gates. Immediately, an outcry went up over the country condemning Obama for injecting race into the incident. It was no surprise that there was a racial divide in white Americans' and black Americans' interpretation of the incident.

The sesquicentennial of the Civil War provides Americans an opportunity to once again confront the issue of race in our history *and* our present. But to seize it, we must be in agreement that the subject merits discussion. At the moment, we are a long way from reaching consensus that the color line still poses a problem for our nation. But if current trends hold—race-baiting politics, racial insensitivity, denigration of those whom we perceive to be different—our opportunity will be squandered, and we will be left to confront its consequences.

Notes

1. W. E. B. Du Bois, *The Souls of Black Folk* (1903; rpt., New York: Penguin Books, 1996).
2. For discussion of the early beginnings of race-based discrimination, see Aristide Zolberg, *A Nation by Design: Immigration Policy in the Fashioning of America* (Cambridge, Mass.: Harvard University Press, 2008).
3. For a discussion of the earliest efforts to deal with the presence of racial minorities from a political perspective, see Edmund Morgan, *American Slavery, American Freedom: The Ordeal of Colonial Virginia* (New York: Norton, 1975).
4. The Dred Scott Decision: Opinion of Chief Justice Taney, with an Introduction/ by J. H. Van Evrie. http://memory.loc.gov/rr/program/bib/ourdocs/DredScott .html.
5. Lincoln had indicated that "If we were to arm [the blacks], I fear that in a few weeks the arms would be in the hands of the rebels." By the end of the war, he had changed his opinion of the black soldier. See Reply to Emancipation Memorial Presented by Chicago Christians of All Denominations, September 13, 1862, in *The Collected Works of Abraham Lincoln*, ed. Roy P. Basler, 8 vols. (New Brunswick, N.J.: Rutgers University Press, 1953–55), 5:423. Hereafter cited as *Collected Works*. For the wartime experiences of black soldiers, see Joseph T. Glatthaar, *Forged in Battle: The Civil War Alliance of Black Soldiers and White Officers* (Baton Rouge: Louisiana State University Press, 2000). Dudley Taylor Cornish, *The Sable Arm: Negro Troops in the Union Army, 1861–1865* (New York: Norton, 1956), although dated, is still useful.
6. For a recent treatment of the Chicago Race Riot of 1919, see Cameron McWhirter, *The Red Summer: The Summer of 1919 and the Awakening of Black America* (New York: Henry Holt and Company, 2011). The statistics for loss of life are found in John Hope Franklin and Alfred Moss, eds., *From Slavery to Freedom: A History of African Americans*, 7th ed. (New York: McGraw-Hill, 1994), 351.
7. Woodrow Wilson, Joint Address to Congress Leading to a Declaration of War against Germany (April 2, 1917). http://www.ourdocuments.gov/doc.php?flash=t rue&doc=61&page=transcript.
8. Brian G. Shellum, *Black Officer in a Buffalo Soldier Regiment: The Military Career of Charles Young* (Lincoln: University of Nebraska Press, 2010), 257–60. For discussion of lynching, see W. Fitzhugh Brundage, *Lynching in the New South: Georgia and Virginia* (Chicago: University of Illinois Press, 1993).
9. Carole Marks, *Farewell—We're Good and Gone: The Great Black Migration* (Bloomington: Indiana University Press, 1989). Nancy Weiss's *Farewell to the Party of Lincoln: Black Politics in the Age of FDR* (Princeton, N.J.: Princeton University Press, 1983) addresses the issue of black rejection of the Republican party.
10. Phillips argued that enslaved people were "by racial quality submissive rather than defiant, light-hearted instead of gloomy, amiable and ingratiating instead of sullen." See Ulrich Phillips, *American Slavery: A Survey of the Supply, Employment*

and Control of Negro Labor as Determined by the Plantation Regime (New York: D. Appleton and Company, 1918), 341–43; and *Life and Labor in the Old South* (New York: Little, Brown, 1929).

11. A good treatment of this subject can be found in Ervin L. Jordan, *Black Confederates and Afro-Yankees in Civil War Virginia* (Charlottesville: University Press of Virginia, 1995).
12. See Edna Greene Medford, "'I Was Always a Union Man': The Dilemma of Free Blacks in Confederate Virginia," *Slavery and Abolition* 15, no. 3 (1994), 1–16.
13. For a discussion of relationships between black women and white men, see Harriet Jacobs, *Incidents in the Life of a Slave Girl* (Boston, 1861); and Deborah Gray White, *Ar'n't I A Woman?: Female Slaves in the Plantation South* (New York: Norton, 1999).
14. David Long, *Jewel of Liberty: Abraham Lincoln's Re-Election and the End of Slavery* (New York: Da Capo Press, 1997).
15. Abraham Lincoln Letter to James C. Conkling, August 26, 1863, *Collected Works*, 6:409.
16. Carter G. Woodson, *The Mis-Education of the Negro* (Washington, D.C.: Associated Publishers, 1933), 84–85.

CONTRIBUTORS

MICHAEL B. BALLARD. Ph.D. 1983. University Archivist, Coordinator of Congressional and Political Research Center, Associate Editor of U. S. Grant Papers, Mississippi State University Libraries. Home: Ackerman, MS.

MARK R. CHEATHEM. Ph.D. 2002. Associate Professor of History, Cumberland University. Home: Lebanon, TN.

THOMAS D. COCKRELL. Ph.D. 1989. History Instructor, Northeast Mississippi Community College. Home: Ripley, MS.

JAMES SCOTT HUMPHREYS. Ph.D. 2005. Assistant Professor of History, Murray State University. Home: Murray, KY.

EDNA GREENE MEDFORD. Professor of History at Howard University. Her publications include *The Emancipation Proclamation: Three Views* (with coauthors Harold Holzer and Frank Williams) and *The Price of Freedom: Slavery and the Civil War—Volumes I and II* (with coauthors Martin Harry Greenberg, and Charles G. Waugh).

STEPHEN S. MICHOT. Ph.D. 1994. Associate Professor of History, Director of Internships—Louisiana Center on Women and Government, Nicholls State University. Home: Thibodaux, LA.

HORACE NASH. Ph.D. 1996. Assistant Professor of History, San Antonio College. Home: Seguin, TX.

TIMOTHY B. SMITH. Ph.D. 2001. Lecturer of History, University of Tennessee at Martin. Home: Adamsville, TN.

INDEX

African American history, overview, 147–51
African American soldiers out West: after the Civil War, 89; as buffalo soldiers, 89, 90–92; Columbus, New Mexico, 90–102; and John J. Pershing expedition, 90–91; relations with whites, 91–93; riot in Houston, Texas, 91–92, 96; in Spanish-American War, 90; sports and racism, 93–102; and World War I, 90
Aughey, John H., 33, 37

Blair, Francis P., 9–10
Buchanan, James, 13, 17
Butler, Benjamin F., 58–60

Commentary on essays, 151–58
Compromise of 1850, 15–16

Davis, Jefferson, 32, 36, 44
Dennis, Elias, 83
Dodge, Grenville M., 36, 38–39
Donelson, Andrew Jackson: brothers killed in the Civil War, 21; Constitutional Union Party, 19; editor of *Washington Union*, 16–17; education, 4; minister to Prussia, 11–13; plantations, 3, 7–9, 11–12, 15–18, 22–23; rift with Andrew Jackson, 10–11; secession and Civil War, 19–20; slavery, 4–8, 13–22
Donelson, Elizabeth, 3, 8–9, 11–12, 22–23

Donelson, Emily, 3, 7–8
Du Bois, William Edward Burghardt, 130–31, 142–43, 147
Duncan, Stephen, 44–46
Dunning School of Reconstruction, 129–30

Eaton affair, 10–11

Grant, Ulysses S., 36, 39, 70, 73–75, 78, 81–83, 85–86

Hayden, Thomas "Speedball," 97–100, 101

Jackson, Andrew, 3–11, 15, 19
Jackson, Andrew, Jr., 4, 11
Jackson, Rachel, 4–6
Johnson, Andrew, 21
Jones County, Mississippi, 31, 40–43, 49

Knight, Newton, 34, 40–43
Knight, Rachel, 42
Know-Nothing (American) Party, 16–17

Lincoln, Abraham, 19, 21, 36, 40, 47–49, 69, 72, 75, 81, 86, 148
Louisiana: African American soldiers in, 56–66; relations between blacks and white Union soldiers, 62–63; Union capture of New Orleans, 57–58; western theater of the Civil War, 55
Lyon, James A., 35

McPherson, James, 86
Milliken's Bend, Battle of, 82–85
Minor, Kate, 46–47
Mississippi: African Americans (slave and free) supporting the Union, 47–48; citizens' attitudes toward blacks, 77; citizens supporting the Union, 35–37, 40, 43–46, 49–50; locations of pro-Unionists, 32–35, 39, 43–44, 49; Unionism-secession debate, 31–35

Naron, Levi H., 37–39, 48
Nashville Convention, 13
National Association for the Advancement of Colored People, 122
Nutt, Haller, 45–46

Pelan, James, 35
Pettus, John J., 32
Polk, James K., 9–10
Port Hudson, Battle of, 56–57

Raymond, Mississippi, 77
Rosecrans, William S., 37–38, 70

Shepard, Isaac, 78–82
Sherman, William T., 36, 42, 70, 78, 85
Shiloh National Military Park, 115–16, 119, 122; African American veterans working in, 115–23; Civilian Conservation Corps, 115–16, 118–20, 122–23; Civilian Works Administration, 116; segregated camps and racism, 120–23
Simpkins, Francis Butler, writing on South Carolina Reconstruction and aftermath, 129, 131–33, 135–43
South Carolina During Reconstruction, 139–43
Steele, Frederick, 78–79

Thomas, Lorenzo, 47–48, 78, 79
Thompson, Toliver T., 119
Tyler, John, 9

Union soldiers: attitudes toward black soldiers, 74–75, 83–86; attitudes toward slaves and slavery, 69–82, 84–86; Milliken's Bend case, 78–82

Van Buren, Martin, 8, 11, 14
Vicksburg campaign, 69; north Mississippi campaign, 70–71; siege of, 84

Woody, Robert Hilliard, writing on South Carolina Reconstruction, 129, 131–32, 134–35, 139–43

www.ingramcontent.com/pod-product-compliance
Lightning Source LLC
Chambersburg PA
CBHW020416230426
43663CB00007BA/1190